Vintage BRITISH Shotguns

A *Shooting Sportsman* Guide

Terry Wieland
Illustrated by Susan Norris

Countrysport Press
Camden, Maine

ISBN: 978-0-89272-774-2

Frontispiece: *Off the Ridge*, oil painting by Susan Norris

Jacket and interior design by Lynda Mills

Printed at Versa Press, East Peoria, Illinois

5   4   3   2   1

Library of Congress Cataloging-in-Publication Data:

Wieland, Terry.
Vintage British shotguns : a shooting sportsman guide / by Terry
Wieland ; illustrations by Susan Norris.
p. cm.
Includes bibliographical references and index.
ISBN 978-0-89272-774-2 (hardcover : alk. paper)
1. Shotguns—England. I. Title.
TS536.8.W55 2008
799.2028'340941—dc22
2008040597

A Shooting Sportsman Book

www.shootingsportsman.com
Distributed to the trade by National Book Network

Also by Terry Wieland

Dangerous-Game Rifles
Spanish Best: The Fine Shotguns of Spain
A View From A Tall Hill – Robert Ruark in Africa
The Magic of Big Game
Spiral-Horn Dreams

For David C. Foster
Editor-in-Chief
Gray's Sporting Journal

1945 – 2008

Contents

Part One: History & Technicalities

Appendices

Acknowledgements

Through a lifetime of interest in British doubles, both rifles and shotguns, the author has met dozens of men with similar interests on both sides of the Atlantic. Each, in his way, has contributed to this book—from Russell Wilkin and the staff at Holland & Holland to the gunmakers at the reconstituted E.J. Churchill, from Paul Roberts at Rigby to Edward Asprey.

In the writing of this book, four experts in the field made a great effort to assist and contribute: Jack Rowe, a well-known English gunmaker now living in the United States, and George Caswell, of Champlin Arms, each contributed directly with information about individual guns and makers.

Steve Denny, of Holland & Holland, reviewed every page of the manuscript, applying his great knowledge of the English gun trade. And Michael McIntosh, America's foremost author in this field, was kind enough to edit the manuscript itself, applying his knowledge of double guns to clarify some points, and his command of English as an Elizabethan scholar to polish the language.

* * *

Susan Norris, an accomplished painter and sculptor, created works of art that impart the atmosphere and romance of English gunmaking, and threw herself into the world of British guns in order to do so. Together, we spent time at Champlin Arms to examine and photograph guns, and visited Jack Rowe to see him working in his shop. In the course of this, Susan also developed a great affection for a Purdey 20-bore over/under. Such is the magic of the English gun.

And, at our publisher, *Shooting Sportsman* art director Lynda Mills once again provided the catalyst that turned Susan's art work and my words and photographs into a lovely book.

* * *

Finally, our thanks to a large group of men, mostly long dead, named

James Woodward, Thomas Boss, Holland, Purdey, Lancaster, Rigby, Westley Richards, and literally thousands of others, whose dedication and extraordinary skills created the fine English double.

Foreword

Of all the world's great gun trades, none is more fascinating than the one that evolved in Britain beginning about 1800, kicked into high gear in the 1850s, and became the world standard by 1900. The modern game gun as we know it is a British invention. The British didn't invent all the concepts, but they certainly perfected the form and established a level of craftsmanship that now is the standard by which guns are judged worldwide.

Michael McIntosh

The typical British gun is a side-by-side double. The trade had some flirtations with over/unders, a few to lasting effect, notably by Boss and Woodward. More recently, Purdey and Holland & Holland have turned out superb over/under guns, and if you want to see one that will take your breath away, have a look at a current round-action over/under by Scottish maker David McKay Brown. Still, the classic British gun is a side-by-side.

British guns hold an allure unlike any in the world. It's difficult to explain, no easier than explaining why you find some women stunning and others not. And not all British guns are equally captivating—but those that are . . . I've had two of them, a best John Wilkes sidelock and a vintage-1886 Purdey hammer gun. The Purdey is still in my safe and will be there until I'm gone.

Simply counting all the books written about British guns would be a daunting task; listing the titles would be even more so. So why yet another? Short answer: This one is different. This one does not purport to be ency-clopaedic, though there is encyclopaedic knowledge behind it. This one is meant to condense a long and complex history into something that is both readable and useful to one who harbors a yen to own a British gun. It scores on both accounts.

And who better to write it than Terry Wieland? Terry and I have been friends for the better part of 25 years. We may not be the winsome lads we were back in those days, but winsomeness, I'm afraid, has only a limited shelf life. No matter. I prefer to think we've added some more substance to the dimples, have become better writers, and deepened our knowledge and understanding of a subject we both love. I know that's true in Terry's case. He has a prodigious talent for wordsmithing to a level I much admire and has untiringly pursued his fascination with British guns.

This is one of those rare books that you'll want to read again and again, even to the point of memorizing it. And if you hanker to buy an older British gun nowadays, committing it to memory is no bad idea. You won't be sorry.

From here I'll put you into Terry's good hands and say only that I hope you enjoy reading it as much as I have.

— Michael McIntosh

Introduction

The late 1990s witnessed a very strange phenomenon: Americans, often clad in tweeds, descending from planes at Heathrow, and venturing in rented cars out onto the left-hand side of England's country roads, seeking out obscure little gunshops. There, they would scan the racks of used doubles, looking for serviceable guns to take back to the States and sell for five or six times the price they paid.

For a while, this was a lucrative practice for a few knowledgeable dealers who understood what Americans wanted, and also knew a bit about the English gun trade.

To borrow a financial term, these venturesome souls were "arbitraging": Taking advantage of price disparities in different parts of the world to buy low over there and sell high back here. They were allowed this opportunity by the fact that a certain type of shotgun—the ubiquitous Birmingham boxlock non-ejector—was almost valueless in modern Britain. In the U.S., however, it was exactly the kind of gun being sought by upland game hunters who had fallen in love, once again, with double guns.

This love affair really took shape in the mid-1980s, but it is more compli-cated than that. Instead of a renaissance, as it is often portrayed, it may have been a case of the prodigal son returning home after a 40-year fling with upstart pumps and semiautos. The pump, the semiauto, and the mid-range over/under are still by far the dominant shotguns found in America, whether hunting pheasants or shooting clays. But the side-by-side double has made a substantial comeback, not just in use but in overall interest. Books have been published, magazines inaugurated, annual events promulgated—all to learn about and celebrate the side-by-side.

* * *

The side-by-side shotgun as we know it today is one of mankind's great-est industrial artifacts. As a mechanism, the side-by-side (especially the London 'best' sidelock) approaches design perfection and, in its highest forms, perfection of execution as well. This is manifested not just in beauty of form and decoration (such as fine walnut, engraving, and inlay) but in the fact that these guns continue to function beautifully a century or more after they left the shop, and after firing hundreds of thousands of cartridges, often under dreadful conditions.

What's more, with proper care and assuming the availability of gunmaking skills far into the future, these guns should continue to function for hundreds of years more.

This is the foundation of our long fascination with doubles. Using a gun made in 1900, which has passed through several pairs of hands during its lifetime, outliving them all, gives today's hunter a connection with the past that is almost ethereal. So there are many aspects to our renewed interest— as fine mechanisms, as art, even as status symbols. But the basic reason for caring about doubles at all is the fact that no gun handles and shoots as well as a finely made side-by-side.

None of the other, more fanciful, explanations would matter a damn were it not for the fact that shooting a well-balanced, properly fitted side-by-side will allow the average shooter to perform better than he ever thought he could. And look good doing it.

Some British guns are legendary for their handling. The first time you pick up such a gun and feel the way it comes to your shoulder is a gunning epiphany. In my particular case, it occurred with a Boss & Co. round-body game gun made between the wars. At that moment, in 1993, I realized what a shotgun could be. Since then, I have handled many guns by dozens of different makers. Some may have been every bit as good as that Boss, but none has made me forget it.

Once bitten, shotgunners often embark on a search for the "perfect" shotgun; some find it, but most do not. A few Americans embarked on that journey in the mid-1980s, and it led them down various paths. There was a general reawakening of interest in the old American doubles, especially the Parker, and prices began to spiral. As they did so, some aficionados attempted to resurrect these old marques. The Parker Reproduction was born, manufactured in Japan. This was followed by the A.H. Fox and the Ithaca. Of the bunch, only A.H. Fox (manufactured by Tony Galazan in Connecticut) is still extant. Galazan, America's foremost expert on the manufacture of double shotguns, also produces the Model 21 under licence from Winchester.

At the same time, interest grew in fine shotguns made in other countries, and a frantic search ensued for guns that were priced below their real value. Spain was a particularly fruitful area, and the remaining small fine gunmakers of the Basque Country enjoyed a long period of solid growth through the

1990s. Italian guns asserted themselves, and we began importing guns from Turkey, the Philippines, Brazil, Japan.

Many of these guns were good, and some were great. Still, the unchallenged mecca for double-gun lovers was London. The greatest London makers, like Purdey and Holland & Holland, have been represented in the U.S. without interruption, with a handful of guns built and sold to the wealthy every year without much notice by the shooting masses. The English gun trade, however, extends far beyond those hallowed names. It is a trade that, in its modern form, goes back to 1850, with roots almost two centuries earlier than that. At its peak it included thousands of gunmaking shops in two main centers (London and Birmingham) and a host of lesser ones (Edinburgh, Bristol, and Manchester, among others).

The question lingers, why write a book about British guns only, and intended for the American market? Why not Belgium, Italy, Germany?

The answer is that Britain is unique. For more than a century, its empire provided a vast worldwide market and the British had a major gunmaking industry to supply it. That industry made guns of all grades and several different types, but the side-by-side shotgun was dominant, and even in its lowest grades, the guns were made to a standard of quality impossible to find today outside of the better custom shops. Through the 1970s and '80s, many of those guns still lingered in Britain—in attics, henhouses, closets, and gathering dust in small gunshops.

As for America, it is by far the world's largest market for guns, and since the 1980s has had a continuing appetite for doubles.

Through the late 1800s and into the 1900s the British gun trade set the world standard, and not just in numbers. The game guns made today in Italy, Spain, Germany, Turkey, and everywhere else, were largely invented in England. The Anson & Deeley boxlock action is reportedly the single most-manufactured mechanism of any kind in all of history. It was invented in Birmingham in 1875.

America's double-gun tradition goes back to the late 1800s as well, but it had different roots and ultimately quite different products. In England, upland birds were king: the red grouse, English partridge and pheasant, as well as woodcock, pigeons, and snipe. In America, into the 20th century, there was a more "democratic" tradition of shooting. Instead of large shooting estates, we had common-land swamps, rivers, and woods. The main shooting game was waterfowl.

A waterfowl gun is quite different from an upland game gun—heavier, with longer barrels and tighter chokes. Generally, stocks have more drop.

When ducks are coming in to decoys, you want a gun that places its pattern a little low; conversely, most upland-game situations require a gun with a straighter stock that shoots a little high. It also needs to be lighter, quicker handling, and more dynamic.

The vast majority of American shotguns manufactured from 1880 through 1940 were either dedicated waterfowl guns or "all-around" guns. The latter were made on the assumption that waterfowl would be the major game.

The rekindled American interest in doubles was for upland guns—guns for quail, grouse, woodcock, and pheasant. A premium was paid for any old American gun in the smaller gauges, especially 20 and 28. Since then, the requirements of non-toxic shot have widened the chasm even more. No one in his right mind would put steel shot through a vintage shotgun, regardless of weight or choke.

When the Parker Reproduction was born, it was made first in 20-gauge, and later in 28, specifically to cater to these tastes. Its configuration was more a game gun in the English style than the blue-collar American all-around gun. Similarly, when Tony Galazan brought back the A.H. Fox (in the opinion of many, the best upland gun America ever produced) it was almost exclusively a game gun, not a waterfowl gun.

What escaped most (but not all) American gun dealers was the fact that across the Atlantic lay a storehouse of good-to-great game guns, tailor-made for American tastes of the 1980s, practically going begging. The United Kingdom was full of shotguns, made between 1890 and 1940, that were beautiful pieces for hunting quail, grouse, and woodcock. And by American standards, asking prices were ridiculously low.

There was good reason for this, and it had nothing whatever to do with the quality of the guns themselves. The British are a nation of shotgunners with a tradition that goes back almost four centuries. After the Second World War, the big estates fell on hard times, demand for shotguns dropped off, and through the dismal 1960s more than one epitaph was written for the English gun trade. Purdey and H&H hung on, but dozens of other great names fell like leaves. With the return of economic prosperity in the 1980s, interest in game shooting, especially driven shooting, returned with a vengeance.

The modern English shotgunner, however, wanted one of two guns: Either a London 'best' sidelock game gun, or, if he was not so well-off, a mass-produced over/under. Interest in old English boxlock non-ejector guns fell almost to zero, and prices fell along with it. English gunshops were filled with side-by-sides at rock-bottom prices that would make an American's mouth water.

Granted, the vast majority were 12-bores. The 12 is the British standard (just as the 16 was the favorite of continental Europe). However, a British 12 —even a Birmingham utility gun—is a far cry from the average American 12. For one thing, it is lighter. It is rare to find one heavier than seven pounds, most run around six and a half pounds even with 28- or 30-inch barrels, and it is not uncommon to find them at six to six and a quarter pounds.

Surprisingly, the second most-common bore size is .410. There was a tradition among wealthy shooting families of buying "bespoke" (custom-made) .410 shotguns for their progeny as soon as they were big enough to sit a pony, graduating to a 12 about the time they turned 12, so .410s (many of outstanding quality) are quite common. Twenties and 16s were next, with 28 bores the rarest. Without a doubt, however, 12-bores of all configurations outnumbered all the others combined.

The British gun trade from 1850 to 1940 catered to more than just the wealthy landowner shooting driven birds. Those land owners all employed gamekeepers, and gamekeepers need guns. Small farmers owned guns for shooting foxes and stoats. And then there were the colonies: Every man leaving for Africa or India needed rifles and shotguns, and the colonizers who owned farms in Kenya and Rhodesia bought guns by the boatload.

As well as high-quality, low-volume gunmakers like Purdey, Britain had large-volume factories like Birmingham Small Arms (BSA), Vickers, and Greener. Although William Wellington Greener is best known today for his book *The Gun and its Development*, and for his production of high-quality custom boxlocks, at one point W.W. Greener claimed to be the largest civilian gunmaking plant in the world—bigger than Remington or Winchester in their heyday!

These companies, large and small, turned out shotguns by the tens of thousands. Most were side-by-side game guns, and if one could narrow it down, naming the one configuration that outnumbered any other, it would probably be the above-mentioned "Birmingham boxlock non-ejector."

The name really says it all, the key being "non-ejector." A gun with only extractors was perfect for a gamekeeper, being extremely durable (almost unbreakable, in fact) and cheaper to produce. It was, however, a decided disadvantage for any kind of shooting where birds come or go in flurries and reloading quickly is vital—hence its unpopularity in modern Britain, where almost all recreational shooting involves bunches of birds.

In American upland-game shooting, ejectors are considerably less important. In fact, many prefer extractors because they do not fling the hulls hither and yon, and more than a few shooters have the ejectors disconnected anyway.

Altogether, Britain constituted a storehouse of guns of great appeal to modern Americans. A boxlock non-ejector that might command £300 (about $450) in 1998 Britain would easily sell for $1500 to $2000 here, depending on how pretty the stock was and whether it had fluid-steel barrels. Some changed hands for $2500 or more.

Naturally, any gun with the name H&H, Westley Richards, or Purdey sold for higher prices on name recognition alone. But that is not the market we are discussing here. The real bargains existed in the realm of names with little or no recognition factor: Williamson & Son, William Golden, C.G. Bonehill, and several hosts of others.

Ironically, a Westley Richards that sells at a 20 percent premium, and a William Golden at a 50 percent discount, might well have been made at the same time, in the same plant, even by the same pairs of hands. Such was the nature of the English trade, especially the Birmingham branch of the family.

The purpose of this book is to provide some guidance to prospective buyers of British guns. It is not a price list. The *Blue Book of Gun Values*, by which American dealers live and die, is impossible in the world of British guns, for so many were unique, bespoke, or produced in such small numbers. Therein lies the trap (and the opportunity) for the modern gun buyer. Our purpose is to help you avoid traps, true. But more important, it is to help double-gun lovers recognize the opportunity, when it is presented, to own a seriously good gun, and a piece of history, at a reasonable price.

— Terry Wieland

Part One:
History & Technicalities

From Manton: *The English trade*

Joseph Manton is the acknowledged father of the modern British fine-gun trade. "But for him," James Purdey once remarked, "We should all have been a parcel of blacksmiths." Purdey himself learned the trade with Manton, and once he was on his own, signing guns with his own name, always added "from Manton." The addendum constituted his credentials as a fine gunmaker —a practice that has endured to this day.

Joseph Manton and his brother, John, came into gunmaking at a time when it really was little more than a specialized form of blacksmithing. By 1780, firearms had completely replaced the bow and arrow and crossbow in the armies of the world, but were considered noisy, dirty, and decidedly low-brow by most upper-class people. They had little or no sporting application; hunting, such as it was, was carried out in traditional ways.

The earliest firearms that could be considered 'fine' were duelling pistols. John Rigby, the oldest gunmaking firm in the English-speaking world, began as a maker of duelling pistols in Dublin in 1735. Dublin became a center for pistols, and other famous makers of the era include Calderwood and, in London, Egg, Mortimer, and Twigg.

The duelling pistol was a unique and deadly tool—possessed only by gentlemen, intended for one sinister purpose: to kill an opponent, face to face, at close range. As such, owners of duelling pistols (especially those who used them on a regular basis) were interested in function far more than form. Specialist pistol makers developed a design and a standard of quality "the like of which had never been seen before," according to firearms historian Geoffrey Boothroyd.

"Instead of the obvious outward display of decoration, their work was possessed of the more indefinable qualities that can only be described by the terms 'feel,' 'balance,' 'coming up,' etc., none of which are adequate to describe the feeling of 'rightness' that the pistol shot of today experiences when he handles and perhaps shoots one of these weapons," Boothroyd wrote in *Guns through the Ages*.

"Such qualities did not appear by accident; they were the result of a painstaking empiricism, a constant search for the ultimate in perfection.

Pistols made by the elite of the gunmaking craft became a natural extension of the shooting arm and, with practice, would come up to bear on the target every time."

Duelling pistols by the finest makers are recognized today as being among the greatest all-time masterpieces of gunmaking. The qualities that made them such were equally desirable in a game gun, and it was only natural that the same standards would eventually be applied to the making of guns for shooting birds.

Almost as soon as hand-held firearms came into existence, someone, somewhere, was using one to kill game, and birds were among the first targets. In *The Merry Wives of Windsor*, written in 1597, Shakespeare makes reference to Master Ford being out "a' birding." Exactly what form this pursuit took, he does not say, although we are later told of Master Ford's custom of discharging his firearm up the chimney to unload it.

So from very early times, hunters had an interest in a gun that could be used on game birds; the first guns, however, were so cumbersome and slow, the best one could hope for was to shoot a bird on the ground or off a branch. The concept of shooting a bird on the wing, either deliberately because it is more sporting, or merely because that is the opportunity that is presented, was a long time coming.

The catalyst that at once made many things possible was the 1807 invention of percussion powder by the Reverend Alexander Forsyth. Primitive ignition systems such as the flintlock were a serious impediment to any kind of sporting shooting because of the noise and the delays involved. The advent of the percussion cap simplified things considerably and made firearms more resistant to moisture and bad weather—critical in the United Kingdom. Forsyth was offered a large sum for his invention by Napoleon Bonaparte (he declined) and the British Army simply adopted it without considering niceties like patent infringement. Probably it was considered a matter of national security, then as now the excuse for any number of legal barbarities.

The art of "shooting-flying" began in France in the 1600s, spread to Britain, and gradually shoulder guns evolved that were intended for sportsmen rather than soldiers.

It was at this point that Joseph Manton arrived on the scene. He looked at the products being turned out in the gunshops of the nation and decided (with astonishing foresight) that here was an opportunity to dominate the trade by making guns that were finer, in every respect, than those of his competitors.

One has only to look at a flintlock from the "Brown Bess" era (circa 1776)

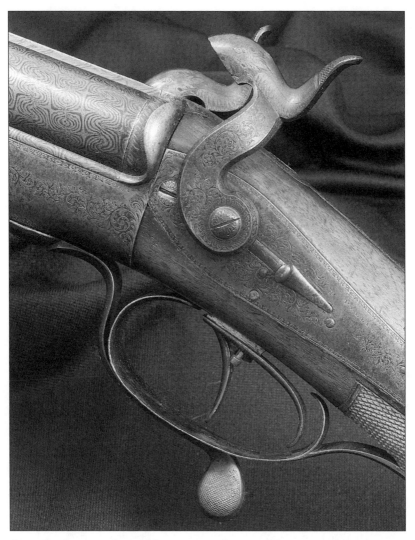

James Purdey was a former Manton man whose name has come to epitomize grace and fine craftsmanship in shotguns. This is an early Purdey 20-bore pinfire double rifle with a Jones underlever, individual sliding safeties for each hammer, and Damascus barrels.

to see how crudely made shoulder guns really were. The stocks are roughly shaped and clumsy, the triggers and trigger guards gross and awkward, the guns themselves heavy and unbalanced. Wood-to-metal fit, as we understand it today, did not exist: Metal met wood and was hammered into place. End of operation.

The arms museums of Europe are full of earlier shoulder guns, from Spain and Italy, that are extremely ornate, but decoration and craftsmanship are not the same thing. Joseph Manton pioneered fine craftsmanship, in which every part of the gun was lovingly shaped, with an eye to creating a whole that was graceful and elegant. Stocks became slimmer, butts narrower; lockplates were made graceful and hammers became objects of artistry, sculpted rather than merely filed. Instead of crude iron tubes, barrels were struck (filed) lengthwise to reduce diameter and weight. The British learned early that the key to fine balance lay in the barrels, and began paying close attention. As for gaudy decoration, that was conspicuous by its absence.

In *Best Guns*, shotgun authority Michael McIntosh summed up the qualities of a fine gun, as defined by the Manton brothers: "The Manton influence was threefold. They defined the style of the English gun and by extension defined the nature of the game gun for all the world and for all time— the slender, lightweight side-by-side double, trimly stocked, with a perfect harmony of form and function in its clean, simple lines.

"The Mantons also established the style and taste of decoration that became the standard by which fine guns worldwide are judged: metalwork filed in graceful curves and engraved in delicate scroll; wood polished to a fine sheen and richly finished in oil; barrels deeply blacked; the whole effect subtle, restrained, elegant.

"Perhaps most important of all," McIntosh concluded, "The Mantons established standards of craftsmanship in which perfection was the only acceptable level of performance, standards that every man who worked in the Manton shop was expected to meet."

"Every man" included some of the greatest names in English gunmaking —craftsmen who learned the trade under the Mantons and went on to set up in business for themselves. Unquestionably, they comprised the greatest and most remarkable generation of gunmakers the world has ever seen: Charles Lancaster, James Purdey, Joseph Lang, Thomas Boss, William Greener, William Evans, and a host of lesser-known names who, together, created the vast and rich tapestry of English gunmaking through the 19th century.

* * *

It was the time of the Peninsular Wars, in which Sir Arthur Wellesley (later the Duke of Wellington) commanded a small British army and collec-

Robert Ringer was a gunmaker in Watton, Norfolk (c.1857-68), whose mastery of his craft shows in every stylish detail of this 12-bore pinfire game gun.

tion of Spanish and Portuguese troops against the Bonapartes. Many British officers returned home with barrels of Spanish steel (Toledo steel was renowned throughout the world) and turned them over to gunmakers such as Manton to become the basis of a fine fowling piece.

The sport of fowling and shooting-flying, and the making of fine guns for the pursuit thereof, grew up together, and the center was London.

So many seemingly unrelated social and industrial trends converged around this time that it is impossible to extricate just one and tell its story divorced from the rest. The Victorian era, the age of exploration, the advent of big-game hunting, the industrial revolution, the introduction of driven shooting, the rise of shooting estates, and the shooting party as a cornerstone of upper-class life—all of these things were taking place concurrently, falling over one another in a rumbling, tumbling revolution.

The turning point occurred in 1851, with the Great Exhibition of London. This was an exposition of all things manufactured and industrial, and attracted exhibits from around the world. Artisans from across Europe converged on London to display their wares. One such was Casimir Lefaucheux, a French gunmaker from Paris. The gun he displayed in London was destined to change the world of shooting, for Lefaucheux had created the first really functional "break-action" gun—a gun in which the barrels were hinged and pivoted down from the breech, allowing practical breechloading.

Various other approaches had been tried; in fact, breechloading firearms had existed in one form or another for more than a century. None, however, had proven practical because they were all slow, awkward, or difficult. Lefaucheux's design was the breakthrough for which everyone had been waiting, and it had the effect of a bursting dam.

First out of the gate, according to legend, was Joseph Lang, a gunmaker who had been in business in London since 1821 and who, in fact, had acquired the assets of Joseph Manton when that company went under. Within a few months of the Great Exhibition, Lang was displaying a break-action gun of his own. At that precise moment, all other systems, including muzzleloaders themselves, became obsolete. They did not immediately disappear, of course, and adherents continued to fight a rear-guard action for years thereafter, but the writing was indelibly on the wall.

In one famous case, the Greeners, father and son, fought bitterly over which was the superior system—in person, in print, and finally through third parties. William Greener, a respected old-time gunmaker, was a die-hard supporter of muzzleloaders, and proclaimed loud and long that breechloaders were a flash in the pan that could never compete in terms of accuracy with a good muzzleloader. His son, William Wellington Greener, espoused the breechloader. Relations reached a nadir when the two refused to speak to each other, a situation that persisted for some years.

Just as the invention of the wheel did not immediately spawn an Aston-Martin, purring at the curb and ready to rip, Lang's break-action gun left many questions unanswered. First of all, now that we have the breech open, what will we stuff into it to shoot? Obviously, lead and gunpowder would have to be contained in some sort of package, along with a method of igniting same. And it was fine that the barrels hinged up and down, but a workable method of locking them closed, so they could be fired safely, was a high priority; and, almost as important, a quick, easy method of unlocking them, in order to eject the empty hull and insert a new one.

Those were just the big questions. Behind them came a host of lesser ones, all requiring some sort of ingenious technical innovation. Fortunately, the British gun trade was up to the challenge, and it was met by men bearing names that are so familiar to us today. Purdey, Scott, Anson, Deeley, Webley, Greener, and a score of others contributed this bit or that part, and over about a 40-year period of frenzied development, they perfected the side-by-side double as we know it today.

There were false starts, blind alleys, and good developments that were immediately superseded by better ones. Around 1860, the rifle and shotgun parted company, each going its separate way. Their development was intertwined, of course, but some companies became rifle specialists (Rigby, Gibbs, and W.J. Jeffery, for example) while others became makers of shotguns— "game guns," in the British usage. Riflemakers continued to produce shotguns, and vice versa, but there was a definite parting of the ways.

The first really practical cartridges (derived from the French *cartouche*) for break-action shotguns were pinfires. These cartridges looked not unlike a modern shotshell except the primer was inside, and it was fired by a pin that extended out the side of the base. The cartridges had to be inserted carefully, with the pin in a slot where it could be struck by the falling hammer.

The system appears awkward, but in fact it worked quite well. Pinfire guns were simple to make, lent themselves beautifully to external hammers, and they hung on for many years. Pinfire ammunition was manufactured well into the 20th century, and several English shooting writers have recounted how, in their poverty-stricken youth, they were able to shoot only because they could afford a used pinfire gun, which in the 1920s and '30s sold for very little.

* * *

If you examine a modern side-by-side shotgun, whether sidelock or boxlock, studying the function of each familiar part, you realize just how simply and beautifully integrated the whole mechanism is, and why non-shooting industrial historians have applauded the near perfection of the design.

There are three basic parts: the barrels, the forend, and the buttstock and frame. "Lock, stock, and barrel" is an expression denoting "everything," and this is its origin. The three components can be assembled or disassembled in seconds.

The forend acts as a fastener that holds the gun together and provides certain vital mechanical functions. Even when it is made as a beavertail or semi-beavertail, it is not a hand-grip, for the simple reason that the forend is too far back for the leading hand in the English manner of shooting. The forend is attached with a spring-loaded latch that grips a lug (the English call it a 'loop') under the barrel. The forend iron may also contain the ejector mechanism, which drives the extractors (in England, 'luggers'), which are mounted in the barrel lump under the forend. And, as the gun is opened and the barrels rock down, the forend iron pivots the cocking levers, which cock the tumblers.

The forend is far from insignificant, and it houses many of the seemingly small but ingenious innovations that have become part of the traditional double gun.

Because the muzzleloader was a hammer gun, the first break-action guns also had hammers, whether for pinfires or the centerfire cartridges that followed. The hammer was part of the lock, which consisted of several small moving parts and springs, all attached to a lock plate that fastened onto the side of the frame behind the barrels. Between 1860 and 1875, various modifications were tried. Traditionally, a shooter would close the action and then cock the hammers manually. In driven shooting, this was too slow. The answer arrived in 1875, when William Anson and John Deeley patented their boxlock action, using the falling barrels to cock the tumblers. This one feature was adapted to hammer guns and sidelock guns as well.

This was followed, logically, by safety systems that would allow the shooter, if he did not fire the gun immediately, to leave the hammers cocked but prevent them in some way from falling accidentally.

If the hammers were cocked by the pivoting of the barrels, then obviously there was no longer any need for them to be on the outside, with large ears for the thumb, and it was not long before different approaches were tried to move them to the inside of the lock plate. In some early designs, small projections from the tumbler (as it came to be called) extended out through the lock plate, allowing manual cocking or de-cocking, and instant knowledge by view or feel of whether the gun was cocked.

These constituted some of the blind alleys mentioned above, for not one of these systems survived long once the major sidelock designs were perfected, most notably by Holland & Holland, Thomas Boss, and Frederick Beesley. By 1890, the sidelock with internal tumblers, a cocking indicator, and safety mechanism had shouldered aside the traditional hammer gun. Hammers hung on for some years, but only because there were shooters who refused to abandon the familiar. Among them was King George V, one of the best game shots of his era, who famously remarked that a gun without hammers "looks like a spaniel without ears." The influence of such notables can be significant.

Even royal disapproval, however, could not hold back the hammerless revolution in the intensely competitive world of the British shooting estate, circa 1900. This was the era of Lord Ripon, probably the greatest game shot of all time, his rival Lord Walsingham, and others who aspired to be renowned as game shots. It was a social phenomenon that shaped a nation as well as an industry, and bears a closer look.

* * *

The Victorian shooting party has long been an object of both fascination and derision. Like fox hunters on horseback with red coats, trampling crops and shouting "*Halloo!*", it is more criticized than understood, more parodied than appreciated, condemned for its excesses without acknowledging its many and varied benefits.

Oscar Wilde called fox hunting "the unspeakable in pursuit of the inedible." No comparable epigram exists, alas, for the shooting party that dominated English country life from the 1870s until the outbreak of war in 1914. Queen Victoria's consort, Prince Albert, was an enthusiastic shooter, and his interest was a major reason for its growth. This enthusiasm was passed on to his sons, and the Prince of Wales (later King Edward VII) was an excellent shot. As the arbiter of English social life, the Prince's tastes and preferences largely dictated the activities of the upper classes.

The British have long loved country life and its many pursuits. The general movement of the population from rural areas to cities during the industrial revolution, combined with less labor-intensive farming, left many large estates with land that could be put to other uses, such as breeding and fostering game birds. With the coming of trains, groups of people could move about the country quickly and easily, from estate to estate. From the Home Counties of the south to the northernmost tip of Scotland, shooting became a passion.

The red grouse of Scotland, northern England, and parts of the west country, is the unchallenged aristocrat of British game birds. The grouse roams wild in the heather, and can be neither pen-raised nor domesticated. The hills it inhabits are useless for almost anything else—the key word being "almost." During the Highland Clearances, Scottish clan chiefs forced their own people off their estates in order to make room for sheep, which at the time were more profitable. When sheep farming lost its financial allure, there were few alternatives. One was forestry—planting evergreen trees for pulp and lumber.

Landowners who wanted to keep the heather in its pristine form, rather than ripping it out to make way for trees, needed to find some way to make the heather pay its way. This challenge was met by fostering the red stag and the red grouse, harvesting this new crop with rifle and gun, charging for the privilege, and then selling the resulting venison and grouse to fine restaurants in London.

This is a brutally truncated description of a complex economic arrangement, but it conveys the idea. The survival of much of the Scottish Highlands, and the heather moors of Derbyshire and points north, depends to this day on the continued economic viability of the red grouse.

Grouse season opens on August 12 every year, and "The Glorious Twelfth" has been celebrated in song and story for well over a century. Even now, the success (or lack thereof) of opening day of grouse season is front-page news in England. For many years, there has been an intense competition to see which expensive restaurant can be the first of the season to offer grouse on its menu—a race that was made considerably less romantic when express trains to London were replaced by hovering helicopters picking up the day's first brace.

The other great British game bird is the English partridge, which is (or was) found on estates throughout southern England and Wales. It has been augmented by infusions of French partridge ("Frenchmen" in the deliciously incorrect idiom of English country gentlemen, who have delighted in shooting Frenchmen since Agincourt, Crécy, and Waterloo). And then there is the ring-necked pheasant, transplanted to England as it was to America, and now the dominant game bird for commercial shooting estates, at least in terms of numbers.

Ah, yes—numbers. Since the halcyon days of the Prince of Wales, Lord Ripon and Lord Walsingham, and the other "Big Shots" of the late Victorian era, numbers have been a matter of ego, obsession, and economic viability. For the shooting estates, each day's bag was critically important, for the birds were sold in the game-meat markets of Europe. Landowners needed "guns" who could deliver, and top shooters were coveted guests. In a class-conscious world of social strivers and *arrivistes*, being a good shot could be a ticket to the upper realms of society.

With shooters competing against each other for total numbers of birds bagged, and estates competing for records in birds delivered to the game dealers, and all with the Prince of Wales at its head, it is no surprise the high society of the shooting party excited the intense interest of society columnists combined with equally intense condemnation of Laborites, Utopians, and anti-vivisectionists.

News from the grouse moors was mainstream and front page; a decline in the red grouse population incited questions in Parliament and the establishment of a parliamentary committee to investigate. The term "grouse-moor look" became a derisive description of an upper-class politician.

* * *

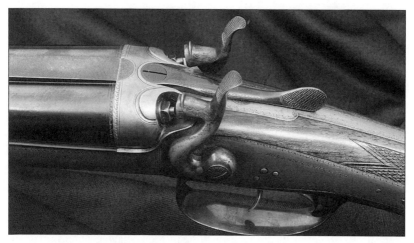

An early Holland & Holland central-fire double rifle, chambered for the .450 BPE 3¹/₄". With both rifles and shotguns, lines were important, as shown by the gracefully carved fences. This hammer gun has back-action locks.

Seen from this vantage point, the frantic competition among English gunmakers in the late 19th century snaps into focus. The fortunes of a gunmaker were reflected in the household names who shot his products on the grouse moors, setting records and astonishing the crowds.

Developing guns that were more reliable, more durable, faster to fire and reload, all became matters of economic survival for gunmakers. Any development that gave shooters an edge was devoutly to be pursued. This was the imperative that drove the revolution in gunmaking from 1860 to 1900.

Individual guns progressed from hammer to hammerless, from blackpowder to smokeless, from Damascus barrels to fluid steel. Safety mechanisms were perfected, including secondary safeties like the safety sear found in all fine sidelocks today.

In driven shooting, birds usually come in clusters (red grouse fly in "packs") and top guns quickly discovered they could get two coming in, and two more going away, if they used a pair of guns and employed a loader to look after that chore and keep handing them a gun ready to fire. From there, it was a short step to the matched pair. As the English perfected the well-balanced game gun and moved into the teaching of proper shooting techniques, they realized that a shooter would perform better and chalk up a better score if his two guns were identical in every way—identical to the point where even the most doting master did not know which of his two guns he was holding.

Some shooters went even further, and had three guns made (a "garniture"), or four, or five. One was limited only by imagination and money, and the London gunmakers were more than willing to accommodate any harebrained idea, provided there was money to pay for it.

There developed a whole new nomenclature around sets of guns: matched pairs, assembled pairs, and so on. Generally, guns were identified by a digit (1, 2, 3) engraved or, more usually, inlaid in gold, on barrels and frame. It was at this time that gunmakers adopted the practice of embedding a gold escutcheon in the underside of the buttstock, just up from the toe, engraved with the owner's initials. As with virtually everything in English shooting that is so mysterious to Americans and often seems like affectation, this had a perfectly practical reason: When the owner was a member of a shooting party with a dozen other "guns," each with two or three guns and all looking very similar standing in the rack in the gun room, having one's initials on one's guns made identification easy.

The competitive atmosphere and economic pressures to deliver the birds regardless forced landowners to adopt practices that were sometimes very hard on both the shooters and their guns. In the United Kingdom weather is always a factor, but when so much money is at stake, a shoot will be cancelled only when the winds hit hurricane force and the downpour becomes biblical. This is true even to this day: When an estate has guests each paying $3,000 a day to shoot, cancelling a day of shooting represents a huge direct financial loss, never mind the contract for hundreds of birds undelivered to the game dealer. It is also a major and expensive feat of organization, with loaders, game keepers, beaters, pickers-up and their dogs, cooks, maids, and drivers.

I have long suspected that it was familiarity with this kind of situation, and a cheerful determination to go ahead regardless, that caused the British generals to be sanguine about proceeding with the Normandy invasion, even while General Eisenhower was agonizing over the approaching weather.

Shooting parties have proceeded with a stiff upper lip under the most bizarre of conditions. August 12, 1998 was one of the worst days on record in northern England. I was part of a shooting party at Knarsdale, which was then enjoying bumper crops of red grouse and vying for various daily and annual bag records. The rain set in days before, continued all through the night of the 11th, and was still coming down in sheets when we gathered for breakfast. Through five drives in the morning and four in the afternoon, the downpour never paused. More than once I saw a shooter up-end his gun to dribble rainwater out of the barrels, and when we got back that night, we

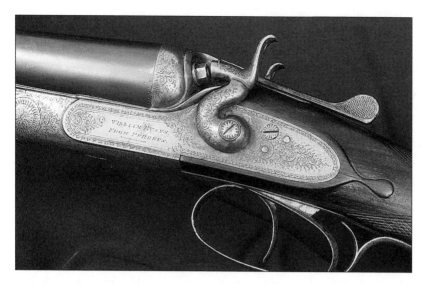

An early William Evans 12-bore hammer gun. Evans was a salesman, first for Purdey, later for Holland & Holland. When he set up on his own, he adopted the practice of signing his name "From Purdey's." This gun is an early Evans, made in the trade and sold from his London shop. It employs a bar-action lock.

poured water out of our rubber boots where it had wicked in through our clothing.

The guns in use that day bore names like Stephen Grant, John Wilkes, Boss & Co., H&H, and Henry Atkin. Some were a century old. That night, the loaders stripped them down, dried them off, oiled them, and the next day they were ready to go again. As were we.

This is not an unusual situation. Especially as the season wears on and winter approaches, the weather deteriorates but the drives and the game harvesting go on. Since the days of Queen Victoria, English shotguns have been built to withstand such outright abuse and keep shooting, regardless.

Naturally, in terms of mechanical features, anything that failed or did not perform up to expectations was quickly reported to the gunmaker by its irate owner, and gunmakers modified their designs accordingly. If a top-flight shot like Lord Ripon had an idea for a modification based on his unparalleled experience as a game shooter, his gunmaker (in this case, James Purdey & Sons) listened intently and either implemented his suggestions or had good reasons for not doing so.

In this way, guided by experience and hard use, the English game gun evolved into the masterpiece it is today.

English usage of the game gun also evolved. Sending a gun back to its maker for an annual "strip-and-clean" became general practice. A professional strip-and-clean is a major operation; it does not consist merely of an apprentice running a cleaning rod down the bore. A skilled gunmaker takes the gun completely apart until no two pieces are left fastened together. Each part is checked carefully for rust, signs of wear, and potential trouble. The gun is then reassembled by the gunmaker, who dips his fingers into his own secret formula of gun grease and lightly coats each piece as it goes back together. When the gun is in one piece again and he is satisfied that it is ready for another season and thousands more rounds of ammunition, it is returned to its owner.

To give an idea of just how much abuse an English game gun is capable of enduring with nothing more than a happy smile, consider the Boss & Co. side-by-side that was used by the original Eley Brothers for decades to carry out random tests of cartridges coming off the line. It is estimated that particular gun fired about one and a half *million* rounds during its career, with little more than routine maintenance. This was reported by G.T. Garwood (Gough Thomas), who lamented the fact that the gun disappeared when the cartridge company was absorbed by another. As far as anyone knows, it is still happily shooting away, somewhere.

* * *

Obviously, high-volume driven shooting was not the only type of shotgunning for game in the United Kingdom, but the intense demands of shooting driven birds dictated the general form of the English game gun. This pattern is eminently adaptable to most forms of rough or walk-up shooting over dogs, as well as flighting ducks, migrating woodcock, and even marauding predators.

By 1910, all the major technical innovations had been made and the game gun had taken the form that endures to this day. But there was more than form involved. Method was equally important, for the great English gunmakers had adopted the principle of the 'best' gun.

A 'best' gun is defined as follows: It is a gun upon which no further improvement can be made. It is absolutely and in every way as good as its craftsmen can make it—with no constraints of time, money, or effort.

Boss & Co. was founded by Thomas Boss, who learned the trade with Joseph Manton and worked with James Purdey before setting up on his own.

The company's case label reads "Makers of 'best' guns only." This is the company that made the test gun that Eley Brothers used for quality control, firing one and a half million rounds in the process.

There is a connection: The London gunmakers discovered that durability and extreme longevity could be built into a gun if it was made as close to perfect as human hands could do. By hand-fitting every single tiny part, normal wear and tear was reduced to an absolute minimum or even eliminated altogether.

The great destroyer of lesser guns is allowable tolerances. When parts are machine-made to generous tolerances, different sized parts work on each other in different ways at varying speeds, eventually breaking or wearing down to the point where they no longer function. As parts become increasingly sloppy through use, they begin acting adversely upon other parts, leading to an overall domino effect and ultimate failure.

To American eyes, the lengths to which an English gunmaker will go are unfathomable, and in the opinion of many, simply uncalled for. But the British don't see it that way. Take, for example, the timing of the ejectors. A craftsman will work on the ejectors for hour after hour, assembling the gun, testing, disassembling, making a single file stroke, reassembling, and testing again, until the ejectors will toss two empty hulls exactly the same distance away and have them land side by side.

The rationale is that if this effort is expended on such a seemingly trivial function, it helps ensure that all the more important functions will also be perfect. It also fosters pride in each of the craftsmen and inspires them to produce perfect work.

The proof is in the longevity: There are today tens of thousands of guns in everyday use that were made in England and Scotland more than a hundred years ago. Most of them are (or were, when they were made) 'best' guns. The vast majority were bespoke (custom-made) guns intended for shooting driven game. They have survived, and continue to function, because they are so extraordinarily well made. It could be argued that an expensive best gun will survive where a lesser gun will not because its various owners would have lavished more care on it, and that is certainly true to an extent. It does not change the fact, however, that some of these guns have fired hundreds of thousands of rounds over their lifetimes, and are still perfectly functional.

Let's assume an English gentleman of serious sporting bent orders a matched pair from, say, Charles Lancaster, one of the upper echelon of London gunmakers. He takes delivery in the year 1900, at the age of 25. Being energetic, popular, and a good shot, he receives many shooting invitations and for the next 15 years he averages 30 shooting days per season. That sounds like a great deal, but people like Lord Ripon often shot three or four times that number. Keep in mind, grouse season opens August 12 and closes in early December, but partridge and pheasant open later and run later as well, so there is serious shooting in the United Kingdom for a good five months a year—potentially 150 days.

On a good day of drives, with many birds, a shooter will easily fire 200 shots, which is 100 per gun. That is 3,000 shots per gun per year. It is now a century later. How many cartridges has each of that matched pair fired? And these, remember, are very conservative estimates that do not take into account any practice rounds fired at shooting grounds during instruction.

The great American single-barrel trap guns were renowned for their durability, being capable of firing a quarter-million rounds during their lifetime. An English 'best' game gun will top that effortlessly, and under much worse conditions.

One cannot build a gun with such attention to detail and not learn a great deal about how a gun works, and what contributes to keeping it working, and this knowledge was put to use in building lesser guns as well. A second-tier gun from a first-rate maker might have its internal parts every bit as well made as a 'best,' but display less engraving, lower-grade walnut, the name not inlaid in gold, and similar gestures to economy. If the Lancaster name was engraved on the outside, then Lancaster quality was installed on the inside.

Some makers, such as Boss, took the position that a craftsman could not switch from grade 'A' work to grade 'B' and back again, without the overall quality of his work suffering. This is a dispute that has never been resolved and will not be settled here. Each great gunmaker, and there were many, had his own views.

There are those, the author among them, who believe that the greatest age of the English gun occurred in the years between 1890 and 1914. While many would argue in favor of guns made "between the wars" (that is, between 1918 and 1939), it seems to me that during that period too many other factors were coming into play, affecting the quality of both game guns and rifles.

Before 1914, all the greatest gunmakers were under glorious full sail, competing madly, and the most formidable game shots were in full swing, shooting on estates that were then at their height. After 1918, the horrendous financial and manpower drain of the war took their toll, along with economic depression and labor problems. Many gunmakers folded or merged with others, and the goal was to hang on rather than forge ahead.

Whatever the cause, workmanship suffered in minor ways. If you examine a gun made in 1895, and compare it to a similar gun from the same maker 30 years later, you will find tiny corners being cut. For example, instead of a minuscule doll's-head rail on the ejector guide, there will be a simple slot and blade. Instead of tiny, exquisite, full-coverage scroll, there will be larger scroll, or only partial coverage. The passion for third bites (which are, admittedly, not necessary for strength) has given way to simplicity—and reduced manufacturing costs.

Certainly, a best gun from between the wars, when orders were few and craftsmen had all the time in the world, is the equal of any. But there is not the same broad range of makers, of gun types and grades and fascinating variations, and all displaying wonderful workmanship, that there was before the world came to an end in September 1914.

Worlds Apart: *London & Birmingham*

The most fashionable of addresses, engraved on the barrels of that most fashionable of London guns, a Holland & Holland.

The English gun trade can be divided loosely into two worlds: London and Birmingham. Some would say "London and all the others," and certainly there were other fine gunmaking centers: Edinburgh; Dublin, for a time; a few in Manchester. But above them all towered the capital of the world, London, and its great industrial rival in the "black country" to the north, Birmingham.

A London 'best' is world renowned and requires little explanation. All the most famous names were London names: Holland & Holland, Purdey, Boss, and so on. While there were a few Birmingham companies that vied for attention, such as Westley Richards, W.W. Greener, and William Powell, they were generally known for products other than the typical London 'best' sidelock.

The boxlock, as great a design as any sidelock, was invented in Birmingham at Westley Richards & Co., and became a Birmingham standard.

Greener adopted the boxlock as his own and made some of the most exquisite examples ever created.

The purpose of this chapter is not to argue the case for either London or Birmingham, but to look at the different methods of making a gun that were used in those two centers. In terms of industrial processess, they were quite distinct.

The London method of building a bespoke gun is to gather the disparate basic parts (the frame, the barrel blanks, the lock blanks, the stock wood) in one shop, distribute them to the appropriate craftsmen, and fashion the gun step by step under the watchful eye of the shop foreman. Virtually every process, from soldering the barrels, to filing the action, to engraving and checkering, putting a London finish on the stock and blacking the barrels, is carried out in-house. In the old days, even regulation of the barrels was generally done at a company's own shooting ground outside London, where all the big names maintained their own field shop with craftsmen skilled in the black arts of making two barrels shoot to the same spot.

When completed, the guns were sent back to the shooting ground where a fitter (the most skilled and unforgiving of craftsmen) would test it exhaustively and tune it minutely, until it was letter perfect in every respect.

For a London shop, catering to kings and princes, various royal dukes, the Lords Ripon and Walsingham, and all the would-be "big shots," such an approach worked well. Personal relationships between a gunmaker and his moneyed clients were as important as to a Savile Row tailor.

It should be added that this personal continuing relationship also played a major role in the overall quality of guns produced by the London shops. One did not sell a gun and watch the customer carry it out the door, never to return. The gun or guns came back, year after year, for routine maintenance. A satisfied client might eventually buy a second pair of guns, refer his friends to do the same, bring in his son to be fitted for his first .410, and later his first matched pair of 12-bores. It was in the gunmaker's best interests to make guns that were first-rate in every way.

Holland & Holland had a continuing relationship through the late 1800s with the greatest big-game hunter of his era, Sir Samuel White Baker. Baker's ideas and experience were important to H&H in making their big rifles and designing cartridges for them, and Baker's celebrity among the people of England, to whom he was a national hero, reflected well on Holland & Holland.

In an era when the exploits of the best game shooters were reported in the daily press, being known as gunmaker to Lord This or Prince That was great

With British guns, one should never say never. For a long time, it was believed H&H never made a Paradox (Fosbery patent) gun in 28-bore. Yet here is one.

publicity, and adding "By appointment to . . ." on one's shop sign or case label added great cachet. As well, some gunmakers were natural showmen. W.W. Greener was always outspoken, at times outrageous, and a shameless self-promoter, as well as being a first-rate gunmaker. The more well-bred London firms, like Purdey, preferred to let their guns do the talking, and in the hands of a man like Lord Ripon they spoke very eloquently indeed.

It is impossible to separate the London gunmakers from London society. Birmingham, on the other hand, was quite different. The dominant city in a part of England known as the "black country," from the layer of factory soot that covered every surface from the gravel on the roads to the leaves on the trees, Birmingham has always been gritty, forthright, and unpretentious. It was also arms maker to the British Empire, and looked upon London as effete and pretentious. Competition to be the best is never a bad thing, and neither great city would give an inch to the other.

As a major industrial center, Birmingham had its own way of doing things. Where the London gunmakers clustered in and around Mayfair, the cultural and social West End, Birmingham gunmakers congregated in an area of the city known as the "gunmaking quarter." It encompassed several well-known streets that today are either paved over as part of a motorway, or built up into housing developments. In the late 1800s, however, they were narrow, inter-

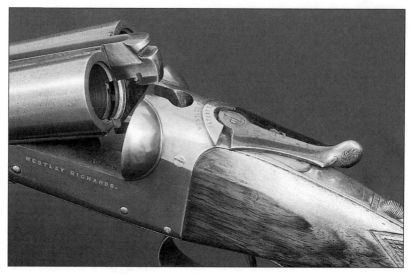

The world's greatest boxlock, the Anson & Deeley, was invented at Westley Richards in Birmingham. Westley Richards not only made many boxlocks with its own name, it also supplied them to other makers. The distinctive shape of the action, with its unique lever and doll's-head third bite, make a Westley Richards instantly recognizable.

twining streets lined with shops, and each shop had its own specialty.

One might be an action filer; another a barrel maker; a third would specialize in blacking barrels, or case-hardening frames and locks. A gunmaker would take an order for a gun, or a dozen guns, and then farm out the individual functions to subcontractors.

In 1900, the greatest Birmingham names were Westley Richards and W.W. Greener. This is interesting, because Westley Richards was not a typical Birmingham gunmaker. Its shop was not in the gun quarter of the city, and its practices more closely followed those of London than of its "Brummy" compatriots.

Greener was a fine gunmaker, but also a major mass-producer of firearms. At one time, William Greener could claim that his factory was the largest civilian gunmaking plant in the world. Other prominent names included Birmingham Small Arms (BSA), Vickers, and Webley & Scott. The latter was a merging of P. Webley and W&C Scott, both companies famed for their work with Birmingham's Anson & Deeley boxlock and variations thereof.

W.W. Greener was, after Westley Richards, Birmingham's greatest proponent of the boxlock action. As an inventor, he contributed the now-ubiquitous Greener crossbolt third fastener. Much less successful (quite rare, in fact) is the Greener "Watershed" rib, shown here.

William Powell & Son is often referred to as the "Purdey of Birmingham," a nickname that is not unjustified. The company traces its roots to 1802, and has occupied its premises at Carrs Lane for almost 150 years. Powell still makes fine guns, although today its mail-order catalog of shooting clothing and equipment is the dominant part of the business. What is very unusual is that the company was, until early 2008, run by two brothers who are direct descendants of the founder. At that time, the company was purchased by Mark Osbourne, one of the partners who resurrected E.J. Churchill in the mid-1990s.

Powell, however, is not a typical Birmingham gunmaker and it is significant that the two Birmingham companies that have survived, and are thriving in the 21st century, are the two that most closely copied London methods.

If one were to generalize about Birmingham, aside from the methods used to produce guns, it would be to call it a military center, a mass-production center, and a maker of a wide variety of guns, but specializing in none. London specialized in best sidelock shotguns and double rifles, with a few bolt actions, and today that is all that is made there. Birmingham did not specialize except, perhaps, in boxlocks, and bit by bit the Birmingham gun trade crumbled in the face of changing world demand, new designs, social evolution, foreign competition, and not least, the demise of the empire it served.

Unarguably, the finest Birmingham guns were the equal of almost anything made in London. Equally unarguably, there were far fewer of these guns than there were lower-grade weapons of all varieties.

In the halcyon days of the late 1800s, gun ownership in Britain was largely unencumbered. Any countryman could own a shotgun, and most did. For that matter, rifle shooting was a national passion for several decades, with long-range rifle teams crisscrossing the Atlantic to challenge the Americans, the Irish, the Canadians, and the Australians at 1000-yard matches. Greener, John Rigby, and George Gibbs of Bristol were major names in target rifles.

With shooting so popular, every local blacksmith and ironmonger (the English term for hardware store) was also a gunshop, and many sold decent shotguns with their own names engraved on the ribs or the side of the frame. These guns were made mostly in Birmingham, whose gunmaking specialists did a thriving trade in such guns.

Exactly where the term "in the trade" originated is not known, but it may well have been Birmingham. Today, many shotguns and rifles emanating from London are made in the trade. William Evans, a famous London name for more than a century, has never had a factory of its own, and every gun and rifle bearing the highly respected Evans name has been made in the trade.

"In the trade" denotes a gun made more or less in the Birmingham fashion, with independent craftsmen working from their homes or small shops, each performing a different function. The unfinished gun travels from shop to shop, and home to home, gradually evolving into a finished gun. Since these craftsmen all apprentice with a company like H&H or Purdey, and are highly skilled enough to survive on their own, such a gun can be the equal of any.

There are currently tens of thousands of guns in circulation, boxlocks and sidelocks, that bear unfamiliar names. Some may be small provincial gunmakers, but the majority are the names of long-disappeared local companies whose guns were made for them in Birmingham. Such a gun can be of a quality that belies its mysterious origins. More than one such gun bearing an obscure name was actually made, in the trade, by Westley Richards, and some of these are recognizable by the distinctive shape of the Westley Richards frame, with either a long, graceful top lever, or a doll's-head third bite with a sliding bar operated by the lever. Not all, but some.

This is part of the fascination of English shotguns. A Purdey may carry a 20 percent premium on its name alone, but another gun, just as desirable in its own way, may command an abnormally low price because its maker is an unknown. Most of the latter began life in Birmingham.

Essentially English:
Elements of the game gun

The English game gun is the most graceful of firearms, as this E.M. Reilly London 'best' boxlock clearly shows.

The British call their definitive shotgun a "game gun." The term differentiates a high-quality gun from a "keeper's gun," a waterfowling gun, or even a punt gun.

While British shotguns come in every imaginable shape and size, the game gun is the standard from which the others deviate. It is also the pattern that is most desirable to American hunters and shooters who are seeking a nice English side-by-side.

In broad terms, a game gun can be described as follows: A 12-bore, with 28-inch barrels choked 1/4 and 1/2, double triggers, and a straight stock with minimal drop. It weighs from 6 1/4 to 6 3/4 pounds. It can be either sidelock or boxlock, but when picturing a game gun, most conjure a sidelock. The gun has 2 1/2-inch chambers and is proofed for a 1 1/16-ounce load. The gun will be regulated with #6 shot (the equivalent of American #7) and will pattern best with that shot size and load.

When you consider it, there is not much that flies and is shot on the wing, anywhere in the world, that could not be handled more than adequately by such a gun and load, in the hands of a good shot.

The game gun is intended primarily for shooting driven birds—red grouse, pheasant, partridge, woodcock—but is equally sound for birds flushing over dogs, walked-up snipe, and flighting ducks. This is the standard pattern that evolved in Britain during the heyday of estate shooting, from 1890 to 1914, when there was intense competition among estate owners for total bags, among individual guns for shooting records, and among gunmakers themselves to produce the guns that made it possible. It was a crucible that quickly devoured anything that did not work.

This is not to say there were not differences of opinion, and some gunmakers deliberately—and even flamboyantly—flouted collective wisdom and tried marketing something completely different.—Robert Churchill and his 25-inch barrelled 'XXV' springs to mind. But by and large, tribal knowledge was collected, accepted, and shared. The greatest competition among gunmakers was to do the same things, but do them better.

The gun described above, with a few minor cavils, is almost the ideal upland gun for North America. With such a gun, one could hunt woodcock in the thickest cover, chukars on a mountainside, pheasants in cornfields, and bobwhite quail bursting from the briars.

Compare this now with a typical American double gun from the same era. The American gun will be heavier, the barrels may be longer and they will almost certainly be more tightly choked, and there will be considerably more drop in the stock. The reason is simple: The typical American side-by-side was intended as an "all-around gun," and at the turn of the century, the major wingshooting target in America was ducks. The vast majority of Parkers, A.H. Foxes, and Ithacas were duck guns first, and upland guns second at best. Because you have to make such a gun to the lowest common denominator (proofed for the heaviest loads, choked tightly enough to concentrate the shot and reach out), they are generally poor grouse guns.

There are, of course, exceptions. All the good American makers built smaller-gauge guns as well, and many (particularly Foxes) were built as upland guns. The best examples of these bear an uncanny resemblance to an English game gun.

One could paint all kinds of sociological pictures of why and how this divergence in taste and style came about. Essentially, though, three elements went into American shotgun design: The German heritage of many American gunmakers (to this day, Germans favor multipurpose guns), the "hunting for food" motive of American gunners, and Americans' background as a "nation of riflemen."

For the British wingshooter of the late 1800s, shotgunning was recreational, and their guns reflected this. They were not looked upon as mere tools with which to gather food. For the modern American shotgunner, for whom wingshooting is purely recreational, an English game gun can be just the ticket.

* * *

There are myriad technical niceties in a fine shotgun, all of which can be studied, analyzed, and debated into the ground, but the qualities the English sought in a gun can be summarized quite simply: Fine, responsive handling combined with reliability and extreme durability.

Handling is a combination of weight and balance that ensures the gun comes to the shoulder, swings smoothly, and shoots where you are looking. Reliability and durability are the result of a combination of the best basic materials and first-rate workmanship.

Just as a gun can be too heavy, it can also be too light. Through experience, the British arrived at the "96 times" formula. This rule states that the optimum weight of a gun is 96 times its intended shot charge. Conveniently, 96 divides nicely by 16, the number of ounces in a pound.

So, for example, a 16-bore shooting one ounce of shot should weigh 96 ounces (96 x 1) or exactly six pounds. A six-pound 16-gauge double? What could be nicer?

A 12-bore shooting $1^1/_{16}$ ounces of shot should weigh 102 ounces (96 x $1^1/_{16}$), or six pounds, six ounces. For an upland 12 this is very nice indeed. A 28-bore with a $^3/_4$-ounce load would come in at four and a half pounds. Too light? Probably. For most people to shoot well, that is not heavy enough—at which point the English gunmaker starts to make adjustments. With smaller bores for normal adults, the usual approach is to lengthen the pull by up to a half inch, often combined with longer barrels. This moves the weight forward and compensates for their inherently light barrels.

In a shotgun, weight is a factor to be considered in relation to several things: How it dampens recoil for the shooter and saves the gun from taking too much punishment, how it affects balance and swing, and how difficult it becomes to shoulder a gun through a day of shooting at hundreds, or even thousands, of driven birds. One could argue that any of these is the most important consideration, but probably most shooters would choose the effect of gun weight on swing as the most critical. After all, swing is what kills birds and break targets; if a gun won't do that, what else matters?

The average American, picking up a high-quality English gun for the first time, is struck by how light it feels. The key word is "feels." It may not actually be all that light, but it feels lighter because of its fine balance, or weight distribution. Reams of copy paper and gallons of ink have been expended by shooting writers over the past century trying to define balance, or measure balance, or come up with a formula for balance. The English writer Gough Thomas (G.T. Garwood) even experimented with a pendulum-type device, trying to accomplish this. Since Garwood was a devoted shooter, a student of the gun, *and* a professional engineer, if he could not do it, I certainly do not expect to.

All one can say is that, when you pick up a beautifully balanced gun, you will know it. For the author, that "road to Damascus" moment came in 1993 when, for the first time, I was handed a Boss game gun from between the wars. I had handled fine guns before, and have handled many more since, but nothing—*nothing*—approaches that Boss. The only thing standing between me and it was the $50,000 price tag for the pair of them. The moment had a lasting effect because it set in motion a search for a gun that I could afford, that had that same balance, that same feel. In 2002, I took delivery of a gun from Grulla Armas in Spain, the fourth gun I had had made there as part of this search, that finally came close.

Two years later, I happened upon an English gun of obscure make, an E.M. Reilly from around 1890, that had that "Boss" feel. The Reilly was from the golden age of English gunmaking and it showed. The Reilly is a boxlock, and was originally made as a gift for a Scottish gamekeeper, so technically I suppose it is a "keeper's gun." I mention this just to show that a gun need not be a $50,000 Boss in order to have this elusive quality of perfect balance.

The Reilly has 30-inch barrels, but weighs just 6 lb. 4 oz. Therein lies the key to its wonderful balance. Long barrels, but light barrels, with the weight moved forward. Boss's artisans achieved their legendary handling by skillfully striking the barrels until the walls were as thin as God and the proofhouse would allow. This painstaking work cannot be done by machine, it can be done only by a highly skilled craftsman with a file. It takes time, and time is money.

This side of the fabled Boss, however, are thousands and tens of thousands of guns that offer balance and handling that make the mouth water and put to shame anything mass produced today.

* * *

The question of weight as it relates to recoil is a concern because it affects longevity. The surest way to retire a gun permanently is to subject it to a steady diet of loads that are too heavy and too powerful. It is not the extra pressure that hurts the gun. It is the jarring recoil that eventually causes fatigue, loosens parts, and increases wear.

Stay on the civilized side of loads for which the gun was intended, however, and it will last virtually indefinitely. In Chapter 1, we told the story of the Boss that stood duty at Eley Brothers for decades, test-firing one and a half million rounds.

A Joseph Lang sidelock made in 1906, with 27-inch barrels. Built as a typical game gun, it is almost ideal for upland game in America or, as in the case of this greywing partridge, South Africa.

Of course, recoil also affects the shooter. A gun that is light as a feather and easy to carry will also kick like a mule. This may not matter much when hunting ruffed grouse, where the hunter walks a lot and shoots only a little, but it certainly matters in any kind of high-volume shooting, whether it is driven pheasants in England or doves in the Southwest.

Every shooter has his (or her) limits, within which a gun is comfortable to carry *and* comfortable to shoot, easy to mount and smooth to swing, sometimes for hundreds of shots. Exceeding those limits is a mistake that will result in various bad things, from a chronic flinch to an inability to hit anything.

Felt recoil is governed by more than weight of gun and power of load. Fit is also important. How many times have we read of kids who were handed an old L.C. Smith double, and were almost put off shooting for life because it kicked like the devil? Most of those old guns were heavy, but they also had excessive drop. In a duck gun, more drop is desirable because it causes the gun to shoot naturally low. When ducks are coming in to decoys, that is a good feature.

English guns have much straighter stocks as a rule, because when shooting driven game that is coming toward you, you want the gun to shoot ahead of the bird, which amounts to shooting high. The same applies with walked-up birds that flush ahead of you. They are rising, so you want the pattern high rather than low.

Coincidentally, a straight stock that gives a slightly high pattern also has the effect of dampening recoil by directing it straight to the rear, whereas a gun with excessive drop acts as a fulcrum. The muzzle jumps and the gun rears up into your face. In combination, a lighter gun but with a straighter stock can be more comfortable to shoot for long periods than a heavier gun with more drop.

Similarly, by American standards, a British gunstock is longer (greater length of pull), which moves the weight forward, improves the swing, and reduces felt recoil.

* * *

It is standard practice in England for beginning shooters of every stripe to get professional shooting lessons, and to be measured for their gun. The gun is then made to measure. English terminology for such a gun is "bespoke," just as it is for a tailored suit or a pair of boots.

It is safe to say that the vast majority of high-quality English shotguns were originally bespoke guns, and were made to dimensions that range from fairly normal to wildly unusual, depending on the physical characteristics of the original owner. There are, however, no "standard dimensions" for a custom-made gun.

In America today, a shotgun off the rack will have a stock that is straight (that is, no cast-on or -off), with a length of pull around 14^1/4 inches and drop at heel of 2^1/2 inches or a little more. This stock is usable by almost anyone, but ideal for almost no one. But there is really no alternative for a company that is turning out thousands of guns a year, and selling them to gun stores by the bushel.

Conversely, high-quality English guns were turned out one at a time, for a specific client, and the stock was tailored to that gentleman's particular requirements and physical characteristics.

The most obvious consideration in gun fit is whether the shooter is right- or left-handed and, to a lesser extent, whether the dominant eye is right or left. This determines whether a stock will have cast-off (a slight bend to the right, seen from behind) or cast-on (a slight bend to the left). Cast allows the gun to come to the shoulder with the shooter's eye more closely aligned, looking straight down the bore instead of across it at a slight angle.

After cast, the most usual variation is length of pull (it can be long or short), followed by amount of drop at comb and heel, and the amount the toe of the stock cants to right or left.

When the original owner dies or sells his gun, and a new owner acquires it, it is standard practice for the British to alter the stock to fit the new owner. It can be shortened by cutting or lengthened by adding a recoil pad or ebony stock extension; it can be bent to left or right to eliminate cast, increase cast, or change from cast-off to cast-on. Bending is done by heating the stock and applying linseed oil, all the while applying pressure in a jig until the stock takes its new shape.

Lower-grade guns produced in England, such as the thousands of boxlock non-ejectors produced by W.W. Greener and BSA, were made to standard dimensions, but their buyers may have subsequently had the stocks altered to fit them. A man who could not afford a full-blown bespoke London gun could afford a production boxlock, and then a few pounds' worth of fitting to make it shoot well for him.

The result of all this is that any given British gun, pulled off a gun rack in middle America, might or might not fit the prospective buyer. But even if it doesn't, it can be made to fit through professional, skilled stock alteration. For the majority of British-gun buyers today, this is almost an automatic course of action simply because the chances of finding a gun you like, that you can afford, that fits perfectly, are very, very slim.

And, what is the point of spending thousands of dollars on a gun that does not fit you, and not trying to do something about it?

Through a Hundred Seasons:
What makes a 'best' gun best

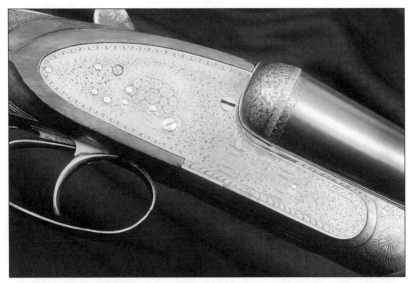

Rose and scroll engraving on this H.J. Hussey Imperial Ejector (c. 1910) sidelock is typical for a London best. Note that the case colors have all but disappeared on the surface metal, but still lurk in the depths of the engraving, imparting dark shadows and giving the lock a pleasing appearance. Greener's "beauty of newness" is long-since gone, replaced by the beauty of use.

As far as I can determine, the concept of the "best" gun originated with the British gunmakers, and they are still its supreme practitioners. Undoubtedly, the Italians, Basques, French, and Germans make some superb shotguns, and a few are in the same league as an English best. But the overall principle remains British, and it also remains largely misunderstood.

A best gun is not merely the finest model a gunmaker happens to produce. This seems to be the modern interpretation, and I have seen it applied to some guns that were anything but. Nor does ornate presentation have anything to do with it. Taking a ho-hum gun and slathering it with engraving and gold inlay does not make a best gun; all it makes is a gun that is in questionable taste.

With shotguns, what is on the outside should reflect what is on the inside.

A best gun is always made to be used—always. It is not made to put on display in a glass case. And, one should add, it is made to be used in the worst of conditions. An English best does not get the day off simply because it looks like rain.

For the past century, the concept of the best gun has been the foundation of the English gunmaking industry. Knowing what goes into a best, even makers of less expensive guns tried to incorporate as many essential features as they could. Gunmakers who produced a range of models, including a best, often ended up making less profit on their cheaper models than they wanted to because they found themselves making them to higher standards. When a gun is hand-made, even a low-end one, the craftsmen can make it as well or as poorly as they choose that day. Most chose, when time allowed, to make it better than required.

Pride played a very large role. For more than a century, Purdey has been acclaimed as England's greatest gunmaker, partly perhaps because Lord Ripon, among others, shot Purdeys. But the title was not unchallenged. Holland & Holland would have disputed it, as would Boss & Co., Charles Lancaster, James Woodward. The competition was intense, and pride in their work drove every company and every craftsman to produce the best—in every sense of the word.

In 2007, the editor of *Guns & Ammo*, Richard Venola, asked me to explain a best gun for his readers. What follows appeared in *G&A*, in somewhat truncated form. Here I have expanded on some points, but overall I felt the best way to explain a best gun was to show what they could do under the worst of circumstances.

* * *

August 12, 1998—the "Glorious Twelfth," irrevocable opening day for red grouse in England—dawned in a monsoon of sweeping rains.

A North Atlantic gale struck the Scottish coast, driving heavy clouds across the grouse counties of Scotland and England, and the BBC was reporting flooding across the north. It was hardly a day to go shooting, but in the big-money world of the red grouse, the Glorious Twelfth is sacrosanct —to say nothing of the fortune riding on the day's success.

The "guns" (shooters, to an American) have paid ten thousand pounds each to be there, and the gamekeepers, loaders, beaters, stoppers, pickers-up with their dogs, and bird-wagon drivers are standing by. Not only that, helicopters (or, on this socked-in day, eager trucks) are waiting to carry the day's first bag to the fashionable restaurants of London, and long-term contracts with game dealers across Europe mean the estate owner's finances ride on the daily bag of grouse from now until December.

So shooting we went, clad in oilskins and rubber boots.

After a long day pouring water from our gun barrels and stabbing at grouse that materialized out of the fog, trudging from one line of butts to the next knee-deep in mud, we returned with 64 brace (128 grouse) to show for our efforts, to empty the water from our rubber boots and repair to a blazing fire and some steaming tea.

In the gun room, the loaders gathered around an ancient, heavy wooden table strewn with cleaning rods, cloths, oil, and the bits and pieces of shotguns. There lay forends from Churchills, barrels from Holland & Hollands, and stocks and frames of a dozen revered names ranging back a century and more.

My friend Tom, a freelance loader, was humming away as he stripped down a matched pair of Stephen Grant sidelever guns belonging to a surgeon from Denver, mopping pools of water from the frames. Loaders today are professionals in the world of driven shooting, driving their Land Rovers from shoot to shoot, providing dogs and expertise to the guns who hire them. Some carry engraved business cards in the vest pockets of their J.J. Cording tweeds. Many loaders come from the world of gunmaking, and thorough gun care is second nature.

"Not the first time this old gun has seen a day like this," Tom grinned. "This rain is unusual for August, but come November . . ."

I was inspecting the bits Tom had laid out on the table. These guns had done spectacular duty that day: I saw the surgeon deck a pair of birds at a dozen yards as they came pounding in, dropping one into the butt beside Tom as he stuffed shells into the second gun.

"How old are they?" I asked.

"Not sure," Tom said. "Close to a hundred years. Before the first war anyway."

"And they've been shooting all this time?"

"All this time."

* * *

There are many misconceptions about the English game gun, which is traditionally a 12-bore side-by-side, either sidelock or boxlock, made to exacting standards and intended for high-volume driven shooting.

One belief is "you're paying for the name." You're not. Another is that a new gun costs $50,000 because of the engraving in the steel or the walnut in the stock. Not true. Even coated in stove paint and stocked with a two-by-four, a Holland & Holland would still cost a mint.

Why? Hand labor. A standard game gun requires 900 hours of skilled work. Multiply that by the hourly rate for a craftsman. At $40, that's $36,000. Plus materials. Plus overhead. It adds up quickly.

And why pay for this hand labor? One major reason: To get the kind of meticulous fit and finish that allow a gun to go into the field, day after day, in rain and sleet, take the pounding of thousands of rounds, season after season, and continue doing so without breaking down, without a pause, for a hundred years.

Back between the wars, the British shotshell maker Eley Brothers had a Boss & Co. game gun they used for random ammunition testing. Their tester would take a pair of cartridges off the line, go into the tunnel, fire two shots, and go back for more. This went on for years. During that time, this "ordinary" Boss fired an estimated 1.5-million rounds. It did so, reportedly, requiring no major repairs. When the original plant closed, the gun disappeared. For all anyone knows, it is still out there, shooting away.

That is phenomenal endurance for any gun. For a game gun weighing six and a half pounds, it is unbelievable. The secret lies in hand-fitting the parts so closely there is no play, no tolerance, and no built-in self-destruction. Guns that rattle soon rattle more, and eventually rattle themselves to pieces. Not a fine game gun: Its parts work closely together almost as one. So hand labor contributes durability. It also creates the legendary handling qualities.

Boss guns, for example, were renowned for their light weight and exceedingly fine balance and swing. They achieved this by using long barrels with walls struck as thin as the proof house would allow. This cannot be done by machine, only by a highly skilled, meticulous man with a file. It takes many hours, and hours cost money.

The result, however, is a gun that, when you hold one for the first time, reveals in a blinding light what a fine shotgun can be. It is a life-changing experience for a shooter. I know because it happened to me. I have never owned a Boss, but I have longed for one since the day I first held one.

* * *

A British best gun (and this applies to best guns made anywhere) is one that is finished to the ultimate level. It may not be perfect in the absolute sense, but it is as good as human hands can make it, and no amount of further work will make it better. The gun is, of course, the sum of its parts, and its parts are made by specialists: the stocker, the actioner, the barrel maker. It is put together and made to work by the fitter, whose job it is to assemble the gun piece by piece and ensure that everything works as it should.

In the case of Holland & Holland, the gun then goes to the shooting ground at Northwood, where Steve Cranston, the resident barrel regulator, puts the gun through its paces.

"Each gun is fired a minimum of 250 rounds," Steve told me. "Every couple of hours I take a break from the bench, pick up a gun, and put a few more rounds through it."

Each time, he checks opening and closing, trigger pull, extraction and ejection, looking for the slightest fault.

One arcane feature of a best gun is the timing of the ejectors. The ejectors should throw the two hulls in a parallel arc and leave them lying side by side in the grass. If they fall far apart, it is a sign that one ejector or the other is not right. Does this matter? Only in the sense that Steve Denny, formerly with Churchill and now director of the H&H Shooting Ground, once explained.

"By concentrating on these tiny details, you ensure the overall mechanism is perfect," Steve said. "It is a way of instantly testing the standards to which a gun has been made."

A best gun is made up of tiny details. If you know what to look for, you can take a strange gun off a rack and know within seconds how good it was originally. And, it is useful to know, if a gun was a "best" to begin with, it can almost always be a "best" again if you are willing to spend some money.

For example, something as simple as the escutcheon in the stock, with the owner's initials. It's there for a reason. After my loader friends finished cleaning the guns at Knarsdale that rainy night in 1998, they placed them on a long rack in the gun room. This is standard practice on any shooting estate. When the loaders come to get their "gun's" guns the next day, from a row of 20 or more that all resemble one another, it is easy to check the initials. Very practical, and it saves your gun from being pawed by strange hands.

A "treble-bite" is a good indication, too. Although the double underlugs invented by James Purdey are amply strong even for double rifles, many gunmakers like to put a third locking lug somewhere. The Greener crossbolt is the most common. Purdey uses a hidden bite that fits a notch in the standing breech. These are finicky to fit, and not found on any gun intended to sell for a low price.

Then there are sideclips, the little wings on the standing breech that keep the barrels from flexing from side to side. Properly fitted, they are almost invisible when the gun is closed.

An added benefit of a rib-extension bite such as the Greener or the various doll's-heads is that they provide a rail that can be used to support and stabilize the extractors as they move in and out. How this rail is fitted (or not) is an indication of just how exacting the barrel maker and actioner were in making the gun.

Inside the locks you may find gold-plated parts or engine-turned (jewelled) flat surfaces. The gold, often dismissed as an affectation, serves the serious purpose of preventing rust. Jewelling helps hold oil, preventing rust and assisting smooth operation. When you remove the lock, you may notice little touches of decoration, such as an artistically crafted bridle (the main component to which others are attached). Some parts will be left with their case colors intact after hardening; sometimes screws will be nitre blued, giving them that bright, hard, translucent blue that is so attractive, and which contrasts nicely with an old-coin or rust-blued finish. When you see these touches, you know that the man who filed the locks took great pride in his work—even work that would rarely be seen by human eyes. If such care was taken over its appearance, you know that its functioning will be flawless.

On any gun, screws have an alarming tendency to back out under constant recoil. Tiny, almost invisible, set screws prevent them from coming loose. A fine maker will then engrave the screw heads in such a way as to camouflage the set screws.

Another good indication of quality on double-trigger guns is an articulated, or hinged, front trigger. This acts as a shock absorber when the rear trigger is pulled and recoil slams the front trigger into the shooter's finger.

One of my favorite features are the gas-escape holes in the standing breech. These are incorporated into the striker disk, a small round steel plug with a hole in the center through which the striker protrudes. Additional holes in the disk serve the dual purpose of diverting escaping gas and allowing the use of a two-pronged tool to remove them. Should a striker break, it can be replaced without disassembling the entire action.

And speaking of strikers, a really fine gun from years past will have tiny bevelled notches on the extractors to gently cam the strikers back into the standing breech and out of the way, if one should happen to stick when the gun is opened. Since the advent of spring-loaded strikers this is unlikely, which is why the feature is seldom found on newer "best" guns.

Every tiny feature, it seems, has its purpose rooted in long experience.

Take the standard practice of having all the screw slots aligned. Pointless affectation? Not at all: The shooter can tell at a glance if a screw is backing out.

* * *

August 13, 1998 was not quite so bad. The rain came and went. The fog came and went. The birds came, and a few—but not that many—flew on. Ten guns delivered almost triple the bag of the day before, the estate owner's bird wagons rumbled back fully loaded, and the continental game dealers and their grouse-loving restaurateurs were happy.

The surgeon and his matched Stephen Grants were methodically deadly on this, the first of seven weeks of driven shooting he had booked in England, Spain, and Hungary.

For a pair of guns crafted lovingly at a bench a century ago, by hands long dead, it was a performance both splendid and routine. Those guns have been doing it, wielded by a succession of hands also long dead, season after season, and will continue to do so long after the Denver surgeon has gone to his reward and the two Stephen Grant guns have passed to a new (temporary) owner.

That's what makes a best gun best.

* * *

When the conversation turns to best guns, the subject of engraving inevitably comes up. Aside from the misconception that a large part of the price of a London best is for the engraving, there is a general misunderstanding about the role of engraving, not just on a best, but on any gun.

Firearm engraving is more a natural subject for a photo essay than for the written word, and therein lies the problem: In any discussion of engraving, the viewer is all too likely to become absorbed by the beauty of what he sees, and pay no attention whatever to its utility.

Utility? Yes, utility—because engraving has a definite function beyond decoration or self-indulgence. In fact, it has two purposes: One is to reduce glare off a shiny surface, and the second is to help retain oil to prevent rust. Forget all the claptrap about "personal totems" and turning your game gun into an expression of your individuality: Essentially, engraving serves the same purpose as a good coat of stove paint.

Bluing does the same things, but in a different way. And I suppose you could say the same about case-coloring, at least in part. W.W. Greener said that engraving served a third purpose: To soften stark lines and ugly joints, and to give the gun a pleasing appearance after the "beauty of newness" was long gone.

Even when Greener wrote *The Gun and its Development* (beginning in 1881 and continuing, through nine editions, to 1910), engraving as an art form was starting to grow beyond its original purpose and border on decadence. It was becoming so elaborate that it hindered, rather than assisted, not only in its own purpose, but in the purpose of the gun on which it was found. In extreme cases (some Austrian monstrosities come to mind), a gun can have engraving that makes it fragile or even physically difficult to handle; it can also be so ornate the owner is afraid to use it for fear of damaging the engraving.

As the game gun was developed and perfected through the late 1800s, each gunmaker adopted certain features and refinements as being distinctly his own. Stephen Grant espoused the side lever, Purdey the triple bite, Thomas Boss the round action. Similarly, each had his own preferred engraving style. Since every best-quality gun was made to order, and most clients had their own ideas, patterns were found anywhere and everywhere. Still, some came to be identified with a particular maker.

Boss-style engraving is unique and recognizable at a glance. By today's standards, it is understated to the point of obscurity. Although technically "full coverage" engraving, it consists of islands of scroll with considerable areas of blank steel. The scroll surrounds rosettes, and is tiny, tiny, *tiny*—so small and delicate it demands a magnifying glass. Viewed from a distance, the lines of scroll dissolve into broad brush strokes that soften yet enhance the lines of the sensuous Boss round action.

The word "sensuous" is not used lightly. A good shotgun, like a good dog, longs to be stroked. It not only looks good, it feels good when you run your hands over it. Over the years, engraving smooths out, and this is pleasant to the touch.

Greener points out that, on a new gun, case hardening provides all the beauty that is needed. As the gun ages, however, the case colors fade, leaving the steel "dirty white" (his term), at which point you need engraving to keep the gun attractive. You will notice we use the term "case hardening," whereas many makers today refer to "case colors." There is a difference. In the former, a process is used to harden the skin of the steel, and the colors are incidental; in the latter, no hardening takes place, only the imparting of the colors. It is, in effect, a kind of chemical engraving that serves no functional purpose.

Signature engraving pattern on a Thomas Boss: Round clumps of roses, surrounded by scroll. This gun dates from about 1885 and has been well used, but its engraving has embraced the years, been softened but not defaced, and is more elegant than ever.

To backtrack for a moment, most shotguns are made of relatively soft steel. A century ago, a gun was shaped by chisel and file, then hardened and tempered to give the desired qualities. Bluing, case hardening, and even engraving all played their parts in this. With the emergence of stainless steel (which is generally nickel steel), all of the above became more difficult. Nickel was originally called devil's copper (or Old Nick's copper, hence the name) because it was so difficult to work with. Alloying steel with nickel or chromium may make it stainless, but it also makes it much more difficult for the craftsman to shape with a file—and shaping with a file is the only way yet found to create a best gun that will endure for centuries.

As the gun neared completion, the actioner passed the locks and frame to the finisher, who assembled it, regulated the triggers and ejectors, and polished it in preparation for engraving. The locks and frame were "in the white" when they were turned over to the engraver, who, working on the soft, buttery steel, could create a work of art with no more than a gentle tapping of the chaser, or even palm pressure on the bulb of the graver. Only then were the parts sent to be case-hardened—baked in a devil's concoction of charcoal, bits of bone and leather, and a tuft of a virgin's flaxen hair. Every craftsman had his secret formula, with the result that the colors resulting from case hardening were as individual as engraving.

Functionally, case hardening introduces carbon into the steel, creating a glass-hard skin that resists scratches and rust. The colors range from deep blue to light straw in rippling waves. These colors eventually wear away, because in this case beauty is not even skin deep, but the hard skin of carbon steel remains. This was Greener's point about the beauty of newness. Where the steel is engraved, however, the colors are protected in its minute ravines. The unengraved steel around it turns a muted gray, while the engraving remains dark and mysterious. This is one reason why, short of structural damage or serious mutilation, refurbishing the frame of a shotgun is questionable. A gun that has acquired its patina through love and use should be allowed to keep it.

Today, with harder steel alloys that require no hardening for corrosion resistance, case colors are imparted using chemical baths. The result is what one might expect.

* * *

The world has changed since Greener's day, and engraving with it. Where he pointed out that engraving was but a tiny part of the expense of a fine gun, today engraving can cost as much as the rest of the gun put together. This would seem to contradict my earlier statement that a major part of the price of a best gun is the engraving, but it really doesn't.

There is the base price of the gun and then, if the buyer wants something other than the standard offerings of various scroll patterns or game scenes, he pays for it separately. Sometimes, prices are even quoted "engraving extra," because who knows what it will cost to send the gun to one of the handful of *artistes* whose backlogs extend into years. The engraving patterns they produce beggar belief. Fortunately, few of the guns that leave their studios will ever actually be used in the field, so their magnificent art is safe from the ravages of time.

The 1980s saw the beginning of an engraving fad called *bulino*. Bulino is much older than that, but that is when it really became popular in the United States. It is the art of reproducing birds and animals using tiny cuts that each raise a chip of steel, and the play of light and shadow creates a picture. The first great practitioners of the art were the Italians, and some of their creations were breathtaking. As bulino gained fans, its use filtered down to cheaper and cheaper guns. Two decades later, one comes across these from time to time—and time has not been kind.

The ghastly truth is that a bulino-engraved gun will never again look as

This newish Purdey has typical Purdey rose-and-scroll engraving, and the post-war case colors are still vivid. This gun was made for an American client (hence the gold-inlaid "London: England" to go with the rather self-conscious quail). The gun itself has a pistol grip, single trigger, and a monstrous beavertail forend.

good as the day it comes out of its protective box. Every scratch and bump will deface the engraving until it looks like a fly-specked lithograph in a cheap saloon. At which point, a coat of stove paint might not be a bad idea.

Greener again: "The greatest beauty of all is the elegant contour of a well-designed gun." Nowhere is this more true than in the side-by-side game gun, and the purpose of well-integrated engraving is to enhance those lines, not obscure them. Too often with bulino, the gun itself is but a piece of awkward canvas for the engraving, rather than the other way around.

Properly executed to begin with, engraving can add to the beauty of a gun no matter how much hard use it receives. Alas, the tiny scrolls that were inexpensive in Greener's day now cost as much as bulino and gold inlay Boss-pattern engraving, with its microscopic scrolls, is so difficult and time consuming, engravers all charge a premium for it—if you can find one to do it at all.

Just this side of Boss-style, however, are the small-scroll patterns that were found routinely on guns made in England from 1890 to 1914. In those days, any gun that aspired to be a best had full-coverage engraving. That meant the entire frame, except perhaps for some areas left as islands of natural steel for

Full-coverage engraving helps soften the somewhat abrupt lines of this Jeffery boxlock, which also retains a smattering of its case colors. This is a relatively new Jeffery— certainly post-war—and the ill effects of England's post-1945 world are evident.

artistic reasons. The forend iron and the steel tip would be engraved; the tang and lever; the trigger guard, to an extent. Sometimes the engraving extended out onto the breech end of the barrels. Whether a gun was a best (by our definition above) or not, full-coverage engraving usually indicated that this gun was the best you were likely to see from that particular shop.

This holds particularly true, in my experience, with boxlocks. There was a thriving trade in boxlocks made for a local "gunsmith," who was often the local ironmonger who sold the odd gun. He would place an order with Greener or Webley & Scott and a few months later take delivery of a boxlock made to his specifications with his name engraved on the barrel. Often, such guns would be for the vicar or magistrate, and they would have full-coverage engraving of tiny scroll. And, usually, it was very well done. In the years before 1914, special-order, high-quality work was routine; today, such engraving would cost a fortune.

If a man loves engraving as well as nice double guns, then older English guns of obscure name, especially boxlocks, offer an opportunity to own both at a fraction of what a comparable new gun would cost today.

My E.M. Reilly is typical of a gun from that era. It was made, I believe, in the early 1890s. It was a gift for a gamekeeper from his landowner, and the landowner obviously thought highly of his trusted employee, for he went to a London firm, on Oxford Street no less, and purchased their finest boxlock. I don't believe it is going too far to say that the gun was, for E.M. Reilly, a best boxlock. And E.M. Reilly was an established firm of impeccable credentials, occupying, at one time, premises adjacent to Purdey, and supplying guns to both Sir Samuel White Baker and Frederick Courteney Selous.

After I acquired it, I had the Reilly refurbished. Its indescribable French-walnut stock was completely reworked, after decades of use by a gamekeeper who valued the metal but disdained the wood. The frame of the gun, however, blanketed with tiny scrolls on metal that long since ceased to have any case colors, was not touched. More than a century of use has given the frame a beauty and character that money could not buy. While it was in his care, my gunmaker, Edwin von Atzigen, told me, he would take out the frame and just gaze at the engraving, or finger the bits and pieces—so intricately made, so commonplace in 1890, so rare, costly or simply nonexistent today.

The scroll engraving—tiny, dark, and mysterious, more beautiful now than the day it was executed—is a big part of that, but still only a part. That is what engraving should be.

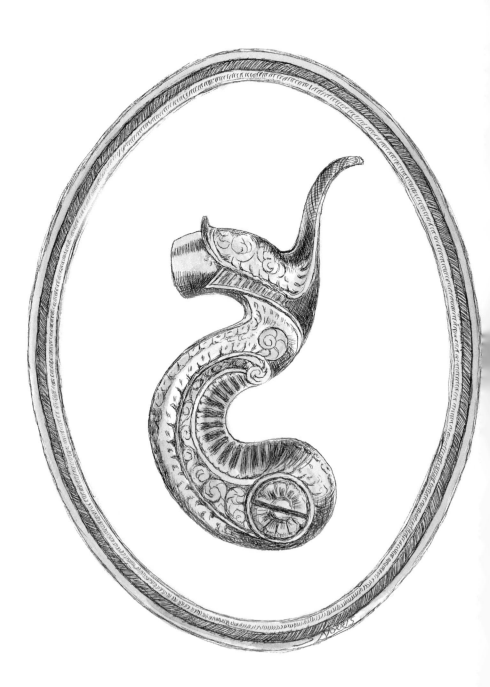

The Hammer Gun:
A glorious anachronism

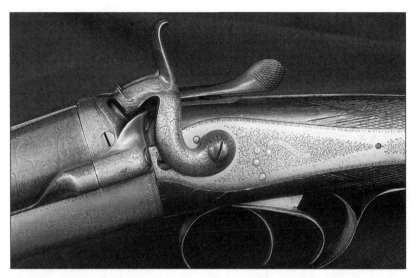

An H. Holland 12-bore hammer gun from the very early days of break-action guns, employing Scott's patented breech bolting system. Although hammer guns later became somewhat standardized, early guns often utilize arcane bolting systems and other features, making them that much more fascinating.

Hammer guns. Ah, hammer guns!

According to Michael McIntosh (and he should know), "God the Father shoots a Purdey hammer gun." And King George V once remarked that a gun without hammers "looks like a spaniel without ears."

Obviously, hammer guns are romantic artifacts that are revered in the highest circles. While some modern shooters may dismiss hammer guns as anachronisms, old-fashioned and inefficient, others treasure them for their history and their almost mythical fine handling. It has been written by more than one authority that the finest-handling gun of all time was a James Purdey with hammers and Damascus barrels.

Whether this is strictly true is open to question. What is unquestionable, however, is the fact that today hammer guns with Damascus barrels can almost always be obtained for considerably less money than a hammerless gun with fluid-steel barrels from the same maker—even from James Purdey & Sons. As such, the hammer gun represents an opportunity for the gun lover of average means to own and shoot a small bit of rich history.

In the closing years of the 20th century, hammer guns enjoyed a brief flare in popularity in the United States. This was due to a number of factors. One was the influence of the Order of Edwardian Gunners, or Vintagers. Another was the search among shotgunners for something different. Others, historians at heart, liked to hunt grouse and woodcock with a hammer gun simply because of its connection with a distant age.

The price spike that accompanied this surge in interest has now largely passed, and hammer guns are once again for sale at prices considerably lower than comparable "modern" guns.

The prospective buyer of a hammer gun is faced with almost countless variations. There is no standard hammer gun design, any more than there is a standard sidelock (although some are more common than others). From the early era of break-action guns, through the pinfire to the centerfire cartridge, up to and including the displacement of Damascus barrels by fluid steel and blackpowder by smokeless, hammer guns underwent a continuous evolution.

Essentially, the hammer gun uses external hammers, one on each side, attached to a lock plate, to hit the striker and fire the primer. Each hammer has its own trigger and the hammers are usually cocked by the shooter's thumb. In 1867, the lock maker Stanton patented rebounding hammers—hammers that return to a partial-cock position after firing—making it faster and easier to open the gun. This is an extremely useful feature to look for if you are in the market for a hammer gun.

From 1851, when Joseph Lang produced the first break-action gun in England, until 1875, hammer guns were the norm. In 1875, William Anson and John Deeley designed the boxlock action, specifically to produce an alternative to the hammer gun and move the firing mechanism inside the receiver. Hammer guns lived on, however, even after the parallel development of the sidelock gun, in which the hammers are inside (and renamed tumblers), but still attached to a plate on the side of the gun.

Some shooters resisted the boxlock and sidelock and clung to hammer guns because of familiarity; others preferred the appearance; still others admired their handling. Whatever the reason, British gunmakers continued to make hammer guns long after the boxlock and sidelock had largely taken

A James Purdey & Sons pinfire 20-bore double rifle with Damascus barrels and sliding hammer safeties. This gun dates from the period when rifles and shotguns were in the process of going their separate ways.

This 12-bore by William Griffiths, who was in business on his own in Manchester from 1855 to the 1870s, has both great style and some very interesting features. Of the latter, perhaps the most unusual are the retracting strikers, held in place with set screws, and the shape of the hammers. The sweeping, rounded fences flow beautifully from the top strap.

over—and hammer guns are still being made to this day.

Practically speaking, the hammer gun enjoys certain advantages over its more advanced cousin, the sidelock. First, it is a simple mechanism that is easy to make, very durable, and can be considerably cheaper. There are fewer moving parts in the lock, and some other functions, such as a cocking mechanism and a safety, are dispensed with altogether.

The mechanism on the inside of the lock plate consists of a spring and sear, and not much more. Hammers are cocked by the thumb, which is almost foolproof and eliminates cocking dogs. The shooter and those around him can tell at a glance if the gun is cocked, and therefore a hazard. The barrels can be cocked one at a time, as needed—another safety feature. And speaking of safeties, since there is no need of a safety mechanism *per se* (although some hammer guns do have them), the whole gun is that much simpler again, with less wood cut from the butt stock to make room for a safety.

With the firing mechanism on the outside of the frame, the frame itself can be slimmer and more graceful. The wood of butt and forend is also more graceful because it is mating with the sveldt frame.

One consideration that should not be ignored is pure beauty. The hammers themselves were pieces of sculpted steel that were often artistic masterpieces. Distinctively shaped hammers became a signature of some gunmakers and ranged from the purely utilitarian to the exotically fanciful. One finds hammers shaped like animals, or dragons, or birds; the thumb piece can stick straight up like a rabbit's ear, or lie back like a horse's mane. Most have a seahorse profile that is always racy and makes the gun appear eager to hunt something.

While beauty was desirable, however, function was vital, and making a hammer that would work perfectly, shot after shot, year after year, required masterful gunmaking skills. On the surface, fashioning a proper hammer looks simple. But consider the demands on this one piece of curved steel: At one end, where the hammer strikes the firing pin, the steel must be hard enough to withstand peening for thousands and thousands of blows. Yet, it must be tough enough that it will not shatter. Similarly, at the other end where the hammer fits onto the axle, the steel must be exactly hard enough that it does not wear on the axle, and the axle does not wear on it and become loose. In the stem, the hammer must be tough enough that it will neither deform nor crystallize and shatter. Meeting all these (sometimes contradictory) demands in one piece of steel is a serious challenge to one's ability to fashion steel and then heat-treat it appropriately.

Yet British gunmakers were able to make hammers that would stand up

A 12-bore from William Evans's very early days in the London gun trade. With its long top lever and beautifully shaped fences, this is a very graceful gun.

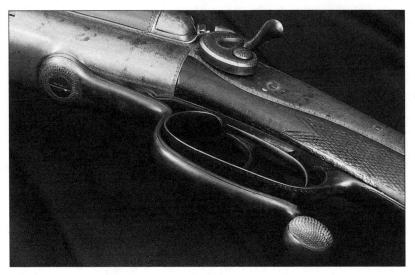

Because so many hammer guns are early, they range in shape from later examples of the percussion era, like this one with its Jones underlever, round frame, and back-action lock, to early examples of the sidelock era with bar-action locks and a squared frame.

to such wear, and still be beautifully shaped, and often beautifully engraved as well. British gunmakers were artistic, creative, sometimes fanciful, and almost unfailingly egotistical. A gunmaker who prided himself on the grace, beauty, and originality of his hammers was not about to give them up just because a couple of Birmingham upstarts (Anson and Deeley) had invented something better. *"Better? And just who's to say . . . ?"*

And so the hammer gun in various forms remained in common use right up until the outbreak of war in 1914.

* * *

There are some common variations among hammer guns. They were made in every bore size; today one sees a surprisingly large number of 10-bore hammer guns, and 8-bores are almost all hammer guns. Among the upland gauges, however, the 12 is most common; while hammerless 16-bores are relatively rare, there are quite a few 16-bore hammer guns floating about.

Hammer guns were made with both Damascus and fluid-steel barrels. While this subject will be explored in more detail in a later chapter, suffice to say that regardless of whether the barrels have been nitro-proofed (proofed with smokeless powder), a hammer gun with Damascus barrels may be perfectly safe with modern smokeless loads provided they are the correct length for the chamber. Most shooters either don't know that, or refuse to believe it, and as a result a hammer gun with Damascus barrels may sell at a serious discount compared to the same gun, by the same maker, with fluid steel.

Moving back toward the frame, we find quite a variety of bolting systems on hammer guns. Since many were made before the invention of the Scott spindle in 1865, or at least before its use became almost universal, many hammer guns have Jones underlevers. The Jones rotates to the side, and is shaped to cup the trigger guard. As a locking system, it is extremely strong, camming the barrels down tight as it is rotated into position. The Jones underlever was used on many heavy double rifles.

The drawback of the Jones system is speed. It is slower than most other bolting systems, since the barrels cannot be simply snapped shut. Nor does it lend itself to self-cocking mechanisms where the opening of the barrels powers the cocking dogs to cock the tumblers. But on a hammer gun this is generally not a consideration.

Other makers, most notably Stephen Grant, liked a side lever. This lever is usually on the right side of the frame, and is pressed down with the thumb to release the barrels. A side lever is very elegant.

Finally, there are hammer guns that utilize a Scott spindle and top lever, just like a boxlock. These are generally bolted shut with Purdey double underlugs. As hammer guns battled to stay alive, their makers tried to update

Isaac Hollis was a Birmingham gunmaker who also had a London branch at various times. This gun looks like a bar-action lock, but is actually a back action, with the spring behind the hammer. However, it has the overall shape of a later bar-action hammer gun, with its square frame. Yet another hammer gun variation!

This W&C Scott & Son 10-bore epitomizes the beauty and attraction of the hammer gun. This is a bar-action lock, whose engraving and case colors complement the pattern of the Damascus barrels. The lines of the hammers mirror those of the beautifully sculpted fences, and the result is an aesthetically integrated whole that is a pleasure to behold.

them, and one way of doing this was to make "self cocking" hammer guns. In these guns, the pivoting of the barrels cocks the hammers exactly the same way they cock the tumblers of a hammerless gun.

With such a mechanism installed, of course, the maker then needed to devise some sort of safety to prevent accidental discharges. Usually, this took the form of a sliding metal bar that fits into a notch in the back of the hammer itself. To fire the gun, these safety bars would be individually slid back. As systems go, it was awkward at best, but then a relatively tiny number of these guns were built.

The earliest hammer guns had "back action" sidelocks. That is, the lock plate extended to the rear, down the grip of the gun. The mainspring was attached to this long portion of the plate. This design is descended directly from flintlocks. The other design is the "bar action" lock, in which the mainspring is on a bar of the lock plate extending forward of the hammer.

When hammers were moved inside the gun to make them into "hammerless" sidelocks, both the back-action and bar-action approaches were retained. Each system has its advantages and disadvantages. Devotees of the back action sometimes claim it has a faster, more positive lock time because the spring is longer. Devotees of the bar action claim their stocks are stronger through the wrist because less wood is cut away; back-action people respond that their design leaves a stronger frame because less metal is removed to accommodate the spring.

Most people buy a hammer gun because the price is right, or because they like its appearance and balance, and do not let such considerations as the positioning of the mainspring sway them one way or the other as long as it works. Since nothing can really be proven conclusively in favor of either, there is no point belaboring it. It is worth noting, however, that hammerless sidelock double rifles are generally back-action locks (even though they may look like bar actions from the outside) because the added recoil and pressure of a rifle demand the strongest possible frame.

* * *

Although the usual motive for shooting a hammer gun today is nostalgia, or a desire to connect to the past, hammer guns can be extremely effective game guns.

For example, George Calef, a good friend of mine, bought two English guns. One was a William Evans boxlock, the other a William Needler hammer gun with Damascus barrels. Both were well made, and rejoiced in very

Graceful as only a Stephen Grant 16-bore side-lever hammer gun can be. Note how the lever fits around and with the hammer, easily accessible yet unobtrusive, both physically and visually. Aesthetics were extemely important to British gunmakers. Looking at this gun, one understands how some shooters of that day were extremely reluctant to give up their beloved hammer guns and move to the newer hammerless designs.

W.J. Jeffery 12-bore hammer gun. Not a best gun by any means, but solid and dependable. This gun has nitro-proofed fluid-steel barrels.

pretty walnut stocks. At the time, George expected to shoot the Evans most of the time, and take out the Needler only occasionally—when the weather was right or he felt the need for a change.

That was not at all what happened. Having obtained some light Kent shotshells that fit the Needler, George quickly found that it not only fit him like a glove, but was also extraordinarily deadly. Instead of taking the Needler out only for snipe or grouse, he ended up shooting most of the season with it, and hunting ducks, geese, and everything smaller.

"I bought the Needler on a complete whim after reading Steve Bodio's story in *Double Gun Journal*," Calef wrote me. "Saw it at Vintage Doubles and liked it much better than the Purdeys and Hollands he had there. The description said 'shoot a Purdey on a beer budget.' It is choked .007 and .029 with 30-inch barrels.

"I love the Needler and, had I bought it and shot it for a season first, would never have bothered with the Evans. The really amazing part is that the Needler at over seven pounds feels the same and carries more comfortably than the Evans at a pound lighter.

"Similarly, even with one ounce of shot, the Needler kills birds cleanly at 40 yds with the IC barrel. The pattern must be fantastic from the Needler, although I'm afraid to test it since it could only undermine my already unshakable faith in the weapon.

"In addition, there's something challenging about having to cock the hammers on the Needler that makes it that much more fun to hunt with. If someone told me I could only have one shotgun in the world and it would be the Needler, I wouldn't feel bad, especially if I could get some 2½-inch buffered tungsten #2's at a psi of, say, 7500. Such a load would kill even big Canada geese at any range that I could hit them."

* * *

Potential buyers of hammer guns do need to take some extra precautions. Almost any British hammer gun one is likely to encounter today would have been made more than a century ago, and a large percentage will have Damascus barrels. That alone should be enough to ensure the buyer will consult a qualified gunsmith before using modern (smokeless) ammunition.

Most hammer guns were proofed with blackpowder and, while a particular gun may well have been proofed subsequently with smokeless, that does not mean it is still in proof. Guns go out of proof in a variety of ways. The most common is that the barrel walls become progressively thinner until they

A prototype hammer gun, modern production, from John Rigby in California. The company is tentatively planning to offer hammer guns once again. Although employing the overall shape of a bar action, this is also a back-action lock.

are no longer in proof by the definition of the London or Birmingham proof house. If the gun were for sale in the United Kingdom, it would be required by law to be re-proofed before it could be sold.

In the United States, obviously, these rules do not apply. However, any sensible person will follow rules of self-preservation, and those rules dictate taking the gun to a gunsmith to ensure the barrels are sound and capable of withstanding modern loads—or even blackpowder loads, for that matter.

Another important consideration is chamber length. Since many hammer guns were built before British chamber length was standardized at 2¹/₂ inches, they may be shorter or longer. At one time, 2⁵/₈ inches was a common chamber length. Either way, it is best to know and tailor one's loads and shooting accordingly.

If a gun has been in the United States for very long, the chambers may have been lengthened to handle 2³/₄-inch shotshells. In the United Kingdom, that alone would put the gun out of proof. Lengthening chambers is not as simple as it sounds and, in some cases, should not be done at all because it may make the barrel walls forward of the chambers dangerously thin. Again, the eye of a qualified gunsmith is required to tell you if such a gun is safe to shoot, and good to buy.

The Sidelock Gun: *The pride of London*

Holland & Holland back-action sidelock that began life as a 10-bore, was later converted to .577 Nitro Express, and finally to .600 NE. Although H&H is renowned for its Royal, which is built (either rifle or shotgun) on a bar-action sidelock, throughout its history H&H has made rifles and shotguns with back-action locks, usually under the Dominion name, or as a 'C' grade.

The sidelock British game gun is the aristocrat of shotguns, and a sidelock commands a premium over almost any boxlock, even those from the same maker. As with every rule concerning British guns, there are exceptions, but in this case the exceptions are few and usually concern unique boxlock designs such as the Dickson round action and the Westley Richards droplock.

Sidelocks are a London specialty, whereas boxlocks were invented in Birmingham and adopted by such Birmingham stalwarts as Westley Richards and W.W. Greener. The greatest London names—Holland & Holland, James Purdey, Boss & Co., Woodward—were known for their sidelock guns.

Holland & Holland's new round-body gun, developed in the late 1990s, has a back-action lock. This action is being used as the basis for both a 12-bore shotgun (shown here) and a double rifle. For rifles, such an action has advantages because less metal is removed, strengthening the action bar.

If lineage counts for anything—and with aristocrats, it does—the sidelock can claim direct descent from hammer guns going back several hundred years. The sidelock is simply a traditional hammer gun with the hammer reshaped and moved from the outside of the lock plate to the inside. As with most design advances, this did not happen all at once and there were several

A James Woodward game gun, with its distinctive arcaded fences. This is the epit-ome of elegance in a London best.

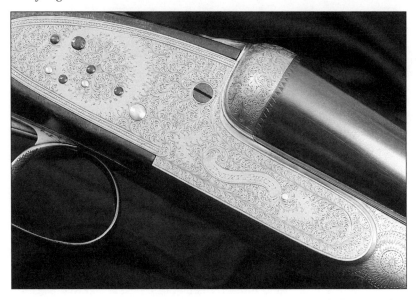

Henry Atkin apprenticed with Purdey, learning to build guns on the Beesley action, and when he set up his own shop, was noted for using the Beesley action, which he called his "spring opener." This gun, however, is built on a standard action.

interim steps along the way. None of those interim designs is any more than a curiosity today, although most would still be functional and usable.

One such interim design moved the hammer inside the lock, but a spur protruded out through the plate to allow the gun to be cocked by hand. This design was neither fish nor fowl, and had the distinct disadvantage of leaving an opening by which dirt and moisture could get into the lock. In the typically rainy weather of British driven shooting, this was a serious drawback.

Once the hammers were moved inside the locks, they were called "tumblers," and so they remain. If the tumblers were completely enclosed, obviously, then some sort of cocking mechanism was necessary. Such a system was in place by 1875, when Anson and Deeley patented their boxlock design, so it was not a major obstacle. Sidelocks then developed in step with boxlocks, and together they relegated the hammer gun to obsolescence.

* * *

When the race to move the hammers inside really got underway, each major gunmaker developed his own design. Holland & Holland had two—a bar action and a back action.

In hammerless designs, bar- and back-action locks function almost exactly the same way they do with hammer guns. The mainspring powering the tumbler is a long, horizontal 'V' spring. In a bar-action gun, it lies in front of the tumbler, fastened along the bar of the lock plate. In a back-action design, the spring is behind the tumbler. In some back actions, it extends along a long, bottle-shaped plate that is inletted into the wrist of the gun; in others, the spring is shorter, stouter, and perches on the inside of a conventional lock plate, above and behind the tumbler.

At H&H, the bar action was used in its Royal shotguns, while guns bearing the Dominion name had back actions. Some people assume the Dominion guns were a lower grade, but they were never intended to be. They were simply built on a different action; quality of materials and level of workmanship were the same for both.

The H&H bar-action pattern has become the world standard for sidelock guns. All high-quality guns made in Spain today use the H&H-pattern sidelock, and the same is true of many guns from Italy. There is no question the H&H is a fine design, and it has certainly proven itself. But that does not necessarily mean it is the best design. (Interjection by Steve Denny of H&H: "Yes, it is the best!")

Traditionally, English sidelocks use 'V' springs to power the tumbler, but

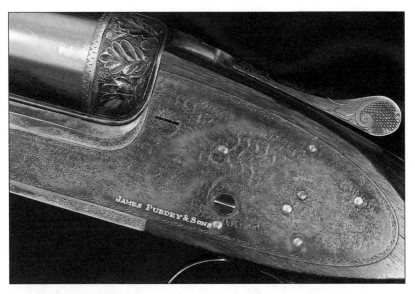

A relatively recent James Purdey. Purdey-style rose and scroll engraving is so rec-ognizable, it has become a standard pattern used on all manner of guns, all over the world. Guns built on the Beesley action can be identified by the placement of the pins in the lock plate.

An early Boss & Co. with Damascus barrels and a sidelever. This gun has Boss's trademark lovely engraving, and the handling of an Aston Martin.

Holland & Holland invented the detachable lock, which has since become a luxury feature on double guns around the world. This is an early model, with the lever on the right side of the gun, and the knurled knob to the rear when tightened. Today, it is usual to have the lever on the left side, with the knurled knob facing the muzzle. The ability to remove locks easily for cleaning is one of the advantages of a sidelock over a boxlock, but many sidelocks with this feature suffer from excessive wear because the locks are removed improperly.

any engineer will tell you that a coil spring will do the same job better and more reliably. What's more, a coil spring on a rod will continue to work even if it breaks (it simply becomes two short springs, working in concert). Many continental sidelocks, especially those from Germany, use coil springs everywhere possible, instead of 'V' or leaf springs.

Regardless of why British gunmakers persist with 'V' springs for newly manufactured guns, however, the fact is that most older British guns will have such springs.

When you hear the term seven-pin sidelock versus a five-pin sidelock, it simply means that the lock design employs seven pins (the English term for screw), and these can be counted on most lock plates. The extra two pins are used to secure the secondary leaf spring that powers the sear.

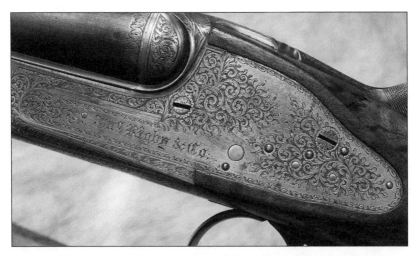

An early John Rigby double rifle with Rigby's signature hump-back lock plate.

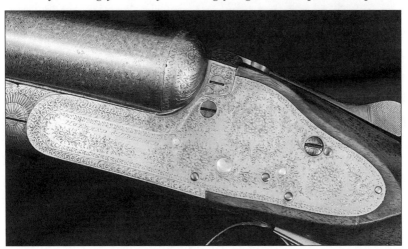

While the hump-back lock came to be associated with John Rigby, it was not exclusive to Rigby by any means, as is shown by this early Holland & Holland.

Boss & Co. developed their own lock design, but it was not adopted by others and remains peculiar to the Boss.

Purdey took a different course. They adopted the Beesley action, invented by gunmaker Frederick Beesley, and it remains the Purdey standard to this day. The Beesley action employs an ingenious system in which the mainspring is used to make the gun a self-opener. Once the tumblers have been tripped, spring pressure comes to bear; as the bolting system is released by moving the top lever, this spring pressure causes the gun to spring open on its own.

Other gunmakers have also used the Beesley action. For that matter, Frederick Beesley himself was in business as a gunmaker, and some Beesley guns (made after the patent expired) have the so-called "Purdey self-opener," a misperception that must cause Beesley to gnash his ghostly teeth.

As well, a few ex-Purdey craftsmen set up shop on their own and then made guns the way they had learned to do it at Purdey's, on Beesley actions. Henry Atkin was one such, and an Atkin gun from before its merger with Grant & Lang is almost always a self-opener.

Sidelocks were also used for over/under guns (under/over, in British parlance), and the two most famous are the Boss and the Woodward. These are also the two over/unders a buyer is most likely to see for sale on a used-gun rack. They will be at the expensive end of the rack, too, by the way

I well remember the very first time I handled a Woodward over/under. It was at the Safari Club convention in 1991, and Michael McIntosh came looking for me. There's a gun you have to see, he insisted. It was a Woodward 28-bore with 30-inch barrels—a magnificent creation if ever there was one. It came to the shoulder like a cloud and swung like a dream. Neither Michael nor I had the requisite $75,000 asking price, so it stayed where it was, although as of that moment our tastes in guns had moved over a couple of notches.

While the Boss over/under is better known, the Woodward is generally considered to be a superior design. In 1948, James Woodward was bought out by James Purdey & Sons. In taking over their distressed rival, Purdey was doing everyone a service, themselves included, for the Purdey over/under up to that point had been a disappointment to everyone. Immediately, Purdey discontinued its own over/under and began making the Woodward under the Purdey name, and so it remains to this day.

Alas, the great Woodward side-by-side game gun was allowed to die, but in retrospect one can understand Purdey's thinking. Fine as it was, the Woodward would have been a competitor to the Purdey, and inevitably would have become the company's second-quality gun—and Purdey prides itself on making only the best. This has not always been strictly true, but it has been company policy for a long time.

Still, the Woodward, with its trademark arcaded fences, somewhat angular lockplates, and the thick mound where the tumbler axis protrudes, was one of the greatest of the London sidelocks, and instantly recognizable.

The traditional English sidelock uses leaf or V-springs, but there are exceptions. These are experimental locks produced for John Rigby in California, using new alloys for the springs, or employing coil springs, and coating moving parts with titanium hydride. A century ago, William Baker in Birmingham advocated the use of coil springs for locks, which are more reliable since they continue to operate even if broken. Traditional gunmakers, however, insist V-springs are "crisper." Baker locks were used on the Vickers Imperial sidelock.

* * *

In recent years, Americans have developed a strong preference for round-action side-by-sides, or more accurately, rounded-action (or round-body) guns. Mechanically, in a sidelock, there is no difference between the function of a round-body and a traditional action. The difference is strictly appearance. The round-body has no square edges, no bead along the bottom of the frame, and no drop points on the stock behind the locks. It is rounded, sleek, and serpentine.

Of the major London makers, only Boss is noted for making a round-body gun, and because the Boss game gun is renowned for its handling, some of this cachet has rubbed off on round-body guns generally. (Of the British makers, the only true round-action is the Dickson, which is a trigger-plate design. And the Dickson is not unique to itself: it is based on an earlier MacNaughton design, perfected by Dickson.)

As each gunmaker established its own sidelock design, they also adopted trademark engraving patterns. Purdey-style rose and scroll has become almost a cliché, found on all manner of guns from around the world, some good, some less than good. Holland & Holland had its own broad scroll engraving pattern, while the Boss pattern consists of tiny, delicate scroll. Churchill's signature engraving pattern was even, full-coverage scroll, with no blank spots.

So well known were these patterns that they were copied worldwide. During the 1950s and '60s, when Spanish companies like AyA and Victor Sarasqueta were marketing many different grades of sidelock guns, the terms "H&H-pattern" and "Churchill-style" were ubiquitous, and applied to everything from stock lines to engraving patterns. In the 1960s, Pedro Arrizabalaga (the "Purdey of Spain") made three different styles of sidelock gun. One was H&H style, from its locks to its engraving; another used a Beesley action, and was made to look like a Purdey; their very best gun, however, was patterned after the Boss, complete with rounded action, real Boss-pattern locks, and Boss-style engraving.

It should be noted that the British have never (well, almost never) used the "side plate" configuration to make a working-class boxlock look like an upper-class sidelock. This is a practice that is very popular on the Continent. A boxlock will be inletted and shaped on the outside to accommodate plates that look like a sidelock, but they are merely dummies. The usual explanation is that it affords more area for engraving. Since most side-plate guns are cheaper, the level of engraving is not of such a quality that one would want more of it.

A side-plate gun is instantly recognizable by the fact that there are no pins protruding through the plate, as there are on a standard H&H sidelock. This would be a dead giveaway, except for two things: Some manufacturers have taken to even putting dummy screw heads in their plates, to make them look authentic. By the same token, some makers of genuine sidelocks make them with "blind" pins (the screw holes do not go all the way through the plate), leaving an unsullied surface for the engraver to work with. This was standard on the Asprey guns, and is usually done to accommodate highly detailed bulino engraving.

There is no foolproof method, no infallible rule, for determining at a glance which is which, although trigger position can be a good indication to the practiced eye. For most, it should suffice to know that British gunmakers very rarely used side plates. (The Cogswell & Harrison Konor boxlock is an exception.)

Finally, a note on the lock mechanisms themselves. The blanks—that is, the semi-finished components that make up a lock, including the sear, tumbler, triggers, and so on—were supplied by small companies that specialized in producing these mechanisms. The best-known were Chilton, Stanton, and Brazier. These three supplied locks to the trade throughout England. A gunmaker would buy a lock blank, file and fit it, heat-treat the metal, and it would go out the door as anything from an Atkin to a Woodward.

Virtually every gunmaker started with the same raw materials, made from the same steel. If a difference existed in the performance of one gunmaker's locks versus another's, it had nothing to do with the steel, and everything to do with how the parts were filed and, more importantly, heat treated to give the right degree of hardness.

The Boxlock Gun:
Birmingham's favorite son

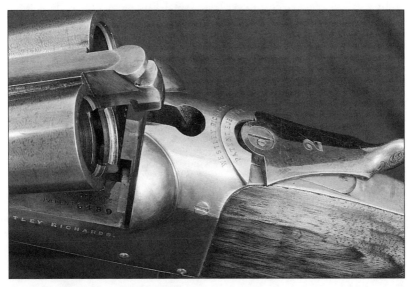

Westley Richards is the home, genetically and spiritually, of the English boxlock, and a Westley Richards, incorporating their various patents, is instantly recogniz-able. This gun has the Westley Richards doll's-head third bite, with a sliding bolt under the short, broad lever. The action body extends back from the fences farther than we are accustomed to today, and there is a distinct shoulder.

The classic British boxlock is the Anson & Deeley design patented in Birmingham in 1875, but the term also applies to any number of other mechanisms invented both before and since. Loosely, it describes any design that sought to create an entirely new mechanism for a double-barreled shotgun, starting with a clean slate, and placing the lock mechanism inside the gun.

Where the sidelock was a logical step in the evolution of the traditional hammer gun, the boxlock took a radical new direction owing nothing to the past.

For the modern shooter, seeking a gun for upland game hunting and clays shooting, the Anson & Deeley boxlock is the most desirable action because it is simple, dependable, and rugged, and if something does go wrong it is easy to repair. Any good gunsmith can work on one.

This is fortunate, because the Anson & Deeley is the most common box-lock by an overwhelming margin. Walk into a gunshop and look at a hundred British boxlocks on the rack, and 99 of them will be A&D actions. The Anson & Deeley's complete dominance is confirmed by the fact that, according to one report, the A&D is the single most manufactured mechanism in history. It has been made all over continental Europe as well as the United Kingdom, and as far away as Russia, Brazil, Japan, and the Philippines.

The Anson & Deeley boxlock action is brilliant in its simplicity, its ruggedness, and its ease of both manufacture and repair. At least as important as these virtues is the fact that a skilled gunmaker can start with an Anson & Deeley action and build a custom gun that is every bit the equal of a fine London sidelock in its handling and deadly dependability. And beauty, too; we should not forget aesthetics, for aesthetics matter a great deal.

William Anson and John Deeley were skilled gunmakers and talented designers who worked for Westley Richards in Birmingham. Anson was the foreman of the "Gun-Action Department;" Deeley was the commercial manager. Interestingly, each went on to design other mechanisms either on his own or in partnership with someone else. Ironically, the two dominant mechanisms for fastening a forend to a gun were invented independently by these same two men: the Anson plunger and the Deeley latch.

* * *

As soon as the pinfire gave way to the centerfire cartridge, a new vista of possibilities opened up and many gunmakers began work on hammerless guns. By the time Anson and Deeley patented their famous design in 1875, there were already a few such efforts on the market.

Although some were moderately successful, each had a drawback or weakness of some sort. The Anson & Deeley had no weaknesses and no drawbacks. When it exploded onto the market on May 11, 1875, it relegated every competing design to the dustbin. From that point forward, the inventive genius of the British gun trade was directed largely towards either perfecting a sidelock design or refining the A&D.

If a gun had no external hammers, a number of immediate questions were raised. One, how was the gun to be cocked? Two, how was the shooter to know if it was cocked or not? And three, if it was cocked, what mechanism could be used to prevent accidental discharge?

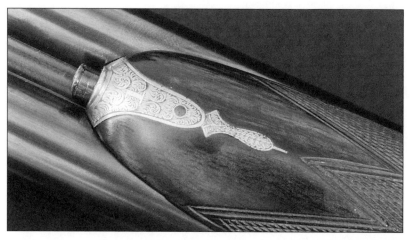

William Anson and John Deeley, the inventors of the Anson & Deeley boxlock, went on to invent other mechanisms that became standard not just in the English trade, but around the world. Coincidentally, they patented, independently, the two most common methods of securing a forend—the Anson plunger (top) and the Deeley latch.

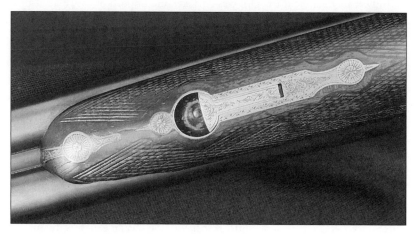

Cocking the gun was the first and most important consideration, and several approaches were tried. One popular method was a lever, not unlike the top-lever now connected to the Scott spindle, except considerably longer to afford leverage. Pushed to the side with the thumb, it pulled the tumblers back until they engaged the sear. Another design used a lever in a similar position, except it lifted upwards rather than pivoting to the side, and at least one gunmaker tried an underlever cocking mechanism.

The problem was complicated by the fact that the gun also needed a bolting system, and a method of opening and closing it to extract fired cartridges and insert new ones. Although hammer-gun devotees were accustomed to making several independent movements to get their gun ready to fire, designers of hammerless guns wanted simplicity, with as many functions as possible rolled into one.

William Anson and John Deeley accomplished this brilliantly by using the force of the barrels dropping when the gun was opened to power levers that cocked the tumblers.

Geoffrey Boothroyd says the A&D was the first hammerless gun to cock the tumblers in this way. So effective was the design, it soon became the standard means of cocking tumblers, not only for boxlocks, but for the emerging sidelock designs as well. Today, there is virtually no other method used for any conventional double gun—side-by-side, over/under, sidelock, or boxlock. The major exception is the use of a sliding cocking lever, found mainly on German and Austrian double rifles.

The shooter was required to do only three things: Press the lever, depress the barrels, and close the gun, and it was once again ready for firing.

Indicators to show if the gun was cocked were important for two reasons. First, of course, was so the shooter himself would know; second was to allow those around him, such as other members of his shooting party, to know if the gun was cocked and therefore dangerous. In the days of hammer guns, it was easy to tell even from a distance if a gun was cocked, but once the tumblers moved inside, it became a real problem.

To deal with the second requirement first, British shooters rather quickly gave up any kind of cocking indicator visible from a distance, and adopted the custom of always keeping their guns open, or "broken," when they were not actually in their shooting positions preparing to fire. A broken gun is absolutely safe, and can be seen to be safe from a hundred yards away. And, since it is foolproof, it is certainly preferable to a complicated system of safety mechanisms and indicators to show the safety is on. Very quickly, the question of cocked or not, and on safe or not, became a private matter between the shooter and his gun. Rendering it safe to those around was done by opening it and carrying it that way.

Having answered the second question, the first question became moot. What did it really matter if the gun was cocked? If you think about it, as far as the shooter is concerned, the question is really meaningless. To those who own a sidelock gun, with the requisite little gold-inlaid cocking indicator on the tumbler's axle, the question is, how many have actually made use of this

An interesting C.G. Bonehill. Bonehill was a stalwart of the Birmingham trade who pioneered the use of machine-made, interchangeable parts, but also made some fine traditional guns. This boxlock is a higher grade, with extensive engraving and checkered panels behind the frame. It also employs a Webley screw-grip treble-bite action in the doll's-head variation. This particular gun has new barrels, modern proof, and 2³/4-inch chambers.

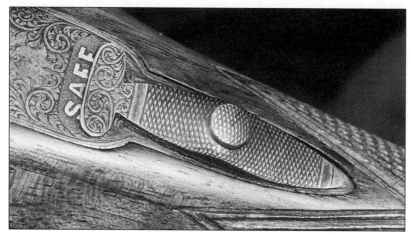

Even a safety can be a thing of beauty on an English gun, as on this Woodward side-by-side circa 1910. The small plunger in the center must be compressed in order to move the safety forward. And of course the word "safe" is inlaid in gold. As with most English guns, this is an automatic safety —a feature that causes many Americans to gnash their teeth, but if you prefer a manual safety, it is easily disconnected.

feature? The answer is, very, very few. And the reason is, once the dropping of the barrels cocking the gun became standard throughout the industry, a gun was assumed always to be cocked if it had not been fired—unless the gun had misfired, in which case the shooter would be well aware of it.

The question itself was a holdover from the age of hammer guns, and just as quickly was relegated to obsolescence. As evidence, consider this fact: The vast majority of boxlock guns made in the last century have no cocking indicator at all. They are simply unnecessary. Cocking indicators cling to existence with sidelock guns as a refinement, as the mark of a fine gun, or as the maker's signature. Practically speaking, they serve little purpose.

There is a whole other area here, wherein a gun might be dry-fired to ease its springs before storage, but the question is quickly answered by doing what every safety-conscious shooter does upon picking up a gun: Checking to see if it is loaded. By opening the gun to check the chambers, you cock the tumblers regardless, and the question is answered. If the gun is disassembled and the springs are eased by cushioning the strikers with a wooden block, you can tell that the tumblers are down by pressing on the cocking dogs. If they resist, you know you have to cock the tumblers by some other means (usually by pressing on a firm wooden surface) before the gun can be reassembled.

In 1875, however, all of this was yet to come, and gunmakers tried different types of cocking indicators. Some were mechanical—little metal protrusions that stuck up or out or through, showing to both eye and feel that the tumbler was cocked. The Savage Model 1899 lever-action rifle, introduced in 1895, is a good example from the rifle world. It was a hammerless design introduced to a hammer-conscious world, and Arthur Savage needed to include a cocking indicator to reassure the skeptical. The cocking indicator on early models was a movable metal piece on the breech block, which was later moved to the tang.

W&C Scott employed one method, which became a signature of their early sidelock gun. The Crystal Indicator was a small round window on the side of the lock. It looked exactly like a ship's porthole, with a heavy crystal set in a stout metal ring. Looking in through this window, one could tell if the gun was cocked. W&C Scott guns employing this device have a very distinctive appearance, with back-action-style lock plates. The system was employed on a vast range of guns, from 10-bore shotguns to, in one case, a .44-40 double rifle! It is a neat system that works very well, but on a sidelock it is easier, considerably cheaper, and at the same time more elegant to put a small gold arrow on the tumbler axle.

The third question—a safety mechanism—was also answered in various

Although the sidelock and its development are mostly associated with London, some Birmingham gunmakers experimented with different designs. W&C Scott & Son developed the Crystal Indicator gun, based on a back-action sidelock. Rather than have an external cocking indicator, the tumblers can be seen through a small glass window similar to a porthole. This design was used by Scott for a wide range of firearms, from this 10-bore shotgun down to at least one double rifle in .44-40.

A relatively plain W&C Scott & Son boxlock non-ejector, of the type that was manufactured by the tens of thousands and shipped all over the world. This gun is a 16-bore with nitro-proofed Damascus barrels.

ways before one approach established itself as the standard. Today, every double gun made has a safety on the tang, where it can be easily manipulated by the thumb of the shooting hand. Again, the exception is German doubles with a cocking lever.

On most British guns, the safety is moved to "safe" by a rod that moves when the lever rotates to the side, the barrels are dropped, and the gun is cocked. This is called an automatic safety. American guns, by contrast, usually require the shooter to move the safety to "safe" deliberately, just as he pushes it to "fire." Automatic safeties are found on side-by-sides usually, but on over/unders rarely. This is one of those anomalies of the shooting world that is ruled by established practice as much as it is by practicality.

Automatic safeties are one of those arcane issues that will cause normally well-bred people to explode in a torrent of invective, condemning them as instruments of the devil. To hear some American shooters tell it, the automatic safety is really some type of Trojan horse—a plot by the British to get even for 1776. Exactly why such a small and eminently practical device should cause such intense feeling has always been a mystery. After all, an automatic safety can be very simply disconnected by a gunsmith, giving the shooter a non-automatic safety should he or she desire. What's so difficult? The reverse, by the way, is not true; so buying a gun with an automatic safety gives you a choice, whereas buying one without an automatic safety restricts you to that system for all time.

Many Americans wonder why the British insist on automatic safeties, and the reason is directly related to the way the British are taught to shoot. Essentially, with the gun held at the ready—butt tucked against the underarm, finger alongside the trigger guard—the shooter locks his eyes on the bird, tracks it with his leading hand, and as the gun comes to the shoulder, pushes the safety off and pulls the trigger.

The safety is never moved to "fire" until the gun is actually coming to the shoulder, and the action becomes part of the overall act of shooting the gun. With enough practice, it becomes so ingrained that a shooter will be thrown off should he bring the gun up and not hear and feel that familiar click. In my case, it is so ingrained that if there is a long delay between birds when shooting report or following pairs at sporting clays, I usually lower the gun and pull the safety back to "safe" before taking the second bird. This is, admittedly, extreme.

The sliding tang safety is so familiar with double guns of all kinds, it is difficult to think of any other. In the British trade, the practice described above became so much a part of shooting itself that no other approach was really practical. But several other designs were tried, and one still sees them today.

The most common is the safety designed by W.W. Greener. It is a sliding button on the left side of the gun, inset into the wooden panel behind the action. The button slides forward and back in a metal frame. The system works very well in terms of preventing the gun from firing, but it is awkward to the person who has learned to shoot in what is now the accepted British style. It requires either turning the gun on its side to move the safety, or reaching far over with the trigger hand and them bringing the hand back to shooting position. Neither promotes good shooting, although much good shooting has been done with Greener guns. W.W. himself, naturally, insisted his system was superior, but the trade did not agree with him, if the number of guns using the Greener safety is any indication. For reasons best known to their Teutonic selves, German gunmakers liked the Greener safety very much, and adopted it with joyous cries much as they did the Greener cross-bolt.

Another interesting safety is that found on the Gibbs & Pitt's Patented Action, a design that came along shortly after the Anson & Deeley, and which is both very attractive and effective. The G&P has a rotating lever on the right side of the frame that can easily be pushed from "safe" to "fire" and back again with either the trigger-hand thumb or trigger finger. This safety is not automatic, and must be set at "safe" or "fire" by the shooter.

Of the safeties described, only the familiar tang safety is completely ambidextrous. It can be used equally well by either a left- or right-handed shooter, while the Greener is actually more convenient for a left-handed shooter, and the Gibbs & Pitt's favors the right-handed.

* * *

The period between 1850 and 1900 was undoubtedly the most fertile 50 years in the history of gunmaking and related inventions. As the double gun evolved, gunmakers invented and produced an astonishing number of variations on themes, and applied different approaches to solve common problems. This includes ejectors, extractors, bolting systems, cocking systems, trigger mechanisms, safeties—virtually every feature now found on a double gun, and a few that no longer are.

Geoffrey Boothroyd, the pre-eminent historian of this period in gunmaking, wrote five books devoted to this one subject. He frequently lamented in print that he could not possibly cover every wrinkle that he knew about, and confessed ruefully that he was still seeing new ones, every year, that he had never suspected existed.

That being the case, a book like this one cannot hope to cover every feature that might be found on an English double in an American gunshop. For those who discover something completely new or mysterious, one can only refer them to Boothroyd's books and hope for the best. The fact that more than a century later, many of these devices are found on guns that are still in use and still being bought and sold, is an indication of the soundness of many of these designs and the quality of their manufacture.

Aside from the Anson & Deeley, a few other non-sidelock patterns did achieve a measure of acceptance. These include the famous Dickson round action, the Westley Richards droplock, and the Gibbs & Pitt's.

The Gibbs & Pitt's Patented Action was produced in the Bristol gunshop of George Gibbs and patented in 1879. The G&P employs a snap underlever to unbolt the barrels, and the movement of this bolt cocks the tumblers. (Unlike the Jones, which rotates to the side, a snap underlever is pushed straight down, similar to that on a falling-block rifle.) The lock work is contained in a metal undercarriage, just forward of the triggers.

By no stretch of the imagination is the Gibbs & Pitt's common, but it is so interesting, and of such high quality, it is worth a closer look. George Gibbs is much more famous for his rifles than his shotguns, especially for large-bore, hard-kicking rifles from the first muzzleloading behemoths he manufactured for Sir Samuel White Baker, to the introduction of the .505 Gibbs in 1911. Gibbs was also active, and successful, in long-range target shooting throughout the late 1800s.

The Gibbs & Pitt's action was used for both rifles and shotguns. The one shown here is a shotgun, and the story of its life says everything one needs to know about the strength and quality of this action. It has 2 1/2-inch chambers, Damascus barrels, and is proofed for blackpowder. In 2006, it turned up in the shop of Edwin von Atzigen, a Swiss-born gunmaker working in Canada. The owner wanted the gun refurbished.

As it turned out, the owner (a man in his 50s) had owned the Gibbs & Pitt's since he was a teenager. It was a gift from an uncle, and for years he shot ducks, geese, and upland game with the gun, oblivious to the fact that it was proofed only for blackpowder. He shot 2 3/4-inch, smokeless-powder, heavy duck loads through the gun, season after season. It cheerfully digested anything he stuffed into the chambers, and when the gun arrived for its restoration, it was still as tight as a vault.

Before beginning the restoration, von Atzigen took the gun out and shot

The Gibb & Pitt's patent is a boxlock only in the sense that it is not a sidelock. Even to use the word boxlock in connection with this sensuously rounded action seems wrong. Patented by George Gibbs in Bristol in 1879, four years after the A&D, this action is extremely strong as well as graceful, and was used on both shotguns and rifles.

a few rounds of skeet with it. It has wonderful balance and shot extremely well.

Around the same time, a Gibbs & Pitt's action was put up for sale at one of the English auction houses. It had no barrels and no stock. The projected sale price was £3,000-£5,000—roughly $6,000-$10,000—and this was for the action alone. Fitting it with a stock and new barrels would be hideously expensive at today's prices, but the new owner would have a wonderful gun to show for it.

* * *

The Dickson is one of the very few true round actions (as opposed to a "rounded" action) that has ever been made, and has acquired cult status in the United States and other countries where double guns are treasured. At one time, one could pick up a Dickson ("strange looking gun . . .") for a few hundred dollars, less than one would pay for an Iver Johnson or an old Parker Trojan. Today, any Dickson commands a premium even compared to fine English sidelocks, and a Dickson in excellent condition with lovely walnut is in the stratosphere.

John Dickson was a gunmaker in Edinburgh, Scotland, and the Scottish makers have always been a little bit quirky. They march to their own drummer, and have produced some truly original designs over the years. The MacNaughton is a classic example. James MacNaughton made his guns with the metal cut away to allow the stock to reach almost up to the fences. For a while, in the 1990s, MacNaughtons enjoyed almost as much demand as Dicksons, and there was even an attempt to resurrect the marque and manufacture the original MacNaughton gun, but it came to nothing.

The Dickson, however, goes from strength to strength, and it is not unusual now to see a fine Dickson sell for $50,000-$100,000. One gunmaker in the United States, Steve Davis of Tennessee, is the acknowledged Dickson expert in this country, from restocking them to full-scale restorations. The Dickson has an almost erotic appeal; it is a gun with the cleanest of lines, no sharp edges, and a serpentine grace. And, I am told by those favored few who have shot with one, they shoot just as wonderfully as they look.

The action itself is a trigger-plate design. All the lockwork is fastened to the trigger plate, which can be removed from the frame for cleaning or adjustment. By putting all the moving parts into the center of the frame, Dickson was able to make the frame itself round, which in turn allows the stock to be round both fore and aft, giving the Dickson its uniquely graceful appearance.

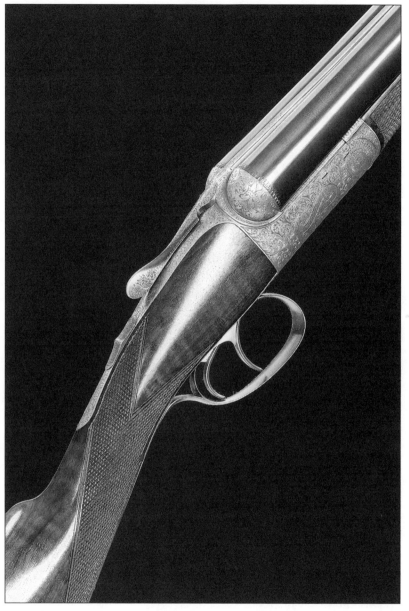

The Dickson round action, developed from the earlier MacNaughton, is not a boxlock but a trigger-plate mechanism. The Dickson's serpentine grace has given it a cult following in the United States. This gun is a 20 bore.

Photo Courtesy Steve Davis and Bill Orr

Geoffrey Boothroyd, who knew as much about these guns as any man living, and admired purity of function as well as form, shot a Dickson in preference to any other gun.

* * *

For more than a century, the question has been argued back and forth as to why London gunmakers never embraced the boxlock the way Birmingham did. Some contend it was merely snobbery; the Londoners themselves say the boxlock is simply not as good as a sidelock (which itself has been widely debated), while others insist it was a case of "not invented here," a malady to which the British gun trade as a whole is certainly prone.

Whatever the reason, the boxlock became a Birmingham specialty. Since William Anson and John Deeley worked for Westley Richards, it is not surprising that Westley Richards became the boxlock's spiritual home, their model became the standard, and Westley Richards also designed variations on the original.

The most famous of these variations is what is now known in the United States as the "droplock," although Westley Richards refers to the locks as "hand-detachable." In this pattern, there is a hinged floorplate ahead of the trigger guard. This plate can be opened, and each lock mechanism, including the tumbler, removed from the frame. Obviously, this system has many advantages. Spare locks can be carried in case something goes wrong. For Englishmen heading for the far outposts of empire, where gunsmiths were notable by their absence, having a spare lock that could be slipped in effortlessly was a huge advantage.

The term "droplock," by the way, comes from the fact that if the floorplate is opened with the gun held upright, the lock will drop out in the hand. Michael McIntosh quite rightly points out that "it's true that the locks will drop out if you open the plate with the action upright, but not necessarily into the hand. Just as often, they'll drop out onto the concrete floor of the workshop, which is not all that desirable. Better, I should think, to caution that one should always open the plate with the action upside down, and lift the locks out with the fingers only."

The familiar hinged version of this action is by no means the only one. The trigger plate (or, as Americans call it, the floor plate) is held on by a screw, and the first Westley Richards detachable-lock action required that the screw be removed to take off the plate. These can be recognized by the absence of axle pins on the outside of the frame, and are extremely rare. In

The Westley Richards hand-detachable (droplock) action, made as a best gun and, in this case, number one of a pair. This gun employs the patented Westley Richards doll's-head third bite and distinctive top lever with sliding bolt.

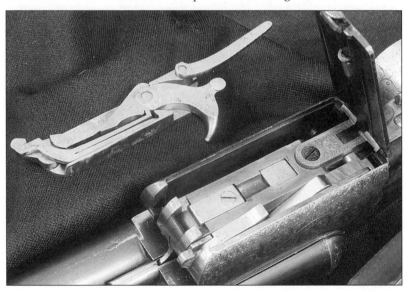

Westley Richards's hand-detachable lock is a thing of beauty to anyone who loves fine mechanisms. It is as finely made as the movement of a watch, and allows an inside look at how the Anson & Deeley boxlock action works. Today, a Westley Richards gun or rifle with this action commands as much as a London sidelock.

another variation, the plate was made easier to remove but still came off altogether. Around 1908, the hinged floorplate with latch became standard.

The locks themselves are little mechanical jewels, like the mechanism of a watch. Each surface is finely finished, and sometimes engine-turned. For the British gunmaker of the 19th century, no part of a gun was too small or arcane to make visually attractive as well as mechanically precise. Making perfect locks was the hallmark of a master.

The droplock design was used in both shotguns and rifles, and today a Westley Richards droplock commands a price comparable to a fine sidelock gun or rifle.

* * *

Early Anson & Deeley boxlock guns from Westley Richards had a very distinctive shape and incorporated a number of features that later fell into disuse.

Some guns did not have underlugs for fastening, but used only the distinctive Westley Richards doll's-head rib extension. The doll's head has a slot facing the standing breech, and a sliding plate underneath the lever slips into the slot as the action is closed. In this instance, the lever is short, very broad at the base, and unmistakably Westley Richards. Other guns use exactly the same system, but incorporate Purdey underlugs as well.

This aside, early Westley Richards boxlocks have a look all their own. Studying one, the average shooter might think "there's something different," but not be able to put their finger on it. The frame extends back from the fences farther than we are accustomed to today, and the shoulder, where the top of the frame becomes the vertical side, extends farther down and is noticeable, whereas in most boxlocks it is not.

Combining these features with a longer, almost serpentine top lever makes the Westley Richards quite distinctive. This is valuable to know when looking at boxlocks from other makers, because it is just possible you are buying a gun made by Westley Richards for sale by some other company. At one time, I owned a William Golden boxlock that Steve Denny (now with Holland & Holland) was almost certain was made by Westley Richards. There was no way of proving it, and I purchased the gun for a lower price; but then, so did the man who bought the gun from me later on.

* * *

Birmingham, with its large gun factories (Greener, Webley & Scott,

Boss & Co. were "Makers of Best Guns Only," and never made a boxlock. Or did they? This boxlock was made for Boss in Birmingham and sold under the name of its guiding genius, John Robertson. Not a best gun, but certainly a very fine 16-bore boxlock.

A William Golden boxlock, almost certainly made for Golden by Westley Richards. It exhibits every feature, from the distinctive shape of the frame to the Westley Richards doll's-head, lever, and sliding bolt. Such a gun offers the opportunity to own the quality without paying for the name.

Vickers), spawned an entire separate class of English shotgun: the boxlock non-ejector or, as it is shown in the gun lists, "B,NE."

No one can even estimate how many such guns were made between 1875 and 1940. It was certainly well into the millions. Thousands upon thousands were shipped out to the colonies—South Africa, Kenya, Rhodesia, Australia, New Zealand, Canada. Tens of thousands more were sold at home for use by gamekeepers and farmers. Some of these guns were the plainest of the plain: Anson & Deeley actions with square sides and little more than the name stamped on them. Many had Damascus barrels. They had straight grips, splinter forends, ample but not overly fine checkering, and, of course, extractors only.

These were not guns made for shooting driven game. They were intended for potting a rabbit or nailing a marauding fox around a henhouse. They were inexpensive at the time they were made, with the price usually measured in shillings, not pounds. Certainly, some were coarsely made, but almost all of them enjoyed a minimal level of workmanship. Of all such guns that I have seen, none were of the execrable level found in the Belgian trade guns that were shipped to America by the millions, and died almost as quickly as they landed.

The British factories, perhaps because they were supplying their own colonies and people at home, established and maintained standards of material and workmanship even in guns intended to sell for a pound or two.

That is one side of the coin.

The other side is the same basic gun, but ordered by one person through his local ironmonger or gunshop, and intended either as his own personal gun or a gift for someone else. In those halcyon days, such a purchaser could stipulate that the gun have some engraving, that the panel behind the frame be checkered as well as the grip and the forend; a recoil pad could be fitted. Some might insist on pretty wood, although that was not really a consideration for most people in those days. At a time when fluid steel was available, but fine Damascus was an option at extra cost, the gun might come with beautiful browned Damascus barrels.

These guns were status symbols for many, or treasured heirlooms (or became such), or gifts to the sons of the unwealthy, going out to the colonies. There are as many stories as there are guns, and not enough paper in the world to print them all even if one knew them.

I have seen such guns that were truly beautiful and which any gun lover would be proud to own. In 1998, I bought one such, with the name Williamson & Son engraved on the frame. Whether Williamson was the maker or mere-

Exactly who Williamson & Son was, or where they were located, is unknown. There were many Williamsons, and several with sons. Regardless, this gun, probably made to Williamson's order for a local squire, is an extremely nice boxlock non-ejector with a lovely walnut stock, 30-inch Damascus barrels, extensive engraving and checkering, and a lovely feel throughout. This gun is typical of the fine-quality English boxlock that can be acquired at a bargain price.

J. Graham of Inverness, founded in 1857 and still in business. This gun was made for Graham in Birmingham, and is a very early gun, since its 28-inch barrels are bored cylinder and full. From the shape of the frame, it is obvious where the term 'boxlock' came from.

ly the purveyor is impossible to determine. There were half a dozen Williamsons in the trade, and at least two separate shops called Williamson & Son. Regardless, the gun was delightful. Browned, 30-inch Damascus barrels, a mouth-watering red-gold stock with end-to-end fiddleback; the panel behind the frame checkered, and all the checkering fine and well done. The frame itself was extensively engraved in tiny scroll. Altogether, it was obvious this gun had been, at one time, someone's pride and joy. I bought it, I later sold it, I fervently hope it found a good home and is once again someone's pride and joy. I don't regret many guns I've parted with, but that one sometimes comes back to haunt me.

That Williamson & Son boxlock non-ejector, to me, epitomizes the finest qualities of the English gun trade in the years leading up to 1914. Even their trade guns were better than almost anything you can buy today outside of a custom shop. There was a pride of workmanship obvious in every one of them. And the inherent quality is unquestionable: Without it, these guns would not have survived for a century, usually in hard use, and still be sound and functional today, just as a London best can be as good now as it was the day it left the shop, a hundred years and a hundred thousand cartridges ago.

Bolting Systems: *Studies in ingenuity*

A back-action 12-bore hammer gun by H. Holland, incorporating both Purdey double underlugs and Scott's patented breech. In the early years after underlugs were introduced, gunmakers firmly believed a third or even fourth fastener was necessary. They were not, but some of the designs that resulted, such as this one with twin sliding bolts and recesses, one on each side of the barrels, are not only fascinating and ingenious, but also delightfully made.

Ultimately, the real story of the English shotgun comes down to the development of a bolting system that made it all possible. Not boxlocks and sidelocks. Not side-by-sides and over/unders. Bolting systems. By "bolting system," we mean the mechanism that holds the barrels closed and withstands the intense stresses of firing, and releases the barrels to be opened and reloaded.

The advent of breechloading firearms did not immediately result in the approach that is so familiar to us today—barrels that drop down on a hinge, controlled by a top lever on the tang that moves from side to side. That whole trim, graceful, efficient, effective, and marvelously elegant arrangement was the end result of a great deal of trial and error, with inventions and refinements contributed by many different gunmakers.

The first concept was that of hinged barrels. Several designs attempted to use barrels that were released and slid forward to open the breech. Others—and the modern French Darne is the best-known—used a sliding breech with fixed barrels. After Lefaucheux, however, the hinged barrel gained ascendancy and never looked back. While a few gunmakers continued to search for alternative approaches, none amounted to anything.

Lefaucheux exhibited in London in 1851, and the break-action concept took off. Just 19 years later, James Purdey & Sons patented their final design for a bolting system of underlugs with a sliding bolt, manipulated by a top lever. The Purdey "double-underlug" bolting system was, by Purdey's own admission, the "making of the company." As soon as the patent laws allowed, the rest of the British gun trade began using it in every type of break-action gun and rifle.

Purdey actually obtained its first patent for a sliding bolt and underlug design in 1863. In 1865, William Middleditch Scott patented the "Scott spindle," which is the under-sung hero of this particular tale. Scott attached the familiar top lever to a spindle that extended down through the action behind the standing breech. In so doing, he created a mechanism that could be made to fulfill an astonishing number of functions with the simple movement of the thumb of the shooting hand. When Purdey connected their sliding bolt to Scott's spindle, they created a mechanism that more than one expert in industrial design has judged to be perfection.

While the Purdey-Scott system eventually reigned almost supreme, it took some years, and during that time other gunmakers continued to look for alternatives, either because of patent laws and the cost of licensing, or out of pride and a desire to market something they invented themselves. Some of the alternative bolting systems were excellent, but not one was good enough to challenge the Purdey-Scott supremacy. Still, today one often comes across shotguns—perfectly good, usable, worthwhile guns—that employ an unfamiliar bolting system.

The Purdey-Scott system had immense influence not only on the gun trade, but on British approaches to shooting, and ultimately, one could argue, on British society itself. To start with the guns, a few decades after the patent expired, it did not matter if a gun was a sidelock or a boxlock, it almost certainly used the Purdey-Scott bolting system. Even over/unders used it, although it had drawbacks for over/unders and alternatives were sought; even the alternatives, however, were really variations on it.

The Purdey double-underlug and top lever was a very slick, fast system of opening and closing a gun. When shooting driven birds on large estates became a national passion, speed of reloading naturally became a major concern. Driven shooting as we know it would never have become possible without guns that could be reloaded quickly, and to this day, the Purdey-Scott combination is the fastest ever designed for a side-by-side double. And out of all this grew the British penchant for matched pairs and garnitures of guns.

As for British society, in the years before 1914, upper-class life (and much of lower-class life as well) revolved around August 12th (the "Glorious 12th") every year, when the season for red grouse opened in Scotland. Special trains were laid on to carry the guns north, and bring the bag south. The gunmaking centers of London and Birmingham hummed, vast tracts of land were given over to the raising and shooting of birds—red grouse in the heather, partridge and pheasant in the south—and questions about the state of this year's grouse hatch were asked in Parliament. If that is not changing society, what is? And a strong argument can be made that it was largely due to James Purdey and William Scott.

* * *

The Purdey underlug did not arrive until 1870, however, and both before and after, scores of different methods were attempted. Many examples of these survive today in the form of early guns by makers both famous and obscure. Some that preceded the Purdey were so good that they continued to be used in specialized applications, and a few others that came after were good enough that they, too, established a following.

When barrels pivot on a hinge pin, every gun needs an underlug to provide the hook to pivot on that hinge. Connecting some sort of bolt to that lug, or "lump," was an obvious place to start. In fact, Joseph Lang's own early guns locked up on the back of the hinge lug, but it proved to be too far from the breech, and leverage from upward pressure at the breech at the time of firing eventually worked it loose.

Before going on, a brief explanation of some terms: While the steel projections from the bottom of the barrels are commonly called underlugs, they are also referred to as "lumps," simply because they are lumps of steel, and have provided another common term in gunmaking: *Chopper lump.* Today, the term "chopper-lump barrels" is a mark of quality in a gun (rightly or wrongly), and the finest sidelock guns from almost every country boast of having chopper-lump barrels.

The term comes from the fact that a barrel forging, with a square steel appendage at one end, looks more or less like an ax, or "chopper." When the barrels are fastened together, the two lump extensions are silver-soldered or brazed together, and the underlugs are then carved out of the solid extension that results. On most guns, if you look closely, you can see a fine seam where the two flat extensions meet.

If the hinge lug was too far forward to provide a solid lock-up, the most obvious solution was to make it longer and move the lock point back closer to the breech. From there, it was a short step to create a second lug, allowing the forward one its primary purpose as a hinge and using the rear one as the main locking lug. This also strengthened the action bar by leaving more steel between the two slots.

One of the earliest, simplest, and certainly the strongest bolting systems was the Jones underlever, patented by Birmingham gunmaker Henry Jones in 1859 and awarded patent number 2040. In this system, the lug fits into a slot in the floor of the action and a rotary underlever pulls a ledge of steel over the lug and locks it closed. The contacting ledge has a gradual slant or "screw grip," and cams the barrels down tight. When closed, the underlever follows the curve of the trigger guard—readily accessible but, at the same time, out of the way.

The Jones design did its job well and was very successful, but Jones inadvertently allowed the patent to lapse in 1862. His invention was seized upon by other gunmakers and became a standard feature in British gunmaking for a half-century. Because of its strength and dependability, it was a favorite for use in large-bore double rifles, and many .600 Nitro Express rifles were so equipped long after other systems had come into common use.

The drawback of the Jones is that it requires four distinct actions by the shooter: Swinging the lever open, pressing the barrels down, raising the barrels, and then swinging the lever closed. This is considerably slower and more awkward than mechanisms that came into use later. It is also rather cumbersome, and ever since the days of Joseph Manton, British gunmakers have striven to make their guns more graceful.

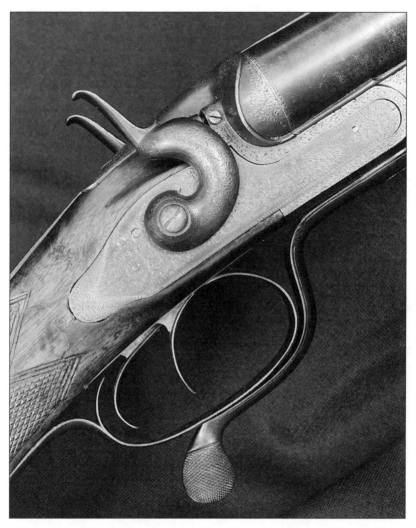

William Griffiths bar-action hammer gun with retracting strikers and Jones underlever. The Jones design is immensely strong and dependable, although slow in action compared to a top lever and underlugs. Dating from 1859, the Jones underlever remained in common use, especially for large-caliber double rifles, until well into the 20th century.

Various other lever systems also employed the lugs under the barrels. In fact, the concept of two lugs in the center of the frame, one behind the other, may seem the only logical approach today, but in 1860 gunmakers were try-

A Westley Richards pinfire gun, dismantled to show the components of the Jones underlever. Although slow to operate, the Jones lever exerts solid camming action to hold the barrels down tightly, and is very strong.

ing everything. There were even systems that used multiple lugs, located under the center of each barrel, occupying parallel slots in the action bar.

Describing in detail the scores of designs that emerged, involving lugs, bolts, pins, and levers that slid, swung, rotated, lifted, dropped, and otherwise moved to release the lock, would require a book in itself. Most of these designs had a brief moment in the sun, a few guns were made, a now-obscure name was engraved on the barrel, and they ended up as curiosities for later firearm historians to puzzle over.

Some designs did have merit, caught on, and were used for a while, and still others became fixtures of the gun trade.

* * *

A number of dynamic effects occur when a shotgun is fired. There is upward pressure on the barrels at the breech end; the barrels want to push forward; there is flexing from side to side. The forward pressure causes the bar of the action to flex downwards as well, which is why the frame, where the action flat meets the breech face, is radiused rather than square. This makes it stronger and discourages cracking.

These various stresses were not all recognized immediately, of course. Trial and error showed where an action was likely to break down, and bolting systems were developed to cope with them.

Early single-lug bolting systems failed for a number of reasons. Sometimes the action bar was too long; since the hinge is at the end of the action bar, this increased leverage. The answer was either to lengthen the lug or shorten the bar. Both approaches were tried, but the shorter bar became standard. It was generally recognized that it was best to have the fastening as close to the breech face as possible; that way, it was merely resisting upward pressure and not having to cope with the destructive force of leverage as well.

Boss & Co. game gun with sidelever. Sidelevers are very elegant mechanisms, especially on hammer guns. They are also robust and dependable, and leave the top strap uncluttered.

A very early Westley Richards boxlock. Note the absence of Purdey underlugs. The sole means of bolting the gun is the doll's-head extension and sliding bolt under the lever. Such a bolting system is more than adequate for a shotgun.

So many developments took place simultaneously it is impossible to give an exact chronological account of what was invented and how it was used. It is even difficult to tell the story in a straight, linear way, because the inventions paralleled each other and were interwoven, twisting like strands in a skein of wool.

Before underlugs became dominant, however, a number of methods were used to lock the barrels closed at or near the breech face. The most common was a rib extension that fits into an opening in the breech itself. This is actually a direct descendant of the proven system of fastening a set of muzzle-loader barrels to the frame, where a stout steel hook between the two barrels locks into a slot in the standing breech.

This concept being so familiar to gunmakers of the time, it was only natural for them to adapt the idea to breechloaders. Sometimes, these rib extensions took the form of a flat blade. Others were "doll's heads," a male extension that fits tightly into a corresponding female opening, and takes its name from the fact that the extension resembled a doll's head.

The doll's head would (in theory) keep the barrels from lunging forward or flexing from side to side. This left the most important stress—the upward movement at the breech—to be prevented by a sliding bolt of some kind that fit into the doll's head itself. The most famous of these systems is that used by Westley Richards. Introduced in the 1860s, it worked so well that, on many Westley Richards shotguns, it is the sole means of holding the gun closed.

This fact tells us something very important about bolting systems, which is that the good ones are adequate by themselves. In 1870, this had yet to be proven and gunmakers seemed to like to pile on the features. Today, Purdey double underlugs are found on the vast majority of side-by-side shotguns and double rifles, and have proven over and over again that, by themselves, they are more than strong enough to handle the pressures and stresses of even the most powerful rifle.

Not knowing this, or not believing it, or simply seeking a marketing edge, British gunmakers embarked on a decades-long search for the perfect "third bite"—a third lock-up to augment the Purdey underlugs. Most gunmakers simply continued to use rib extensions, and this was the most common approach.

Westley Richards stuck with their doll's head; John Rigby developed an intriguing rib extension called a "rising bite," in which a hollow-U-shaped projection from the rib fits down into a cavity in the standing breech, over a post, and the rear part of the post rises up into the extension to lock it solid.

Even Purdey themselves got into the act, with their famous hidden third bite. This is a small projection from the rib, either above or in the center of the ejectors, that fits into a slot in the face of the standing breech. A small bolt slides over the top of it from inside the breech to lock it in place. When the gun is closed, there is no indication that it even exists. Whether a hidden

The famed Westley Richards patented doll's-head rib extension and sliding bolt under the top lever. This very strong design virtually immobilizes the gun's barrels and by itself is quite adequate for most purposes.

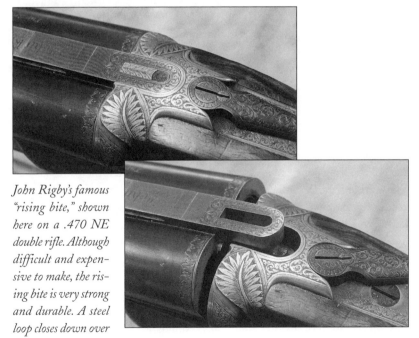

John Rigby's famous "rising bite," shown here on a .470 NE double rifle. Although difficult and expensive to make, the rising bite is very strong and durable. A steel loop closes down over a standing post, the rear part of which moves up as the loop comes down to lock it solidly in position.

third bite adds anything material in the way of strength is debatable, but the presence of such a feature has become a selling point with used guns, and the mark of an extra-special gun by some makers, particularly in Spain.

By far the most common third bite was invented by W.W. Greener in Birmingham. The Greener cross-bolt employs a square, flat rib extension that fits into a slot in the standing breech. The extension has a hole through it; as the gun is closed, a rod in the fence slides into the hole, preventing the barrels from either lunging forward or rising up. The Greener cross-bolt is undoubtedly a very strong system. Subsequent tests have shown that it is sufficient by itself, with no other bolting device. However, William Wellingon Greener, ever the marketeer, teamed it with Purdey double underlugs to create his "Treble Wedge-Fast" lock-up, trumpeted as the strongest bolting system to be found anywhere.

As a feature, the Greener cross-bolt took off like a rocket. It became a standard on Birmingham boxlocks from smaller makers. Across the English Channel, Continental gunmakers seized on it, led by the Germans, who believe that if a thing is worth building, it is worth over-building. The Greener cross-bolt remains in use today, especially in Germany. In fact, so ubiquitous did its use become that it is now almost a reverse status symbol: Guns with Greener cross-bolts are generally considered rather blue-collar by the blue-blooded Londoners and their acolytes.

One further benefit of a rib extension was that it prevented the barrels from flexing side to side. However, some gunmakers began using side-clips for this purpose as well. Exactly when side-clips came along is difficult to say, and whether they actually serve any useful purpose is debatable.

Side-clips are the little semi-circular wings on the sides of the standing breech, each fitting a corresponding semi-circular bevel on the sides of the barrels. Properly done, side-clips are almost invisible when the gun is closed, and sharp enough to inflict a cut if you are not careful. It is like having two little razor blades fastened to the breech to punish the careless. Naturally, the Germans seized upon this, and so the standard German bolting system became Purdey double underlugs, combined with a Greener cross-bolt and side-clips. Nothing like overkill.

Occasionally, one comes across a Spanish or Italian boxlock shotgun similarly outfitted, and there is certainly nothing wrong with it. No one can fault the strength. But to the British, to whom elegance is every bit as important, such an agglomeration of features is not only redundant, but in bad taste as well.

* * *

John Rigby double rifle with another rib-extension variation: A doll's head that incorporates the Webley screw-grip treble bite. This may be the ultimate in overkill for bolting systems. With the flat front surface of the doll's head locking solid in the standing breech, this amounts to four separate bolts holding the barrels closed.

W&C Scott 16-bore with a blind Greener crossbolt.

E.M. Reilly best boxlock with Webley screw-grip treble bite action. In one photo can be seen the underside of the top lever with its interrupted thread; in the other, the slanted surface of the step of the rib extension. The underside of the lever presses on the step and cams the barrels down as the lever moves over. This Webley patent was used on high-grade boxlocks by many famous makers, including William Evans, W.J. Jeffery, and John Rigby.

One British development does deserve a special mention because it was both ingenious and highly effective, and some beautiful guns were built using the action.

While the boxlock was invented at Westley Richards, several other companies are renowned for their boxlocks, including W.W. Greener, W&C Scott, and P. Webley. The latter two companies later became Webley & Scott. Philip Webley may be better known today for his revolvers, which became British Army issue and were used in wars all over the world. But P. Webley was a serious shotgun maker and inventor, and developed a variation called the "Webley Screw-Grip Treble Bite."

To every boxlock maker with the exception of W.W. Greener, the Webley was the epitome of boxlock actions. It combined Purdey underlugs with a rib extension that fitted into a slot in the standing breech. The extension was made as either a doll's head or a flat rectangular blade, but both had a step on the lower part that extended farther into the breech face. A steel projection on the spindle rotated over this step and, because it had a screw grip, cammed the extension down and held it fast.

It was a typical British refinement in that it added a worthwhile feature while actually reducing the number of moving parts. All it required was a modification to the rib extension and an altered spindle. There was nothing to break and nothing really to get out of adjustment.

The Webley Screw-Grip Treble Bite was patented in 1882 and was used to make some very elegant boxlocks. One, by P. Webley himself, graces the cover of this book; another, owned by the author, was a London best boxlock made by E.M. Reilly of Oxford Street. The Webley action was available to any gunmaker that wanted to use it, but because it was considerably more expensive, it was generally reserved for the best guns. Today, if you come across a boxlock with the Webley screw-grip treble bite, the chances are good that it was a best-quality gun by that particular maker, and not merely a production piece.

The British Over/Under: *Few but fine*

J. Purdey & Sons 20-bore over/under, a modified Woodward design, sporting all the elegance one expects of a Purdey.

The over/under shotgun has never occupied a major place in the British gun trade, and very few Americans have ever actually seen a British-made over/under shotgun (or under/over, as the British prefer). British O/Us are both very rare and, in the case of the tiny handful of really good ones, extremely expensive.

The fine British over/unders of the past can really be summed up in two words: Boss and Woodward. Today, with Holland & Holland a major manufacturer of over/unders in two different forms—the sidelock Royal and the Sporting Gun—the situation has changed somewhat. However, these guns are unlikely to appear on any used-gun shelves.

The Thomas Boss over/under is a truly legendary gun, renowned for its original design, exquisite workmanship, beauty, handling, and performance. The Woodward is in the same class as the Boss, but Woodward was purchased by James Purdey in 1948, the Woodward O/U became the Purdey O/U, and the Woodward name faded from sight. Some maintain the Woodward is superior to the Boss, others say the opposite. It is like arguing the relative merits of a Rolls-Royce and a Bentley.

Holland & Holland has made over/under shotguns for many years, but over/unders never established themselves as stalwarts of the company's business until the early 1990s. In 1993, H&H began making the Sporting Gun, a boxlock O/U intended at the time to sell in the range of £18,000-£20,000. Since its introduction, H&H has made more than 600 Sporting Guns, making it, in Steve Denny's words, "by far the most numerous of all English over/unders." As well, he says, in the last ten years, H&H have probably made more O/U Royals than Boss has made in a hundred years.

Those facts alone put the entire over/under question into perspective. Very, very few have ever been made by any modern standard of production.

The reason the over/under is an also-ran in Britain is pure supply and demand. There was never much supply, for the simple reason that there was never much demand. Had British shooters seriously wanted over/unders, one of the hundreds of enterprising gunmakers searching for a market niche in the 1880s and '90s would certainly have obliged. So why did this not happen?

Proponents of over/unders and side-by-sides have sparred for years over which is the superior approach, without ever resolving the question. In my own experience, both forms have undoubted virtues. They also have drawbacks. These qualities make one gun good for one type of shooting, and the other good for other types of shooting.

Broadly speaking, I find a good side-by-side to be vastly superior for reaction shooting where shots are made at unexpected targets, at odd angles, and one is forced to shoot instinctively, letting the gun do the work. This includes hunting ruffed grouse, woodcock, and wild bobwhite quail that are flushing on their own terms, and many forms of driven birds.

The over/under, on the other hand, is better in set-piece situations. Shooting trap, with the gun already at the shoulder; shooting conventional skeet, where the bird's flight is known and it appears on command; live pigeon shooting. In fact, in any situation where the gun is already mounted to the shoulder and the safety is off, the over/under shines.

In a nutshell, the side-by-side reacts well to the unpredictable; the over/under works well in predictable situations.

This is so because, with a side-by-side, the shooter's lead hand is closer to the line of sight, whereas with an over/under it is well below the line of sight. The closer your eye follows the pointing finger, the better your instinctive shooting.

The obvious advantages of the Woodward design, with its trunnions on the lower barrel, reduce considerably the height of the action and the gun itself.

The modern over/under with which Americans are most familiar is the typical Italian design selling in the range of $5,000. It is a boxlock with a single selective trigger and a manual safety. It usually has interchangeable chokes and is intended for a wide range of shooting, from pheasants in cornfields, to skeet, trap, and sporting clays. It almost certainly has a pistol grip and a thick, chunky forend gripped far back by the lead hand. All of this is a formula for deliberate set-piece shooting, not for fast reaction, quick mounting, and pulling the trigger when the butt touches the shoulder and your eye is on the bird.

These are not theoretical considerations. They are very real, with great relevance to the kind of shooting that was done in Britain, and that determined which guns would be used.

The serious shooter in Britain from the 1880s to 1914, and again between the wars, was a red-grouse shooter first and foremost. His guns were made to be ideal for red grouse, both driven and walked-up. Undoubtedly, he also shot pheasants, partridge, and woodcock, and probably snipe and flighting ducks, but he did so with his grouse gun—or guns, if he owned a matched pair.

In traditional driven red-grouse shooting, the one overwhelming drawback of the over/under is its substantial "gape"—the need to open it much wider to eject and reload. In a grouse butt—essentially a hole in the ground with a wall in front and to the sides—space is limited. When the birds are flying thick and fast, it is necessary to shoot quickly, reload, and shoot again. Whether the gun is doing his own reloading, or has a loader, or employs what is called a "stuffer," being able to open the gun quickly in a tight space is essential.

American duck hunters, crowded into small duck boats, often complain of the same problem with over/unders, and this is one reason most still prefer a pump or semi-auto.

The British went to great lengths to make their guns as nimble and convenient as possible in order to facilitate fast repeat shots. This is the reason for the popularity of self-openers such as the Beesley action, and the Holland & Holland system, and for "assisted" opening in which a spring makes the action pop open more easily.

The great shots of the pre-1914 era were interested in huge tallies. So were the landowners who sold the birds to game dealers. Fabled performances, such as Lord Ripon having seven dead pheasants in the air at one time, were reported in the newspapers and talked about on street corners. In order to break into this market, an over/under would have had to display some serious advantages over the side-by-side, and none did.

Boss went to great lengths to make their over/under a contender. A straight grip, a slim profile, unrivalled balance and swing, light weight, a single trigger—the Boss had all of these, and while it gained a few adherents, the vast majority of British shooters, from the best to the worst, stayed with the side-by-side.

* * *

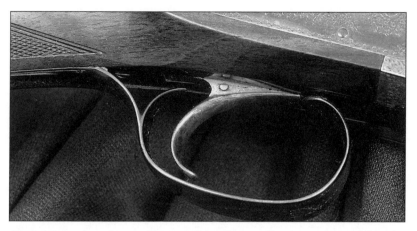

Single triggers have become, if not traditional on over/unders, at least considerably more common than they are with side-by-sides. The trigger on this 20-bore Purdey is slanted and shaped for a right-handed shooter.

It is a matter of historical fact that when guns progressed from the single-barrel blunderbuss stage to twin barrels, the earliest examples were over/unders. Most people believe the over/under is a progression from the side-by-side, but such is not the case.

On the surface, placing the barrels one atop the other is the most logical way of making a double-barreled gun, which is why the earliest specimens did it this way. Where they ran into difficulty was making them fire. How do you arrange a pair of flintlocks to shoot one high, one low? Not easily, if at all. Putting barrels side by side, and then placing a lock directly behind each one, makes far more sense and the side-by-side dominated throughout the flintlock, percussion, and pinfire eras. It was only after centerfire cartridges were developed that the over/under once again attracted interest.

Even then, there still remained the mechanical difficulty of marrying a horizontal lock system to a vertical profile. With a sidelock gun, the locks are where they are, and not easily moved either up or down. So the left lock might be firing the bottom barrel, and having to push the striker down at a sharp angle, while the right lock firing the top barrel has the reverse problem. Ideally, the strikers should hit the primers in line, but no traditional over/under actually does this. Minimizing the angle, to ensure reliable ignition, became a major bugbear for British makers attempting to design an over/under.

The other impediment was a bolting system. Purdey double underlugs could be adapted to over/unders relatively easily, but doing so resulted in a gun that was very deep through the frame. Adding an extra inch or more to the height of two barrels, one atop the other, resulted in a gun that was awkward looking and, to a shooter accustomed to a graceful side-by-side, even more awkward to handle. Conventional rib extensions, that mainstay of side-by-side bolting systems, were of course impossible with an over/under.

All of these difficulties have since been overcome, but in 1900 they were serious impediments, and because the British gunmakers had no real incentive to devote their inventive genius to solving them, the over/under was ignored by all but a few.

Such was the competitive atmosphere of the time, however, a few gunmakers did adopt the over/under and attempted to establish a niche for themselves by touting its advantages, real or imagined. This was in the same vein as Robert Churchill pushing the virtues of 25-inch barrels (the XXV), and W.W. Greener and the boxlock action. Anything to grab attention and market share. To refer to these as gimmicks is probably unfair, but that is really what these companies were doing: Looking for the next big thing, and trying to gain through marketing what they couldn't get through invention.

The argument over whether a sidelock or a boxlock is mechanically superior for side-by-sides may never be settled conclusively, but it is generally acknowledged that a boxlock action is better for an over/under. It puts the tumblers in closer proximity to the strikers, and allows positioning of the strikers themselves at a less oblique angle. In this regard, the fact that the finest London makers insisted on a making sidelock over/unders if they made them at all worked against them. It is not impossible to make a good sidelock over/under (as witness the H&H Royal) but it is certainly more difficult than with a boxlock

The other problem, depth of the action with underlugs, was solved by employing a solution that had been part of gunmaking since Sir Francis Drake and the earliest blackpowder cannons: Trunnions.

Trunnions are the cylindrical appendages on the sides of cannons that fit into round depressions in the sides of the wooden carriages. The trunnion carries the weight of the cannon, and the cannon pivots on it when it is raised or lowered to adjust elevation. By fitting small trunnions on the barrel flats of an over/under, and marrying them to a slot and notch in the sides of the receiver, underlugs were eliminated completely along with the excessive depth of the action. Trunnions have the added advantage that they can be placed virtually anywhere the gunmaker desires, to facilitate opening and closing and to minimize the gape. Or, one can reverse the system and have the trunnions on the

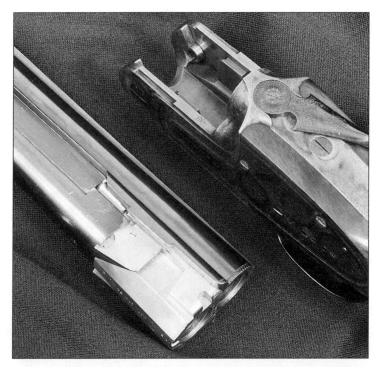

The trunnion system used on the Boss, Woodward, and Woodward-derived Purdey over/unders. The system is now used on the majority of over/under guns made around the world.

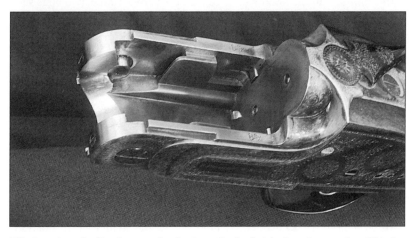

The interior of a Purdey over/under is as finely finished as the exterior. This has been a hallmark of fine British gunmaking since Joseph Manton.

inside of the receiver, mating with notches on the barrels.

Today, trunnions, or a variation thereof, are as dominant in over/unders as Purdey double underlugs are with side-by-sides. It was the use of trunnions that allowed Boss to make its fabled over/under as slim and graceful as it is.

* * *

Boss & Co., as it is properly known, dates from 1812 when Thomas Boss went into business for himself after learning the trade with Joseph Manton and then spending some time with James Purdey. The motto of the company is "Makers of Best Guns Only," and that sums up the approach Boss has always taken. There are no lower-grade Boss guns—and for that matter, not many high-grade ones either. Michael McIntosh estimates that during its almost two centuries of existence, the company has probably not made 10,000 guns of all types.

The history of Boss is covered more thoroughly later, in the directory. For our purposes here, suffice to say that after Thomas Boss's death, his widow ran the company and eventually took into partnership a Scottish gunmaker named John Robertson. Robertson was really the innovative force behind Boss, with a couple of dozen patents to his name. Foremost among these was his patent in 1909 for an over/under shotgun designed by a Boss craftsman named Bob Henderson.

The Boss over/under dispensed with Purdey underlugs and replaced them with trunnions on the lower barrel. To lock the barrels closed, two bolts slide from the standing breech into two bites, one on each side of the lower barrel. In total depth, the gun is barely deeper than the thickness of the two barrels themselves. It is a bar-action sidelock, usually fitted with another Robertson invention, the Boss patented single trigger.

All of this would be enough for most, but not for Boss. The company took this innovative design and executed it with the highest of high-quality craftsmanship. In the words of Geoffrey Boothroyd, a "Boss over/under is not a gun, it is a work of art." By this, he did not mean an assemblage of engraving and inlays. The Boss is one of the most exquisite-handling guns ever made. The company prided itself on the wonderful balance of its guns, and their relative light weight. This was made possible by meticulously filing the barrel walls until they were as thin as they could be and yet still be capable of withstanding the rigors of, first, the proof house, and second, a career of hundreds of thousands of shots in the field.

The term "henhouse gun" refers to a gun that is discovered languishing in a henhouse somewhere, and found to be a rare treasure. Why a henhouse? Because that is where foxes and stoats were often found lurking, and farmers kept a gun behind the door to deal with them. In the late 1990s, Steve Denny, when he was still with E.J. Churchill, encountered possibly the ultimate henhouse gun: A Boss over/under, special lightweight 12-bore. The gun was found by a colleague behind the door of his girlfriend's father's henhouse, and he brought it to Steve for an evaluation. The gun was out of proof, meaning that in England it could not be sold or even returned to the owner until it had been re-proofed.

This, incidentally, is not unusual with Boss guns. Since their barrel walls are razor-thin to begin with, it does not take much wear for them to go technically out of proof, and need to be returned to the proof house for re-testing. This is an expensive proposition and one that, if the gun fails proof (that is, blows up), the owner loses everything. Steve and the owner made a deal on re-proofing, the gun passed, Steve sold it in a matter of days, and it then changed hands repeatedly over the next couple of years, going from dealer to dealer. Each time, the sale price was higher; each time, it took a little longer to sell. When last heard of, it was for sale at an asking price of £35,000— more than three times what Steve originally paid for it.

As he noted with some satisfaction, calling on 25 years in the gun business, "the first profit is the best profit," when you have little time or money invested in the gun. "Each of the subsequent buyers laid out successively larger amounts, and had their money tied up for longer and longer periods."

That, however, is one of the truly exciting aspects of being in the used-gun business. When a widow comes through the door, toting an old gun case and looking lost, you just never know what you will find in it.

* * *

The other really great name in British over/unders, and the only real rival to Boss in reputation, is the Woodward.

James Woodward began in the gun trade with Charles Moore, then formed James Woodward & Sons in 1872. The company became known for the high quality and distinctive style of its guns. Its sidelock game guns had arcaded fences, almost as a company signature, and the axle of the tumbler formed a bulge on each lock plate. The plates themselves were straighter and more angular than other sidelocks, making a Woodward easy to spot even at a distance.

In 1913, Woodward introduced its over/under design, not dissimilar to the Boss in overall configuration, but with subtle differences mechanically.

The Woodward over/under boasted all the quality and style the company had to offer.

For 35 years, Woodward produced over/unders. The company also worked on a single trigger, probably because Boss had one. Because they became the two most illustrious names in over/unders, the tradition of putting single triggers on over/unders probably began here.

Over, now, to James Purdey & Sons. According to Geoffrey Boothroyd, Athol Purdey, then head of the firm, returned from a visit to America in the early 1920s. While there, he was told that Boss and Woodward over/unders sold well, and that Purdey should make one as well. In 1924, he instructed the head of the Purdey factory to do so.

As they had done with the Beesley action, adopting someone else's design as their own, so they did with over/unders. In this case, the gun was designed by Edwinson Green. Green was a Birmingham-trained gunmaker who set up in business in Cheltenham in 1863. He died in 1927 at the age of 89. In the meantime, he built guns of considerable elegance and style, and had many patents to his name. One such was an over/under, patented in 1913.

The Green patent was the antithesis of the Boss and Woodward. It is described as "not the most attractive" design, being bulky and heavy, but it was undoubtedly strong, employing six bolts, or "grips," to lock it shut! And strength, to Purdey, was the paramount concern. The first over/under to leave the Purdey factory was an ungainly thing, weighing 8 lb. 2 oz.

Interestingly, one should add, the gun was built by gunmaker Harry Lawrence, son of the head of the factory, Ernest Lawrence. Ernest worked at Woodward before coming to Purdey, and so he was familiar with over/unders. Harry began as an apprentice with Purdey in 1914, and eventually rose to be director of the company.

Obviously, a gun weighing more than eight pounds was unsuitable as a game gun and efforts were made to slim it down. Reducing the number of grips to four helped, and the redesigned gun weighed 7 lb. 4 oz. Better, but still too heavy. A few of these guns were made during the 1930s, but were obviously no threat to Boss or Woodward.

The Second World War took a heavy toll on England's gunmakers, and the economic malaise that followed the war was even worse. Many gunmakers were on the ropes, James Woodward among them. Around 1947, Woodward approached Purdey about buying the company. Purdey declined, and a year later Woodward offered them the over/under design by itself. Purdey workmen went around and collected the dies and templates, and James Woodward & Sons ceased to exist.

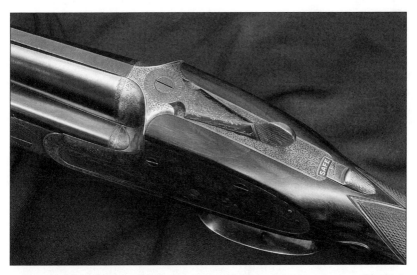

A Woodward 12-bore over/under from 1933. Woodwards were renowned for their elegance, and this gun is no exception.

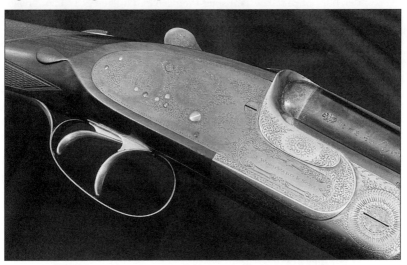

Even in 12 bore, the Woodward has a slim and graceful profile.

By this time, Harry Lawrence was an executive with Purdey, and he seized upon the Woodward over/under. From that day forth, all Purdey over/unders have been either the Woodward design or variations on it. Boothroyd says

Purdey has made three distinct over/under designs since the acquisition of Woodward: The Woodward as made by Purdey, the Purdey-Woodward, and today's Purdey over/under.

One thing all have in common, from the Woodwards from between the wars to the modern Purdey over/under, is that they are rare and expensive. Not many have ever been made, and they appear in the market only occasionally. In 1991, a dealer at the Safari Club convention had a 1930s-era Woodward 28-bore over/under for sale. The asking price then was $75,000, and I have no doubt he got it. And last year, Champlin Arms had a Purdey 20-bore over/under for sale, for which they were asking $90,000.

The chances of finding one of these guns for sale cheap are almost nonexistent, and any that still lurk out there as henhouse guns will be found in the United Kingdom, or perhaps in one of the former colonies such as Canada or Australia, not in the United States.

* * *

Throughout the years, other gunmakers ventured into the realm of the over/under, but none really established themselves. Holland & Holland resisted any temptation to build an over/under until the 1950s, when they made a few dozen and then abandoned them as too expensive to build. In the 1990s, after the company's purchase by Chanel and their adoption of computers and CNC machinery, H&H again began to make over/unders. The aforementioned Sporting Gun came along in 1993, and the Royal Sidelock Ejector, a full-blown, no-holds-barred Holland & Holland bespoke gun for the terminally wealthy.

So relatively few of these guns have been made, and so recently, that they simply do not show up on dealer's shelves and are really outside the limits of this book.

It is worthwhile, however, to give the last word to Steve Denny, who has spent a lifetime in the English gun business. In his opinion, the Boss is a far superior design to the Woodward, especially in its handling. He concedes that, in the smaller gauges, the Woodward and Purdey over/under are more graceful than they are in 12-bore.

So what is the best? Understandably, Steve ranks the H&H Royal well ahead of the Purdey/Woodward in both appearance and handling, but (perhaps significantly) does not compare the Royal to a Boss.

There were other over/unders in the British trade, but none really noteworthy. E.J. Churchill made several over/under designs, including one called

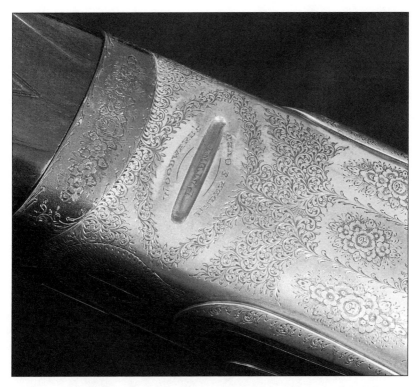

The Woodward Under & Over When the Woodward name disappeared, London lost one of its finest gunmakers, not just in the quality of its guns, but in its philosophy and the aesthetics of gunmaking. Never flamboyant, never embellished, always the soul of austerity and elegance. And, as Edwin von Atzigen says, Woodward guns were the best-made of any of them.

the Zenith. There was the Ovundo, by Westley Richards. The odd Ovundo pops up in gunshops, since Westley Richards, more than most British gunmakers, attempted to make inroads into the American market. As a design, the Ovundo was not particularly distinguished and, unless one is simply enamored of owning a gun with a famous English name on it, they are, for that very reason, generally over-priced for what you get.

The Technical Side:
Nuances of the English gun

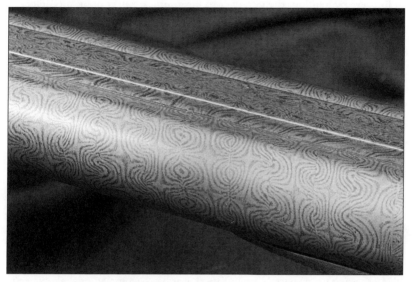

Damascus barrels on a Purdey 20-bore pinfire. One can clearly see the interplay of iron and steel layers, and the seams where the metal was wrapped around the mandrel and welded. This is three-iron stub Damascus.

When George Bernard Shaw described America and Great Britain as "two nations divided by a common language," he might well have been referring specifically to shotguns. The British approach, and the American approach, can be quite different. In many cases, even the terminology is not the same. For example, the British say 12 bore, Americans 12 gauge. The two countries use different methods of measuring, have different standards of shot sizes, and use different-size accoutrements.

For an American in search of a nice English double, navigating through the strange terms is bad enough, although that can be overcome with a little reading. The real difficulty arises in dealing with mechanical differences. For example, the standard American chamber length is 2³/4 inches; in Britain, it is 2¹/2. If you buy a gun with a 2¹/2-inch chamber, can you obtain ammunition? Or can you have the chamber lengthened instead?

These are legitimate questions, the answers to which are not always forthcoming from a gun dealer who wants to sell you a gun. This is a very good reason to deal with an established firm like Champlin Arms; George Caswell not only knows the guns intimately, he also knows what you can and cannot do, what you should and should not do, and can have the work done for you right there by handing the gun over to his gunmaker next door, the Belgian-trained J.J. Perodeau.

There are other dealers just as reputable, of course, but there are also many who have entered the business in the last few years simply because double guns have become a hot item and they want to cash in. To most of them, any English gun without a familiar name is a mystery and anything with "Purdey" on the barrel is worth a fortune.

There are some questions common to all doubles, both big names and obscure companies, whether the gun is a bespoke sidelock or a Birmingham non-ejector trade gun.

Damascus Barrels and Fluid Steel

Walk into a gun club with a Damascus-barreled gun today and the cry will go up, "Surely you're not going to shoot that!" There will be warnings of hell and damnation. Shotgunners have had it pounded into them for so long that Damascus (or twist) barrels are unsafe that it has become an unshakable article of faith.

Looking on the bright side, I have two guns in my vault right now—very nice guns, both of them—that came my way for relatively little money purely because their owners believed anything with Damascus barrels was worthless. The more noteworthy of the two, at least in terms of its acquisition, is a James Erskine 28-gauge hammer gun, circa 1885. I was chatting around a campfire one night in Botswana when the subject turned to Damascus barrels. I opined that they weren't all bad, and one of the participants gave me the gun. I had to collect it from storage near Johannesburg and transport it, without papers, halfway around the world. Three years, two trips to England, £800, and a re-proof later, I brought the gun home. Still, it's worth far more than I paid.

In the second case, I bought a gun with two sets of barrels. Since it was a boxlock with an obscure London name, one ejector wasn't working, and one set of barrels was Damascus, the price was low. I ultimately spent almost four times the purchase price on a complete restoration, but the gun—the E.M. Reilly that appears in various places throughout this book—is now a gem.

Damascus steel has a long history, originating with sword blades from ancient Syria that were lighter, sharper, and stronger than iron blades from Europe. Damascus blades were laminated: Layers of metal were forged together, hammered flat, folded, and hammered again. The resulting steel was tough and durable and had a distinctive swirling pattern created by treating the steel with acid, which reacted differently to the various layers.

In the 1800s gunmakers began using a similar method to create barrel tubes, welding layers of iron and steel together, twisting them into a tight spiral, hammering them flat, and then wrapping them around a mandrel. The continuous seam was welded by hammering the red-hot metal. The tube was struck and polished; the bore was left shiny and bright while the outside was browned. Because the browning agent reacted differently on the iron and steel, a distinctive swirling pattern emerged.

Marrying iron and steel in this way gave the barrels the hardness of iron and the toughness of steel, and it reduced barrel bursts resulting from longitudinal flaws. For almost a century, fine Damascus was state of the art in barrel making. It was only when Joseph Whitworth perfected a method of removing slag (and the resulting flaws) from fluid-steel that all-steel barrels challenged the supremacy of Damascus in gunmaking.

In 1890, the Birmingham Gun-Barrel Proof House tested different barrel materials under strict conditions. The overall winner was a set of Damascus barrels (price, 29 shillings); Whitworth fluid-steel barrels (price, 90 shillings) placed second, and another set of Damascus took third place as well. Even after fluid-steel barrels became commonly available, Damascus barrels were still offered by some gunmakers as an option at a higher price.

Damascus barrels are a fascinating study with as many twists and turns as the barrel patterns themselves. There is a story of forging together the nubs of iron horseshoe nails, then combining this with steel of varying properties. In *The Gun and its Development*, W.W. Greener devotes a long chapter to the methods of making twist barrels and the resulting patterns.

The Belgians turned the making of Damascus into an art form, and assigned names and grades to different patterns which could be identified by the whorls. Today, much of this obscure knowledge has been lost. Only tantalizing fragments remain—references to "sham dam," to bernard or crolle—and occasional illustrations in old catalogs showing the different grades of Damascus steel used in the gunmaker's products. How these grades were made, and what qualities set one apart from another, no one now knows.

Greener points out that using more layers to create ever more intricate patterns ultimately leads to weaker rather than stronger barrels, so an elaborate pattern is no guarantee of original quality.

In the past few years, knife makers have adopted Damascus steel for expensive blades, but it's unlikely Damascus gun barrels will ever again be made. One London gunmaker told me that, if he could obtain Damascus barrels, he could sell every gun he made. The problem is, no one today knows how to make such tubes.

Why, you might ask, would anyone want such a gun? This is a question best answered by handing you a Damascus-barreled gun to put to your shoulder. The very finest examples have a combination of weight and balance that gives the gun exquisite handling qualities. When this is matched with the undeniable beauty of a pristine browned or silver-blue Damascus barrel, it makes your mouth water.

And so why, then, are Americans so suspicious—if not downright antagonistic—when confronted with Damascus barrels?

As mentioned, Belgium was a primary source of Damascus barrels through the 1800s and, the John Browning legacy aside, Belgium has, through the years, made some real dogs when it comes to shotguns. Find a 1900-era side-by-side with a name like "Purdie" or "Barker"—close enough to the real thing to fool the unwary into thinking it's a Purdey or a Parker—and chances are it's a cheap Belgian shotgun made for export. Tens of thousands found their way to America, and many are still kicking around.

Both blackpowder and the early priming compounds used with smokeless powder were highly corrosive and demanded prompt, thorough cleaning. Miss a cleaning session or two and the result was instant pitting. With Damascus barrels, this pitting could be especially severe, eating the iron but leaving the steel, to all appearances, sound.

As well, many were made to withstand only blackpowder pressures, not smokeless. Combine a pitted, weakened barrel with pressures far beyond the level they were built to handle, and the result was often a burst barrel, a damaged left hand (or worse) and a complete mistrust of anything labeled "Damascus."

With European guns, where strict proof laws govern what can be sold, and proof marks give the user exact information on what a gun will withstand, this is less of a problem than in the United States, where manufacturers traditionally do their own proofing.

If you buy an English gun with Damascus barrels and the proof marks show it has been nitro proofed—that is, proven with smokeless powder—you

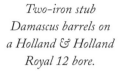

Two-iron stub Damascus barrels on a Holland & Holland Royal 12 bore.

Barrels on a W&C Scott 10-bore hammer gun, of what appear to be stub Damascus.

know it's safe to shoot with loads of the length and gauge marked. Of course, you know neither when the proofing was done nor what has happened to the barrel since, and this is why before you shoot it it's essential to have any Damascus-barreled gun checked over thoroughly by a gunsmith who really knows doubles.

In the case of my Erskine, even after more than a century of African corrosion, an English gunsmith was able to lap the barrels and lengthen the chambers to get rid of pitting in the forcing cone, while still leaving enough wall thickness for the gun to pass nitro proof with flying colors. It is now happily digesting American 2³/4-inch 28-gauge ammunition. I stick to skeet loads, but this is because the gun weighs only five pounds. James Erskine, by the way, was a Scottish gunmaker famous for his Damascus, and the 28-inch barrels on this gun are quite beautiful. They appear to be what Greener calls "scelp" and Geoffrey Boothroyd "stub iron." Such is the difficulty of identification!

The other gun, my E.M. Reilly of Oxford Street, is a London "best" 12-gauge boxlock, complete with Webley screw-grip treble-bite. With 30-inch Damascus barrels ("three-iron stub" or best English, according to Greener), it weighs 6 lb. 4 oz.; with the fluid steel barrels (29³/4 inch) it weighs 6 lb. 5 oz.

My gunmaker, Edwin von Atzigen, immediately decreed that I could shoot the Damascus indefinitely, with proper loads, with no worries. With 2⁵/8-inch chambers, it demands standard English ammunition, which is good because it ensures I won't inadvertently put heavy field loads through it. For the purpose to which it will be put—ruffed grouse, mainly—standard English 2¹/2-inch cartridges with one ounce of #6s (American #7) are almost perfect anyway.

The mystery is why the gun's original owner had the fluid-steel barrels made in the first place. They were fitted and duly nitro proofed around 1925 by George Coster of Glasgow, a barrel maker of considerable renown. The Damascus barrels were proofed only with blackpowder, but could easily have been sent for nitro proof. Yet another question that will never be answered.

As recently as 1990, you could barely give away a gun with Damascus barrels. Today, buyers are more knowledgeable and less likely to recoil in horror. This is good for the dealers, bad for someone searching for a real bargain gun. But there are still bargains to be had, many with (and often because of) their Damascus barrels.

There are no hard and fast rules that allow a buyer to tell immediately if a barrel is safe to fire. Obviously, serious pitting is a warning signal, both inside and outside. But a slight amount of pitting does not render a barrel hazardous. The solution is to take the gun to a gunmaker who really knows vintage double guns and get an expert opinion.

Some Damascus barrels will have been proofed for blackpowder only, while others may have been nitro proofed. Regardless, I would have them checked by a competent gunsmith simply because you don't know where the barrels have been, and what they might have gone through, since the day they left the proof house. By the same token, a set of barrels that has been proofed for blackpowder only may well be perfectly safe to shoot with smokeless loads. My E.M. Reilly is an example. It happily accepts smokeless shotshells, but I am careful to use the correct length and also to limit its diet to low-pressure loads. I do this not because I am worried about the barrels, but because the gun is very light weight, it is at least 110 years old, and I treasure it. I do not want it battered to death by high-pressure, high-velocity loads.

Even if a gun's Damascus barrels are in bad shape, heavily pitted or rusted, with the ribs parting, a gun may still be worth buying. There are all kinds of options open, from sleeving the barrels, to installing steel liners, to lining the chambers. This is highly specialized work, especially if you want the gun to have any semblance of balance and handling afterwards (adding six ounces of steel to the barrels can destroy a gun's liveliness instantly). Also, it is not

Barrels of a Gibbs & Pitt's Patent Action 12-bore shotgun that, with its 2¹/₂-inch chambers and blackpowder proof, withstood a steady diet of 2³/₄-inch smokeless heavy duck loads for 40 years, without wincing. Also three-iron stub.

cheap. But, if it is the only way you are likely to experience owning and shooting a fine English double, it could well be worth it.

CHAMBERS AND CHAMBER LENGTH

Chamber length can be a stumbling block for Americans looking at British guns, and it applies not just to the 12-bore majority but to other gauges as well. In Britain, the 2¹/₂-inch chamber has been standard for about a century. In America, the standard 12 gauge is 2³/₄ inches.

For many years, authorities have warned against using shotshells that are too long for the chamber. The theory is that the crimp, not having sufficient space to open completely, will force the wad and shot load to squeeze through a smaller aperture, dramatically increasing pressures. In recent years, this article of faith has been questioned, with at least one ammunition company reporting that actual tests have shown no dangerous pressure increase. They say the constricted crimp acts as nothing more than an abrupt forcing cone. This may be true; I have not seen the actual report. Regardless, however, I do not intend to shoot 2³/₄-inch loads through any 2¹/₂-inch chambered gun. There are reasons for not doing so, pressures and recoil aside.

The first question any prospective buyer asks, when faced with a short-chambered gun is, can I get ammunition for it? The answer is yes. Two-and-a-half-inch 12-gauge ammunition is now readily available in North America. When it was first imported it was relatively expensive, at least compared to domestic target loads, but today the price is not at all outrageous.

Even if it were, there is always the option of handloading, and if you are shooting large numbers of clay targets, this might be an economic consideration regardless. The components for loading 2½-inch cartridges, and the necessary formulae for doing so, are all available from one supplier or another, and shorter shells are covered in many of the prominent loading manuals. So, for a man serious enough to seek out a vintage English gun, obtaining proper ammunition is not an impediment.

The next question is, if 2½-inch ammunition does become scarce, can I have the chambers lengthened? Yes, that is possible, but it is not always advisable. In fact, I would go so far as to say that in most cases it is inadvisable. In years past, an English gun coming onto the market that already had its chambers lengthened to 2¾ inches commanded a premium price; today, the reverse is true. Modern English-gun buyers prefer their guns in original condition—some because they are infatuated with the idea of "factory original," although that is largely meaningless in the world of bespoke guns, others because they understand the pitfalls involved in lengthening a chamber.

Broadly speaking, any English gun was carefully put together, marrying the correct barrel profile to the frame, making the barrel walls no thicker than they had to be to withstand proof and hard use, but as thin as possible for reduced weight and optimum balance. There is not always enough metal in the barrel walls forward of the chamber to allow safe lengthening, even by a quarter of an inch. If that is the case, however, any competent double-gun 'smith will tell you so.

Buying a gun with the chamber already lengthened is a gamble because you do not know who did the work. It is one more thing that should be checked carefully if considering the purchase of an altered gun. Several years ago I had the chance to buy a really nice Thomas Mortimer boxlock, a 12-bore with 30-inch barrels, weighing 6 lb. 8 oz. I got the gun on a three-day approval and sent it to an English gunmaker for inspection. Word came back, "Don't touch it!" At some point, apparently in an effort to reduce recoil for the slightly built lady who owned it, some ham-fisted rustic had not only lengthened the chambers, but also reamed out most of the forcing cone, in effect giving the gun 3½-inch chambers. The barrel walls were questionable forward of the chambers and, while no one in his right mind would fire three-inch magnum shotshells in the gun, it would have been possible to do so.

In lengthening the chambers, then, you are tampering with the integrity of the gun, just as you would be if you chopped four inches off the barrels. This is, admittedly, a rather esoteric argument and presupposes that every English gun is a work of art that should not be bowdlerized. That is not true, but it is not completely untrue, either. Anyone contemplating such alterations should think carefully before doing anything, and consult an expert gunmaker beforehand.

Aside from aesthetic considerations (and the possibility that posterity will revile you as a barbarian), there are also hard aspects of performance to consider.

My first English gun was a venerable Joseph Lang sidelock, made in 1906. It had 27-inch barrels and the chambers had been lengthened. En route to Africa in 1994, I decided to take the Lang with some buckshot for emergencies. Wanting to know where it would put the buckshot, I patterned it at 15 yards. The left barrel was high and left, the right barrel high and right—not the performance one would want on a charging leopard.

Curious, I obtained some $2^3/4$-inch cartridges and patterned them, alongside comparable $2^1/2$-inch game loads. The $2^1/2$-inch cartridges patterned well, exactly overlaying each other. The longer American shells did not do so well, planting ragged patterns with the centers 12 to 18 inches apart.

The Lang had been regulated with $2^1/2$-inch cartridges and it performed extremely well with them. When I changed the load, performance dropped off. Henceforth, I made a point of shooting only English loads in that gun, and both it and I were happier. This may not be true of all English guns with lengthened chambers, but it is certainly worth investigating if you own such a gun.

Two other special types of 12-bore should be mentioned. The first is the 2-inch, also known as "Greener's Dwarf," the "Pygmy," and various other names. Two-inch 12s were built by various gunmakers, Greener and Lancaster being the two most prominent, and given fanciful names, but the intent was very serious. The object was to create a gun that was lighter and more handy, but did not increase recoil because of that, and which still delivered a fine pattern. The usual shot charge was seriously reduced, from the English standard $1^1/16$ oz. to $7/8$ oz.

W.W. Greener being the promoter that he was, rather extravagant claims were made for his "Dwarf." For some people, undoubtedly, the two-inch was the answer, but not many were made and they are not often seen. In America, they are exceedingly rare—and ammunition even rarer—magnifying the problems presented by a $2^1/2$-inch gun by several orders of magnitude. Finding ammunition will be difficult. It will be expensive. It can be hand-loaded, but that too presents problems. And as for lengthening those chambers to either $2^1/_2$ or $2^3/_4$ inches, it is highly inadvisable.

Two-inch 12s were made to be light, slim, dainty guns. The idea was to reduce gun weight, and one way of doing that was to eliminate metal from the breech end of the barrels. Pushing the chamber of one of these guns forward by half or three-quarters of an inch could be highly perilous. Even if one did it safely, just the thought of shooting large numbers of full-powered cartridges through such a light gun is enough to give one a flinch.

As an aside, one of the enduring mysteries of today's ammunition trade—and there are many things about it the author cannot comprehend—the few manufacturers who make two-inch 12-bore ammunition seem determined to load it so hot that it will match the performance of longer shotshells. Various brands of two-inch that I have tried have been hotter than firecrackers, with a sharp recoil even in a full-weight gun. Small, boutique ammunition makers have even approached the two-inch as a personal challenge, and I sometimes think they are trying to turn a two-inch shell into a three-inch magnum.

The point with two-inch 12s is that they are supposed to be light shot charges, at reasonable velocities, delivering fine patterns from a gun that is light and easy to handle—in effect, a 20-gauge gun with a better pattern. Anyone contemplating the purchase of a two-inch 12 should reconcile himself to that principle, or buy a gun with a longer chamber.

The other special type of 12-bore is the "12/20." Most Americans seeing that designation assume it is a gun with two sets of barrels, one 12-gauge, the other 20, but such is not the case. The 12/20, as pioneered by Charles Lancaster, was a slightly different approach to the goals of the two-inch shotshell. It is a 12-gauge gun, but built on a 20-gauge frame. This reduces the size and weight of the frame, as well as slimming down the barrels at the breech. A 12/20 can weigh about the same as a 16-bore—six to six and a quarter pounds—and with 30-inch barrels can be a pure joy to swing.

Like the two-inch, it imposes automatic limitations on a purchaser. Again, one would have to be doubly cautious about lengthening chambers because the chamber walls will already be thinner than normal. And, with the gun's reduced weight, light loads would be called for because of recoil alone, never mind the likelihood of pounding the gun into oblivion.

The concept of the 12/20 is intriguing, and variations have been tried. I have had a 12-gauge built on a 16-gauge frame, and another on a 20-gauge frame (both in Spain). Both were superb guns. There have been reports of 16s made on 20-gauge frames, although I have never seen one. Going the other way, many Italian 28 bores are built on 20-gauge frames, for the sake of convenience, but I have never heard of the English doing this.

Although the Anson plunger and Deeley latch became the two dominant means of fastening forends, other makers developed their own designs and many clung to them for particular purposes. John Rigby's patent resembles a miniature Jones underlever, and the company continued to use it for double rifles.

With shotshells in the other gauges, the English standard of 2¹/2 inches has been generally adhered to, and most of what has been said about the 12 applies equally in terms of chamber lengthening.

Anyone attending gun shows looking for an English double, or browsing the racks of a gunshop, would be advised to buy a good pocket chamber-length gauge. With more modern guns, you can check the current length against the proof marks on the barrel flats, which should show the original length.

With seriously older guns (say, pre-1900), one may well encounter chambers that are an odd length. My Reilly has 2⁵/8-inch chambers in both its Damascus and fluid-steel barrels, even though 2¹/2 was the standard when the fluid-steel barrels were made.

In the years before 1900, many British gunmakers supplied ammunition as well as guns, and fitted their proprietary ammunition to their own ideas about chambering, chamber lengths, forcing cones, and so on. When the British ammunition companies consolidated, real proprietary ammunition (as opposed to standard ammunition stamped with a company name) became largely a thing of the past. Some guns were left with odd-sized chambers and no source of tailored shotshells. For the majority of these guns, standard English 2^1/$_2$-inch shotshells should suffice.

Another general rule: The older the gun, the more cautious one should be about lengthening the chambers.

Finally, a brief tale about a Gibbs & Pitt's shotgun with 2^1/$_2$-inch chambers (and Damascus barrels!) that, for years, was fed a steady diet not only of 2^3/$_4$-inch loads, but also many magnum duck loads into the bargain. When it came in for a refurbishment, the action was still as tight as a drum. This is a testament to the strength and inherent quality of a British gun from a maker who knew his craft—and George Gibbs certainly did.

CHOKE AND CHOKE DESIGNATIONS

For more than a century, the English and Americans have debated who, exactly, was the first to develop "choke"—constricting the bore at the muzzle in order to give tighter shot patterns. The evidence indicates that English gunmaker William Rochester Pape was first, by several years; he was granted a patent in 1866. In America, Fred Kimble is usually given the credit, but this does not mean he borrowed, copied, or stole the idea; there are many examples of simultaneous developments by gunmakers with similar backgrounds pursuing solutions to the same problems, and that is probably what occurred here.

As with most such developments—and barrel choke must rank as one of the most significant of all time—the system we have now did not spring full-blown from its originator's brain with all the modern nuances. In fact, after deciding on the term "choke" to designate a barrel that had been constricted, for some time afterwards guns with no choke had no markings whatever, while a barrel with constriction simply carried the designation "choke." It is eminently possible, today, to find old guns with one barrel marked choke, and the other with no markings. In today's terminology, you would probably have cylinder and full.

Later, bores left cylinder were sometimes so marked (Cyl.)

The standard American system of choke designation is cylinder, improved cylinder (IC), modified (M) and full (F), with more recent additions of improved modified (IM) and extra full. At the more open end, we also have

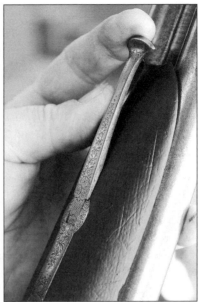

Another intriguing forend latch, this one from W&C Scott & Son, found on a 10-bore shotgun. Beautifully made and engraved, this is the kind of mechanism that makes English gunmaking a source of endless fascination. Undoubtedly, it was abandoned because of the time and expense involved in making it. But it's a thing of beauty.

Skeet #1 (S1) and Skeet #2 (S2). With the advent of interchangeable choke tubes, marketing departments have become involved and there are now so many variations on variations that some manufacturers have taken to grading their tubes by constriction in thousandths of an inch.

British gunmakers, once they moved beyond simply choke and no-choke, designated degrees of constriction in fractions—1/4, 1/2, and full. These correspond roughly to the American scale, with each of the British grades being a few thou tighter. For example, 1/4 is really between IC and M; 1/2 is close to IM.

The author, for one, has long disagreed with the idea that any of these grades is necessarily "improved." Tightened, certainly, but that is not always an improvement.

The prospective buyer of an English gun, especially an older one, may well be faced with some unfamiliar designations, as well as some unfamiliar configurations of choked barrels. So accustomed are we to having combinations like IC/M and M/F, it is puzzling (and sometimes downright disconcerting) to see a combination like Cyl. and Full. The immediate reaction is to ask if the full-choked barrel can be reamed out to something less extreme. When you think of it, however, the combination is really both sensible and useful. How often on a shot does it really make a difference whether you shoot IC or M? Having cylinder and full gives you a real choice of performance, to be used according to circumstances.

Another common approach in America is to match open chokes with shorter barrels. How many different gun models, over the years, have offered 26-inch barrels choked IC/M, and 28-inch barrels M/F, with no option of anything different?

With older English guns, it is quite common to find 30-inch barrels choked cylinder and cylinder, and in between—barrels from 25 to 32 inches long—choked every which way depending on the original purchaser's preference.

Holland & Holland, which makes bespoke (custom) guns only, does not put any choke marks on its barrels. The explanation is that the gun, being made to the original purchaser's specifications, including quality of pattern in each barrel, is made to that standard and the purchaser has no need to be told what the constriction is. This is fine until the gun changes hands, through death, bankruptcy, or legal proceedings, at which point the prospective purchaser is left either to measure the constriction himself or trust the dealer to tell him.

Anyone shopping for an English gun, attending gun shows especially, would do well to carry a collection of instruments with him, including a choke gauge and chamber gauge. Today, the London and Birmingham proof houses mark both chamber length and bore diameter (.729, in the case of a 12-bore) on the barrel flats, but such was not always the case. In the early days, these were not really considerations—just as, before choke existed, there was no need to make any comment because everything was the same: Plain cylinder. In fact, given the plethora of marks found on all modern guns, it is amazing to see how few marks some older guns have. The proof house stamp, provisional proof, definitive proof, and that's it. Today, one finds a maker's mark, bore diameter, chamber length, pressure level marked in kilograms or pounds per square inch, as well as the proof marks themselves.

If one comes across a really old gun with a baffling array of proof marks, some old, some new, some overlapping, you know the gun has undergone serious work at some point and has required, or at least been subjected to, re-proofing.

The first appendix gives a brief history of British proof, of the current requirements for re-proof, and illustrations of the proof marks used by both proof houses over the past 150 years.

TRIGGERS, ONE AND TWO

The traditional British game gun is fitted with double triggers. Usually, the forward trigger fires the right barrel and the rear trigger fires the left. The system is proven, time-tested, and works well. A shooter accustomed to double triggers sees no disadvantage to them at all, and to many experienced guns, two triggers have definite advantages of their own.

Because there are no obvious drawbacks to double triggers, there was never a concerted effort to develop single-trigger mechanisms in Britain. Why bother? There were, of course, exceptions, and if one British gunmaker is associated with single-trigger guns, it is Boss & Co. John Robertson patented a single-trigger design that was used on both over/under and side-by-side guns. Woodward,

Boss was not the only company to market a single trigger. William Evans had its own patent and offered it on its guns for many years.

Boss's major competitor in the field of over/unders, also developed a single trigger, as did W.W. Greener.

Both the Boss and Woodward designs worked well enough but were far from foolproof, and even after the patents expired there was no mass movement to adopt single triggers. Unlike Americans, who see single triggers as up-market and double triggers as down-market, British shooters consider double triggers as good as anything and better than most.

Regardless, most of the major British gunmakers offered single triggers if the client wanted one, which is why one occasionally encounters an English gun with a single trigger. Of course, on a used gun sold in America, a single trigger may not be factory original, especially if the gun crossed the Atlantic immediately after 1945, as many did.

Jack O'Connor, the most influential American shooting writer of the 1960s, hated double triggers and wrote at length about having double triggers replaced by after-market single triggers. The Miller Single Trigger Company of Pennsylvania was most often mentioned as a source of selective and non-selective single triggers that could be fitted by a gunsmith to replace double triggers. The Miller company was purchased by Doug Turnbull Restorations of New York in 2000.

Anyone considering the purchase of an English gun with a single trigger should try to determine, first, if it is factory original, and second, how reliable it actually is. None of the English single triggers have a glowing reputation for reliability. On the other hand, if factory double triggers have been replaced by an after-market single trigger, that may affect the value.

Like lengthening the chambers, discarding the double triggers and fitting a single trigger can be a real drawback for the buyer of today, whereas these alterations were positive selling points 25 years ago.

EJECTORS AND EXTRACTORS

Shooters today are so accustomed to guns with selective ejectors, it sometimes comes as a shock to encounter a gun that has extractors only. Often, ejectors are touted as a positive selling point, while "extractors only" is a negative.

There is no question that ejectors are convenient, but except for driven shooting where speed of reloading is a serious consideration, extractors-only can be equally convenient. This is largely a matter of preference; however, the seeker after a good English gun at a reasonable price should not automatically rule out any gun without ejectors. By doing so, one is ruling out an entire class of gun that is universally priced well below a London best.

Usually referred to as "the ubiquitous Birmingham boxlock non-ejector," these are guns that were made in Birmingham by any number of makers, and sold by small shops throughout Britain, or exported to the colonies in large numbers. They are typically 12-bore guns with Anson & Deeley actions, double triggers, and sometimes Damascus barrels.

Some of these can be extremely handsome guns, more finely made than anything produced today for $5,000 to $10,000. Often, they were special-order guns by the local squire, through his local ironmonger, who would place the order with Greener or Webley & Scott in Birmingham. I have seen these guns with walnut that would be premium quality today, full-coverage tiny scroll engraving, and an escutcheon in the stock. Typically purchased by well-to-do families (or arrant social climbers), it is not unusual to find them in extremely good condition, having been treasured heirlooms.

These are guns for which there is absolutely no demand in Great Britain

A P. Webley best 12-bore boxlock, restored by Edwin von Atzigen, employing the Webley screw-grip treble-bite action (doll's-head variation). Only best guns carried the P. Webley name, and everything about this gun, from the bead on the muzzle to the toe of the stock, says best gun.

The E.M. Reilly frame with full-coverage, delicate scroll engraving. No trace remains of the original case colors, but the frame has the patina of a century of use. Such engraving is simply not found today. The action is a Webley screw-grip treble bite with a blade-variation rib extension.

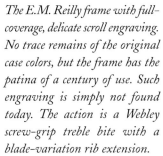

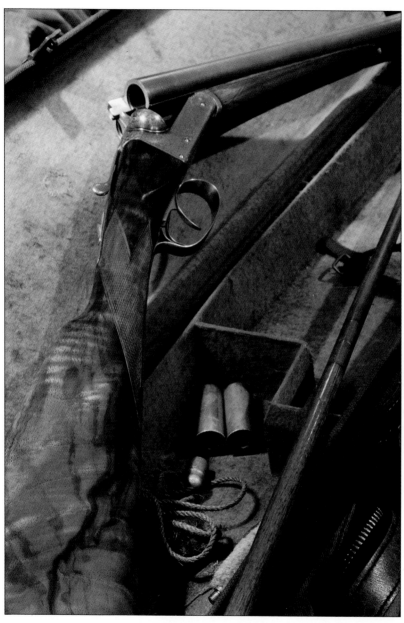

E.M. Reilly 12-bore best boxlock, from around 1890, restored by Edwin von Atzigen. The French-walnut stock is from a bygone age. When the gun was discovered, after 30 years in the rafters of a henhouse, the stock was so discolored with machine oil it took about 18 months to restore, including removing dents, fitting a stock extension, and re-cutting the checkering.

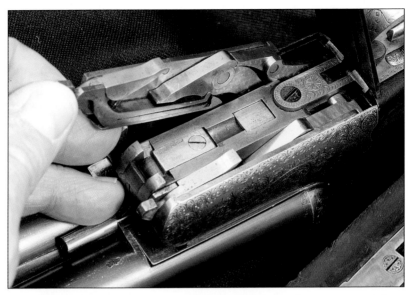

The Westley Richards detachable or droplock boxlock design, here seen on a 12-bore. Today, guns and rifles with this action command as much as a London sidelock.

James Woodward game gun with its signature arcaded fences and raised cocking indicator on the plate. Woodwards are renowned for their austere elegance. Based on his experience, gunmaker Edwin von Atzigen considers them the best made of all the great London sidelocks.

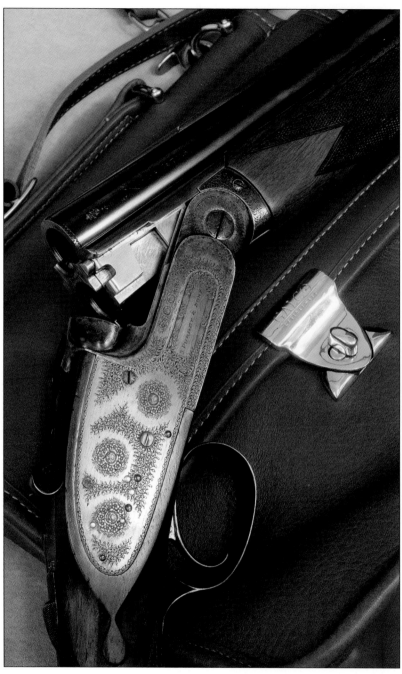

James Purdey & Sons 20-bore over/under, based on the Woodward design acquired by Purdey in 1948.

James Erskine 28-bore hammer gun, restored after a century in the harsh climes of southern Africa. Erskine was renowned for his Damascus barrels.

Immigrants all: These three—a W.J. Jeffery 12-bore hammer gun, a Williamson & Son boxlock, and a Joseph Lang sidelock— are all happily living in the United States, enjoying a renewed lease on life among a growing subculture of English gun aficionados.

Gibbs & Pitt's patent gun. This is a 12-bore, but the action is very strong and was used for both rifles and shotguns. Based on patents beginning in 1873, two years before the A&D, it proved quite popular. Note the snap underlever and lever-style safety on the side of the frame. Variations on the patent include a Jones underlever and separate cocking lever.

Stephen Grant side-lever gun with Damascus barrels, one of a pair owned by an American surgeon that were still embroiled in large-scale European driven shooting a century after they were made. With such a gun, how could one miss?

Damascus barrels are found in many colors, from warm brown to a frosty silver-blue. This beautiful set of barrels is from a W&C Scott 10-bore hammer gun.

A Damascus-barreled, side-lever Boss & Co. Where might the No. 1 gun be today? The sidelever leaves the top strap sleekly uncluttered, available for delicate scroll engraving that invites your fingertips.

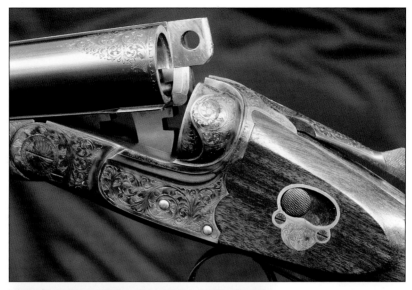

W.W. Greener adopted the boxlock, made it his own, and designed various features now found on boxlocks around the world. The Greener crossbolt is ubiquitous; the distinctive Greener safety, while sound and effective, does not work well with the British style of shooting where the safety is pushed forward as the gun comes to the shoulder, and is found on almost no guns other than Greeners. This beautiful Greener Model FH70 was made in 1936.

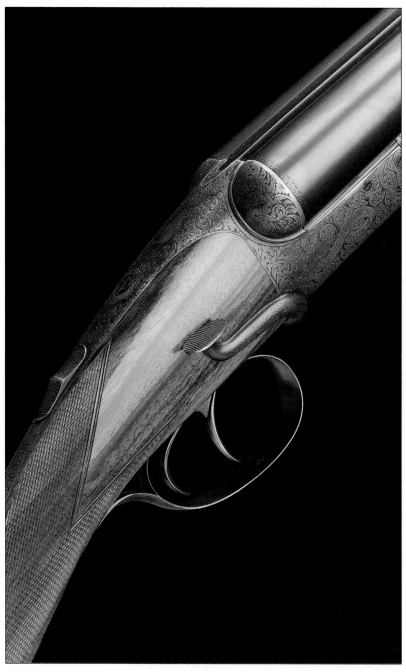

Dickson round-action 12-bore gun. The side lever accentuates the gun's already seductively serpentine lines. Photo Courtesy Steve Davis and Bill Orr

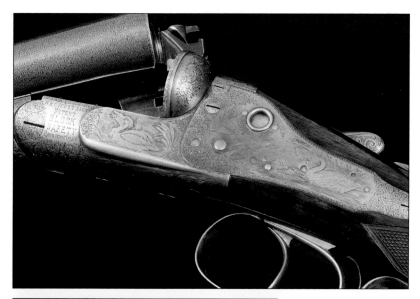

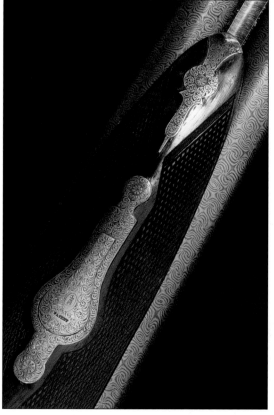

The famous W&C Scott & Son Crystal Indicator gun, with back-action locks. This 10-bore has lovely 30-inch Damascus barrels. Scott used this action for everything from small-bore double rifles to large shotguns. Scott also used a wide variety of forend latches in the years before the Anson and Deeley designs became dominant. Like this one, Scott designs are usually their own patents, elegant in appearance and beautifully made.

A pair of John Dickson 16-bore hammer guns, with Damascus barrels.
Photo Courtesy Steve Davis and Bill Orr

Rigby's signature humped sidelock plate and sweeping leaf motif fences, seen here on a 400/350 Nitro Express double rifle. Although Rigby is most noted for these distinctively shaped plates, other makers also used them at times, including Holland & Holland.

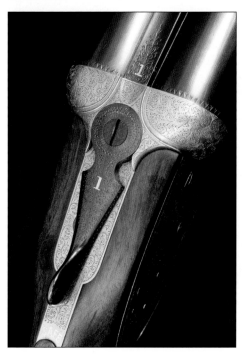

Number one of a set of guns, whether a pair (2) or garniture (3), this Henry Atkin is an elegant gun. Unusual for an Atkin, this is not the Spring Opener (Beesley) action.

William S. Needler 12-bore hammer gun. Needler was a provincial gunmaker, located in the whaling town of Hull. Photo by George Calef

James Purdey bar-in-wood hammer gun. With the decline in popularity of hammer guns over the past few years, such exquisite pieces offer the opportunity to own and shoot a gun with a legendary name at a fraction the price of a sidelock.

James Woodward patent "Under & Over" gun, from 1933. This elegant 12-bore is guaranteed to steal the heart of even the most confirmed side-by-side shooter.

today. In the 1990s, one could find them on racks in England selling for $400 to $600, depending on the maker. Many American dealers raided the Sceptred Isle, buying these guns in job lots, shipping them to the States, and selling them for $1500 to $2000. They were well worth the money, too. That market is largely a thing of the past, but visitors to England can still find good guns— they are constantly emerging from closets —and many of the ones imported to the United States come up for sale as their owners move up or move on.

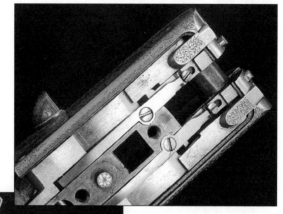

The internal workings of E.M. Reilly's patented ejector system. Geoffrey Boothroyd discovered more than 20 patents for ejector systems taken out by different gunmakers during the 1880s and '90s. The two that came to dominate were the Southgate and Deeley designs, but Reilly's works very well and is found on many E.M. Reilly guns. As with the Southgate and Deeley, most of the mechanism is housed in the forend.

For a grouse or woodcock hunter who also shoots a few rounds of skeet or sporting clays, ejectors are not only not an asset, but they are also an irritation. Speed of reloading is not a concern, and many shooters want to retrieve their hulls, either to reload or avoid littering. This is especially true if the gun has 2½-inch chambers. This is where extractors shine. They don't fling the empties all over creation. What's more, extractors are as close to being foolproof and unbreakable as any part of a side-by-side shotgun, which is no small consideration if you do not have a good double-gun specialist in the neighborhood.

A W&C Scott 10-bore. Note the set screw in the top lever to keep the main spindle screw from backing out. The now-ubiquitous spindle was a Scott patent, invented by the founder's son, William Middleditch Scott. These are the tiny touches that set the great British guns apart.

* * *

One should never say never in the English gun trade, but it is safe to say that every London best produced in the 20th century had selective ejectors, as did the vast majority of lesser sidelocks and boxlocks.

The most common ejector designs are the Southgate, patented by Thomas Southgate in 1893, and the Deeley ejector system, developed by John Deeley for use in the A&D boxlock action and patented in 1886. By no means are these the only ejector systems one is likely to encounter in British guns. Around 1890, many different makers designed ejector systems that were patented and deployed in guns with the proud claim "Patent Ejectors" on the frame. E.M. Reilly was one such maker, and many Reilly guns are found with "Reilly Patent Ejectors" engraved on the side. The Dickson round-action had its own ejector system, installed in the frame of the gun itself rather than in the forend.

Some of these systems are good, some not so good. The thing to remember is that even if an ejector system is defective, it can almost always be repaired by a competent gunmaker; failing that, it is usually possible to disengage the ejector mechanism altogether, leaving a perfectly functional set of extractors.

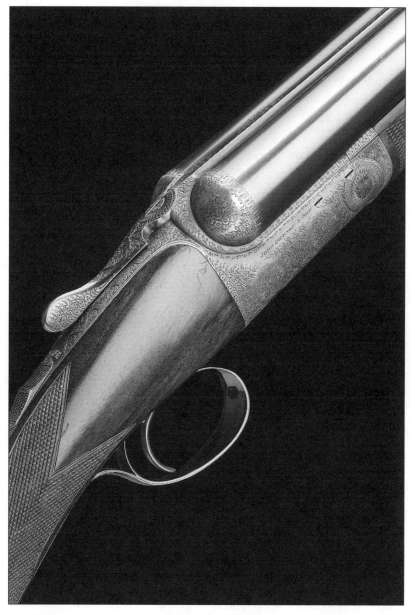

The Dickson round action incorporates some unique features, including its own pattern of ejectors, housed in the body of the action, not in the forend (as with the Southgate). This 12-bore is also fitted with a Boss-patent single trigger.

Photo Courtesy Steve Davis and Bill Orr

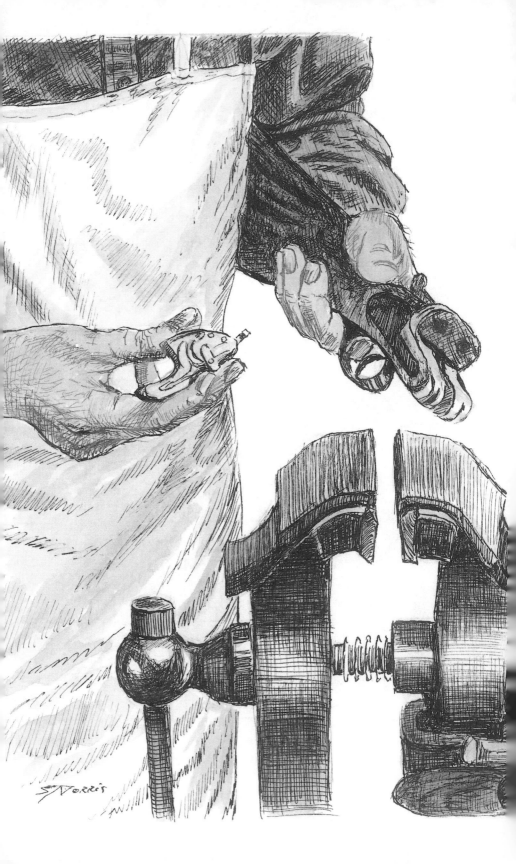

Restoration:
Fitting, refurbishing & modifying

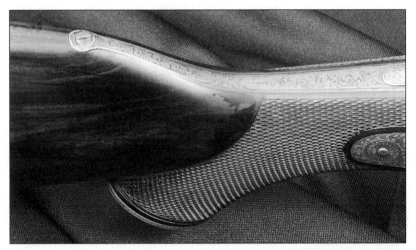

This is a rifle stock now, but it began life as a shotgun—a Holland & Holland back-action 10-bore that was converted, first to a .577 Nitro Express, then to a .600 NE. The stock was probably fitted during the first conversion, since this is obviously a rifle stock with its pistol grip and over-the-comb tang. It is an example of the fine workmanship found on rifles and shotguns from the late 19th century. Although it would be difficult to alter this stock to new dimensions, it can be done.

Just as a British shotgun is quite different from a typical American shotgun, so is the attitude toward used guns, collector value, and the market for older guns. Because most British guns appearing on used-gun shelves in the United States are many years old, and some more than a century, American buyers should approach them from the British perspective, not the American.

Typical rifles and shotguns listed for sale in America are accompanied by terms like factory original, new-in-box, or mint, along with estimates of percentages of original bluing and case coloring. These concepts permeate the used-gun business in America, especially for widely collected pieces such as Winchester rifles and Colt pistols.

Any buyer of a British gun, whether rifle or shotgun, should first rid him-self of any notion that the gun he will buy might be, could be, or even should be, factory original. These concepts are completely foreign to the British atti-tude toward guns and their use—most particularly, ironically enough, with very expensive best guns.

Every London or Birmingham best gun, with the exception of a handful of special commemorative or presentation pieces, was made to be used exten-sively in the hard world of large-scale driven shooting. It was the custom in England that a client would bring his guns back to the gunmaker every year for a full-scale professional strip and clean. This was routine annual mainte-nance. It was part of a client's on-going relationship with his gunmaker, the same as he would have with his tailor.

A professional strip and clean is a major undertaking. The gun is disman-tled until no two pieces are still fastened together. The gunmaker inspects each piece carefully for wear or corrosion, then cleans and lubricates them and reassembles the gun piece by piece, testing it as he goes. Any defective parts are replaced, usually fashioned by hand and file in the gunmaker's vise. When the gun is completely reassembled, every function is tested; if parts have been replaced, the gun is sent to the company's shooting ground where it is test-fired. Only when the gunmaker is convinced the gun is as good as the day it originally left his shop is it returned to its owner to wait impatient-ly for the next Glorious 12th.

When this process goes on, year after year after year, the gun undergoes changes—some minor and routine, others more drastic. Accidents happen. Barrels can bulge; barrel walls get thin; proof laws might require that the gun undergo re-proof, in which case the maker will prepare it for re-proof and submit it. If it passes, new proof marks will be stamped on the barrel flats. If it does not pass proof, the gunmaker might well re-barrel the gun. This, to the British, is all just normal maintenance. Factory original? Surely you jest.

Now let us suppose the gun passes out of the hands of its original owner. Perhaps his son inherits a matched pair, or they are sold at auction. Unless the new owner is exactly the same size and has the same dominant eye and hand as his predecessor, the gun will need to be altered to fit him. If the orig-inal maker is still in business, the gun would logically go there for the neces-sary alterations. These could consist of changing the stock dimensions by bending for more or less cast, or even changing the cast from left to right. The stock could be lengthened, by adding a recoil pad or a wooden stock extension, or shortened by cutting off a half inch or so. While it is in the shop, the stock would be refinished, with the dents and scratches removed;

possibly, the barrels could be re-blacked. The original escutcheon might be replaced with a new one bearing the new owner's engraved initials.

This is an expensive undertaking; it is also time consuming. But on a best gun it is worthwhile, because the new owner will get back, in effect, a perfect gun: Perfectly made originally, and now perfectly fitted to his individual physique and requirements.

A gun that is a century old might have changed hands in this way twice, thrice, or a dozen times, and undergone alterations major or minor each time it occurred. If the gun went back to a company like Holland & Holland, every change would be noted in the record book beside that gun's serial number and be available for inspection by future owners. If the gun was made by a fine maker who subsequently went out of business, such as Charles Lancaster, the records might be lost; as well, many such records were destroyed during the bombing of London in 1940.

The conclusion from all this is that buyers should put any notion of factory originality out of their minds when contemplating the purchase of an English best, or even a mid-range British gun.

Sometimes, guns are sold with "provenance," a history of the gun, where it's been, who owned it, and who did what to it. This is important to some people; others prefer to contemplate the gun and imagine where it has been and what it might have done, or investigate its background themselves and try to piece together the gun's history. All of this can be a fascinating undertaking but it is not in any way necessary when the buyer's primary interest is getting a good gun to take grouse hunting.

Another consideration that should be dismissed immediately is "collector value." Americans are obsessed with collector value and the effect that altering from factory original might have on the value of a gun to a collector.

Broadly speaking, there is no collectors' market for British best guns. Certainly, there are people around who "collect" individual names, like Dickson or Beesley. But this market is tiny, and it is completely unlike the collector market for, say, Parker shotguns or Colt revolvers. The major difference is that Parkers and Colts were listed in catalogs, with definite specifications and prices accorded to individual models, which can then be identified. They came from the factory in boxes, with factory hang-tags and various paraphernalia. British guns come with none of these. Some of the larger companies, like Midland and Webley & Scott, issued catalogs, and made different grades of guns that can be identified and classified, but they were the exception.

James Purdey and Holland & Holland, in recent years, have published catalogs and price lists, but these are really only a starting point. Since every gun is ordered individually, every gun is unique, made to order, with the features its purchaser wanted, and none that he didn't.

While we are on the subject of factory original, one should also mention that alterations carried out later by the original maker qualify as factory original in the minds of most dealers, even if the gun itself is no longer exactly as it was the day it first left the factory. A Holland & Holland rebarreled by H&H commands a premium price over one rebarreled elsewhere, no matter how qualified the secondary barrel maker might be.

Periodically, a British gun, after much hard use, might be sent back to the factory for a complete refurbishment, or "refurb," of both wood and metal. This would involve re-blacking the barrels after removing any tiny dents or scratches. After buffing to remove any rust or pitting, the engraving would be sharpened up where necessary, and the maker's name and address re-cut on the rib. It would include refinishing the stock, either touching up or completely recutting the checkering, a thorough cleaning, and repairing any internal problems.

America's premier restoration specialist is Doug Turnbull, who of course concentrates on Winchesters, Colts, and other American guns. Turnbull objects to the word refurbishment, preferring "restoration." This is an important distinction in one way: Refurbishing may be something of a dismissive term in America, but it is the accepted term in the United Kingdom, so a client buying a British gun from an American dealer needs to know exactly which he is dealing with when a gun is listed as refurbished.

A proper British professional refurb is essentially a restoration. It is not merely buffing and rebluing the barrels and slapping a coat of varnish on the stock.

* * *

For an American buying a used British gun, all three of these processes—fitting, refurbing, and a complete strip and clean—can come together.

Most Americans do not consider the idea of having a gun altered to fit them. I have lost count of the number of people who have said to me "Oh, I shoot okay with standard dimensions." That may be the case, but there is one problem: With English bests, there are no standard dimensions. Since these guns were made to fit the first client, or altered to subsequent ones, chances are that any gun you find that you like and can afford might have to be altered to fit you.

Most British guns were made either with cast-off (for right-handed people) or cast-on (for left). This can be changed—stocks are readily bent—and will have to be if the stock is wrong for you. The other major alteration will be to the length of pull. Shortening is no problem, but lengthening a stock can be.

Of course, in order to have the stock dimensions altered properly, you have to know what your ideal dimensions are, and that means having a stock fitting done by a qualified shooting instructor. A fitting takes a couple of hours and requires the use of try-guns (guns with special stocks in which all dimensions can be adjusted) and patterning boards on a shooting range. Some gunmakers try to get by with charts and check-lists, asking for shoulder width, height, breadth of palm, and so on, but this is haphazard at best. A proper professional fitting will cost about $250-$350, but is well worth the money, both for the man ordering a new gun and one having an old gun altered to fit.

Most buyers want to find a gun that is in good condition at a reasonable price, that fits them at least acceptably, and that works with no alterations. There is, however, a very viable alternative for someone who is willing to spend some time and money: Buying a gun that is down on its luck, refurbishing it completely, and at the same time having it fitted to his exact dimensions and specifications.

Because English bests are so well made to begin with, almost any can be returned to their former glory if you spend enough money. And, they are worth the investment. You will not make a huge profit on a gun refurbishment, but if the gun has a good name and the work is properly done, you should be able to get your money back out of it when the time comes. Even lesser names, and lower-grade guns, can be worth a substantial investment simply because they were basically so good to begin with. The English gun trade did not produce junk. Even a boxlock trade gun from 1910 can be turned into a nice fowling piece, and one that will put most of today's new production guns to shame.

The best way to illustrate what can be done is to look at a couple of specific examples from my own experience. The first is a James Erskine 28-gauge hammer gun, made around 1885, that spent most of its adult life in Africa. I acquired it by accident, took it to England, and left it with Steve Denny. Steve then shepherded the gun through a three-year process of re-proof and then refurbishing.

When I acquired the gun, it had cast-on (for a left-handed shooter), and the walnut stock was dessicated with extensive surface cracking. The Damascus barrels were fine on the outside (although they were an unearthly shade of green), but the bores and 2$\frac{1}{2}$-inch chambers were badly pitted. Obviously, it was out of proof and that was the first thing that needed correction. The firm of Ladbrook & Langton prepped the gun for proofing. To make it acceptable visually (guns first undergo a visual inspection, and can be rejected immediately if there is excessive pitting or visible rust), they lengthened the chambers to 2$\frac{3}{4}$ inches as the best way to eliminate pitting ahead of the chamber. The barrels were polished; since the walls were quite thick to begin with, the polishing left ample metal in the barrel walls.

The strange green hue of the barrels was caused by a coat of varnish that had been applied at some point and, while it was ugly and had to be removed, it probably saved the barrels from external corrosion down through the years.

With proof safely out of the way, L&L set to work making the gun shootable. The stock was rehydrated through steady application of linseed oil until the cracks closed up (none was life-threatening), the dents and scratches could be steamed out, and the stock was once again pliable enough to bend.

An interesting aspect of this particular gun is that its long, slender, back-action locks extend past the point in the stock where it was bent for cast, so the locks themselves are faintly curved, not flat. Bending the stock the other way created problems. To minimize them, we merely bent it to a straight position (no cast one way or the other). Still, the locks themselves are curved and the grip retains its original curve so they will fit, which gives the stock a slightly weird serpentine shape when viewed from the top. However, it is shootable and can always be returned to its original shape if acquired by a left-hander.

The gun has a graceful pistol grip, but the original horn grip cap was chewed by sub-Saharan rodents, so a new cap was installed. The hammers and external pins were nitre blued, the trigger guard and tang re-blacked, and the locks and barrels were left with their century-old patina.

The entire process took the better part of three years. The major factor was the laborious process of allowing the stock to absorb oil, regain its shape, and close the cracks. This cannot be rushed.

Because the chambers were lengthened to eliminate pitting, the gun was re-proofed with 2$\frac{3}{4}$-inch (70mm) shotshells. The entire refurbishment and re-proof cost about £800.

The second example is my E.M. Reilly boxlock, which has been mentioned elsewhere in this book. E.M. Reilly was a highly respected London gunmaker who supplied guns to both Sir Samuel White Baker and Frederick Courteney Selous. For a time, it occupied premises on Oxford Street adjacent to Purdey. Reilly was in business from 1848 until around

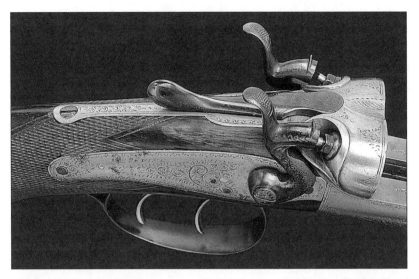

A James Erskine 28-bore hammer gun, dating from around 1885, refurbished and re-proofed in England.

Scottish gunmaker James Erskine was noted for his fine Damascus barrels. These, on the author's 28-bore (c. 1885), are a type of Damascus called 'skelp.' And beautiful they are.

1920, when it was acquired by a non-gunmaking firm and disappeared.

Edward Michael Reilly was a gunmaker and an inventive one, with several patents to his name. The company had a showroom in Paris as well as London, and advertisements dating from 1900 boast of a private shooting ground. The company made and sold everything from keeper's guns to pigeon guns to double rifles.

My gun, which was made in the early 1890s, has a Webley screw-grip treble bite, Reilly's own patent ejectors, a breathtaking stock of French walnut, and full-coverage tiny scroll engraving. These features taken together suggest this was a best boxlock. As far as I can determine, the gun was a gift for a Scottish gamekeeper from his employer. It was originally equipped with 30-inch Damascus barrels, proofed for blackpowder, and $2^5/8$-inch chambers. Around 1925, the keeper took the gun to Glasgow, where George Coster, a well-known gun and barrel maker, duplicated the Damascus barrels in fluid steel. The new barrels were then nitro proofed. The gun passed into the hands of the keeper's son, who emigrated to Canada. There it remained in a farm family until 1975, when the owner died; the gun, however, was nowhere to be found, and his heirs assumed he had sold it.

In 2004, the elderly widow elected to sell the farm. All the buildings were cleaned out and, high in the rafters of the henhouse, they found a burlap bag containing an oil-soaked Brady trunk case with a set of barrels strapped to the top. Inside the case was the Reilly and the second set of barrels.

One glance at the Webley screw-grip action, and the price tag, and the gun was mine. Then began a lengthy process of refurbishment. For the record, and to give an idea of the costs involved, I purchased the gun for $1200 CAD. Less than two years later, I received the finished gun back from my gunmaker. The complete refurbishment cost about $4500 CAD, for a total cost of $5700 CAD.

The gun was not re-proofed, since it was not in England. My gunmaker, Edwin (Edy, pronounced Eddie) von Atzigen, assured me the Damascus barrels were perfectly sound, there was no pitting to speak of (the gun's various owners had not spared the oil) and as long as I stuck to the proper-length shotshells, there would be no problem. And so it has proven.

It was apparent from the beginning that the gun's previous owners had respected metal but disdained wood. The stock was battered, beaten, dented, and scratched; the drop points were gone—worn completely away; the checkering was rubbed down to mere scratches. The entire stock was so black with oil it had no more figure or color than a tarred railroad tie. In fact, when I first saw it, I just assumed I would have the gun restocked. It was only later, exam-

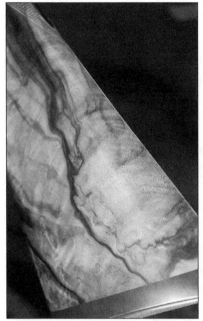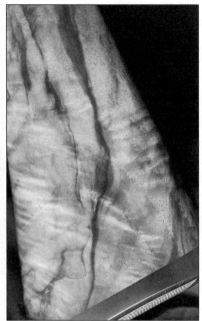

The stock of the E.M. Reilly, after restoration. When Edwin von Atzigen began work on it, the checkering and drop points were gone and the wood was oil-soaked black. After the oil was patiently coaxed out, the scratches and dents repaired, the checkering re-cut, the stock bent from cast-on to cast-off and lengthened with a piece of German rubber that resembles the finest ebony, the French-walnut stock was restored to a glory not seen in a century.

ining the butt under brighter light at an angle, that I detected dark grain running through it and began to suspect it might be worth saving.

Mechanically, there was only one thing wrong with the gun. The Reilly's patent ejectors were malfunctioning in one barrel. The Reilly system is built into the forend iron, and while not commonly found, is in fact a very sound selective ejector. It was quite easily repaired.

On dismantling the gun, Edy found rust in only two places: the pin connecting the trigger-guard extension to the tang, and the steel diamond in the forend that seats the pin holding the forend iron. Elsewhere, the metal was completely free from corrosion, although it was coated in dried oil and grime.

The first step was to begin the repair of the oil-saturated buttstock and forend. Using his own personal and highly secret method, von Atzigen began coaxing the oil out of the walnut. There are various methods of doing this, but some are quicker than others and some are potentially destructive. Edy is of the opinion that you cannot rush it—that if you try to get the oil out too quickly, it can damage the wood. The oil was absorbed slowly, he says, and it has to come out the same way. Altogether, it took more than a year of steady effort to accomplish that.

The buttstock had cast-on, having been made for a left-handed shooter, and was a good half-inch too short for me. I needed it bent and lengthened. As well, Edy needed to recut the panels behind the action (we decided against fashioning and attaching new drop points) and recut the checkering. For a butt extension, we considered ebony but finally decided to use a piece of hard black German rubber that looks like the finest ebony, takes checkering beautifully, and finishes with oil to an ebony-like sheen. This rubber is no longer made because of environmental concerns (the process involves cyanide), but von Atzigen has a stash of stock extensions left, and deemed the Reilly worthy of one.

The reason it was deemed worthy was that, as the oil was drawn out of it and the stock regained its color, we realized it was an absolutely fabulous piece of genuine French walnut. After adding the extension and bringing the wood back to its original state, it was sent to a stock-bending specialist to be bent to my dimensions of cast and drop, after which Edy recut the panels and checkering.

The forend was more of a problem. The inset steel diamond was heavily corroded. Edy made a new one and we sent it to Sam Welch, along with the engraved steel forend tip, and Sam matched the scroll engraving. The wood around the diamond was rotted by oil, so Edy cut it away and filled the gap with an ebony diamond that surrounds the steel one. It was a very effective, and attractive, solution. Some chips in the forend were repaired, and the checkering was recut.

Finally, the frame. Von Atzigen immersed the entire frame in a bucket of solvent and let it soak for 24 hours, then went at it with a soft toothbrush. As the accumulated grime reluctantly departed the delicate scroll, the frame came alive, with the engraving sparkling in the steel's old-coin patina.

The gun was lovingly reassembled. The newly engraved, newly shaped diamond insert for the forend, a new pin between the trigger guard and tang, the buttstock now resplendent in the luster of a London oil finish. The Damascus barrels are a light silvery blue, with no trace of browning left on them; the frame and trigger guard are devoid of case-hardening colors, now just plain steel with a century-old patina. The overall effect is of an old gun lovingly cared for—not a new one, nor even a restored one, since

The forend of the author's E.M. Reilly, in the process of restoration. When found, the checkering was almost completely worn away, the original steel diamond was corroded beyond repair, and the wood around it was unsalvageable. Edwin von Atzigen trimmed away the rotten wood and replaced it with an ebony diamond with a new steel diamond inset. The steel diamond was then engraved in scroll to match the steel forend tip, and the checkering was re-cut.

complete restoration would include browning the barrels, at least.

One can go with restoration exactly as far as one desires. In this case, I wanted to ensure the E.M. Reilly retained all the dignity of years of service, while regaining the spring of youth.

In the end, the obvious question is, how good a gun do I now have to show for all the time, effort, and expense? That is a question that should be asked both before and after undertaking a restoration, so it is worth looking at in some detail.

In terms of sheer beauty, you could not duplicate this gun today for any amount of money, simply because French walnut no longer exists. Of course, you could come close, but it is pointless trying to estimate what it might cost to buy a gun of comparable beauty. Three times the cost? Four? I have seen guns for sale for $50,000 that were not as lovely as the Reilly.

In terms of handling, there is no question: With its 30-inch barrels and total weight of 6 lb. 4 oz., the Reilly's balance is exquisite. It is lively, responsive, alive in your hands, eager to spring to your shoulder and swing through. There is no production boxlock made today that even remotely compares, and very few custom sidelocks, for that matter.

As mentioned elsewhere, my favorite period in English gunmaking history is the years between 1890 and 1914. During that time, gunmakers were both highly skilled and inventive; competition was intense, not to reduce prices, but to produce better, and better, and best. With some makers, time was not a concern; they worked until a gun was as perfect as human hands and dedication could make it. The smallest touches, the tiniest nuances of design and assembly were included in any gun with pretensions to being a best gun, and even those that were frankly not best guns could still boast of fine points that you cannot buy, today, on any gun, at any price.

After the Great War ended in 1918 and the gunmakers who survived went back to their workbenches, this began to change, brought about by any number of economic and social factors.

But, one can look at a gun made in 1895 and pick out some of these subtle features. The Reilly, for example, has a guide rail for the ejectors in the underside of the rib extension. On the original Damascus barrels, made in the 1890s, the groove is a minuscule double doll's head; on the replacement fluid-steel barrels, made around 1925 by George Coster, the groove and head are simply flat blades of steel. Coster was a highly respected craftsman, as good a barrel maker as existed in Scotland—and there were some fine ones in those years. He attempted to duplicate the Damascus barrels down to the last ounce, and he came close (they are actually an ounce heavier than the

Damascus), but the original barrels are still, identifiably, the product of a more graceful time in gunmaking.

* * *

The first step in any restoration, after finding a likely candidate, is determining exactly what will be required and how much it will cost. Actually, the process begins even earlier than that, with an expert assessment of the gun's state before it is purchased.

Today, the majority of fine English guns are sold at a distance. A buyer sees a gun listed in a magazine, contacts the seller, sends a check, gets the gun on a three-day approval. Unless you know the seller very well, or are yourself an expert, the best thing to do is have the gun sent first to a gunmaker who is a disinterested third party and get an objective opinion on the gun's condition and whether the price is fair. This will cost you a little money—probably a couple of hundred dollars, plus shipping—but it may save you a lot.

Having selected a gun upon which to bestow rebirth, you then embark on a long process that may involve many people. You have to find a gunmaker qualified to do the work—and here you need a gun*maker*, not merely a gun*smith*. How do you find one? There is no directory, but one can get references. It would help if the gunmaker is English or European trained, because then you have a firm idea of his background, but that is not absolutely necessary.

James Flynn, a gunmaker who lives in Alexandria, Louisiana, specializes in English double guns, although he was born and lived all his life in the south. But James is part of a web of gunmakers and skilled craftsmen who know each other, refer work back and forth, and occasionally collaborate on a project. Steve Davis, America's foremost expert on Dickson round-action guns, lives in Tennessee. There is a scattering of immigrant English gunmakers, including Jack Rowe in Oklahoma, David Trevallion in Maine, and Dale Tate in California. There is Les Paul (late of Henry Atkin) in Canada, and of course my friend Edy von Atzigen, a Swiss-trained gunmaker, also in Canada, and the Belgian-trained J.J. Perodeau in Oklahoma.

Finding a gunmaker and forming a relationship with him is the most important aspect of any restoration project. As with finding the love of your life, there are no instructions I can give, only suggestions. It helps immensely if the gunmaker is within driving distance, so you can visit the patient while it is in his care, but truly qualified and talented restoration experts are so few and far between that if this happens, it will be pure luck. It is essential that you trust each other, otherwise this partnership—your money, his skill, and a common passion—will disintegrate immediately.

A Holland & Holland restored to life by James Flynn, a specialist in English doubles in Alexandria, Louisiana. When Flynn acquired this gun, the stock was completely destroyed, as one can see from the remaining bits. Restocking was only part of the restoration process, which included extensive metal work and took more than a year to complete. This shows what is possible with a gun that might, at first glance, appear to be beyond repair. Such was the original quality of an English best, almost all can be restored to life—and are worth the effort and expense.

Unless a gunmaker is independently wealthy, and I know of none who is, cash flow is important to them, while getting the gun finished is important to you. Most will expect a deposit to start work—not unreasonably—but it would be a mistake, I think, to pay too much in advance. You then agree on a schedule of payments: So much when this is done, more when something else is complete. This keeps everyone dedicated. He will have costs along the way. If he is not an expert on stock-bending, he may send it to a specialist, which will cost you money. If you want the barrels rust-blued, he may send them to someone like Doug Turnbull. More shipping, and another cost.

If you need engraving recut, this will add considerable time and expense because the best engravers are booked far ahead. On a job like this, you may be able to get your work squeezed in as a small project in the breathing space between two larger jobs. I have had that happen, but I wouldn't count on it. Because each step must be done in sequence, which is dependent on the schedules and work loads of several people, the time required tends to stretch.

A minimum of a year, it seems, is required for a proper restoration and two years is not unusual, but anything beyond three years is probably out of line.

The key for the client, in a restoration project, is to research and learn as much as possible about the gun and the company that made it. If your intention is to restore the gun, as opposed to simply refinishing it or cleaning it up, you would not want to have a standard bluing job on the barrels if they were originally rust blued.

Similarly, you would want to restock the gun with a piece of walnut appropriate to the gun's date and place of birth. Often, one sees an English gun that has been restocked with a piece of wood that looks like it fell off a mid-range Browning—suitable for modern American taste, perhaps, but distinctly un-English. Not all English guns of the golden age were stocked with spectacular French walnut, but many were, and very, very few were outfitted with pieces of boring, mediocre wood. I have seen some Birmingham boxlock non-ejectors with stocks of walnut that would cost you a huge premium today, and almost all best guns have wood that is fine to wonderful. This is another reason to research: The individual companies had their own taste in wood. Some liked it red, some golden; some preferred stocks with very straight grain, others liked smoky swirls of molten caramel. It might not be possible to duplicate that wood, but it is possible to select a piece that looks appropriate.

Bill Dowtin, a gunmaker who imports wood from Central Asia, is an expert at choosing appropriate blanks for particular projects. On one restoration I undertook with Doug Turnbull, we restocked a Winchester Model 1886 whose original stock could not be salvaged. I asked Bill to find me a blank that would look at home on a deluxe Winchester from the late 1800s. The piece he sent was natural rusty red, with straight grain and subtle but extensive feather crotch. The finished rifle looked like it rolled out of New Haven during the McKinley administration and headed west.

We have all seen guns that have been restocked with walnut that is simply wrong for the gun: Winchester 94s with marble-cake Circassian, or a Parker that looks like it should be on display in Milan. By the same token, wood that is appropriate on a Parker looks completely out of place on a Purdey, and the wood we put on that Winchester '86 would be wrong, wrong, *wrong* on any restored English gun, of any grade, made anywhere.

When ordering a brand-new custom gun, it is of course completely appropriate for the client to have it stocked with any piece of wood that strikes his fancy, whether it is presentation Circassian walnut, bird's-eye maple, or a two-by-four from a Douglas fir. But, in my opinion, restorations are different. Most restoration specialists feel it is important to match the wood's overall quality as much as possible with the gun's original stock. That still leaves ample scope for expressing individual taste.

* * *

The metal frame of the gun is undoubtedly the most difficult to deal with. This includes the sidelock plates. It will originally have been case-hardened, but when it left the shop the colors may have been left intact, or polished away to leave it either bright or an elegant gray "old coin." A century later, who knows what it was originally? The patina imparted by a century of honest wear can be very attractive. This patina can be created artificially, and many buyers pay handsomely to have brand-new guns come out of the box looking like that.

It is difficult, if not impossible, to know what the gun really looked like the day it was new. And there is more to the question than just appearance. Altering the frame of a gun is fraught with peril, and my suggestion would be, unless there are mechanical problems that need to be corrected, or egregious scratches and scars, the frame should be left as it is, bearing the dignity of a century of use.

If you have a gun and want the frame and locks to have colors like it had originally, you can either case-harden it or use one of the modern chemical case-coloring methods, in which only colors are imparted and no changes take place in the qualities or hardness of the steel. The first is risky. It involves heat, and heat can cause warping. You do not want a warped frame. The second is wrong simply because it's wrong; it would give you colors, certainly, but they would not be at all like the gun's original colors and could well look hideous, garish, or completely inappropriate.

The frame, or action, is the one part of the gun where problems can be terminal. A cracked or warped frame is difficult, if not impossible, to correct. Stocks can be replaced, barrels can be sleeved, even locks can be duplicated, but without the frame you have no gun. For this reason, your initial assessment of the state of the frame is critical. Obvious indications of either abuse or botched repairs include cracks or signs that the action has been squeezed to tighten it. If word comes back that the frame has been abused, you may well want to abandon that particular gun unless the price is extremely low.

Barrels are a wide-open question. Candidates for restoration may come with pristine barrels or no barrels at all. In between those two extremes lies a wide range of possible conditions and solutions to match.

If a gun has no barrels at all, but has a sound frame and buttstock, immediately you are looking at a very high cost of restoration. Fitting a new set of barrels, in Britain, will cost (as of 2008) a minimum of $10,000. Having the work done in America may cost less, but not by a great deal. This is highly specialized work, and there is only a handful of craftsmen qualified to do it. Even obtaining the chopper-lump forgings to begin the work is an expensive undertaking.

The most common incident that destroys barrels is an obstruction that causes the barrel to rupture. This may destroy one tube or both. If that happens, and the breech end (chopper lump) is intact, the barrels may be sleeved. The barrels are cut off just forward of the forcing cones and new tubes are fitted, leaving the breech, barrel flats, and ejectors intact. This is also a popular approach with Damascus barrels that are questionable, or barrels that have deep pitting and overly thin walls. Sleeved barrels immediately reduce the value of a gun, even if it can be proven that the sleeving was done by the original factory. Unless the sleeving is done by an extremely skilled barrel man, it will be possible to see the seam where the tubes meet the breech.

An alternative to sleeving is to have the barrels lined with a steel liner. Externally the barrels appear to be original, but internally they are new and very strong. This almost always requires going down a gauge. A 12-bore becomes a 16, a 16 becomes a 20. Although proponents insist the balance can be as good as the original, that tells me that either the original was pretty bad, or they don't know what good balance is.

If the barrels are intact and salvageable, but with some rust or pitting, this can be polished away. Provided the barrel walls are still sufficiently thick, you have good barrels. You then have the engraving and maker's name recut and the barrels re-blacked. In England, re-proof would be required, but in America you take your gunmaker's word for it. Sometimes, only the chamber will show pitting, or the forcing cone just forward of the chamber. There are various solutions. Simply lengthening the chamber from $2^1/2$ inches to $2^3/4$ may solve the problem. Or, you can have just the chambers lined. This involves boring out the existing chamber to make room for a steel liner. Again, this is highly specialized work and only a few craftsmen can do it.

When a gun is rebarreled completely, the barrel maker usually engraves his name on the rib, although this is not always the case. Sometimes, the original rib can be salvaged and used with the new tubes. On my E.M. Reilly, the original barrels show the maker's name, while the fluid-steel barrels that were made for nitro proofing show the name and city of the barrel maker (George Coster, Glasgow).

There are so many possibilities and permutations involving barrels, barrel markings, proof marks, and re-proof marks, that it is impossible to list every one. Suffice to say, when considering a gun, this is an area that requires particular attention to determine not only the authenticity of the barrels, but of the barrel markings themselves.

* * *

It is possible to have a complete restoration carried out by the original company, in the case of companies like Holland & Holland, Purdey, or John Rigby, which are still extant, or by reconstituted companies like Atkin Grant & Lang or Watson Brothers.

If a new company legally acquired the company name and records, then it is considered to be, for the purposes of gun valuation, the original company. With H&H, the restoration would be done in the original factory on Harrow Road, where the gun was most likely manufactured; in the case of Rigby, it would be done in California, not in Rigby's original premises in London.

The cost of having such work done would be high, and it would take a long time. It would also lack the personal contact of client and gunmaker. On the positive side, the finished gun would be worth a considerable amount of money—almost as much, with luck, as you paid to have it done.

Some of these companies actively buy old guns of their own manufacture, restore them, and then resell them. Atkin Grant & Lang, now owned by Ken Duglan, has turned this into a significant part of the business at their shooting ground outside London. Henry Atkin, Stephen Grant, and Joseph Lang were all established independent companies at one time. Lang and Grant amalgamated, and later Henry Atkin joined the group. Each made its own style of gun, and even after it became Atkin Grant & Lang, there were no guns made under the combined name. Instead, if you wanted a self-opening sidelock on a Beesley action, you would receive a Henry Atkin; if it was a sidelever gun, then it would be a Grant. The Joseph Lang name was put on a variety of non-specialty guns. So, the current AG&L can buy old Atkins, Langs, and Grants, restore them, and sell them as factory-refurbished guns. Some I have seen have been remarkable pieces, all expertly restored to their original brilliance. Details of the restoration are entered in the original company books, and their provenance is established beyond question.

* * *

At this point, it is only fair to warn readers that firearm restoration is addictive and can be damaging to your financial health. Just as some become hooked on new custom guns, ordering one after another and always having a couple under construction, so others can be seduced, immersed, and finally possessed by the fascination of restoring old firearms to new life.

In the first category, the eccentric Charles Gordon stands alone. Gordon, a wealthy gun collector, was John Dickson's most unusual client. He did not shoot, only collected. Gordon ordered his first custom gun from Dickson in 1875, and his last in 1906; during those 31 years, John Dickson made more than 300 firearms for him. Three hundred! Gordon went bankrupt indulging his passion. Today, his guns occasionally come up for sale, identified as a "Charles Gordon gun."

Charles Gordon is in the same category as Lord Walsingham, one of the premier game shots of the Edwardian age, who bankrupted himself paying for elaborate shooting on his estates. To the best of my knowledge, there is no record of anyone bankrupting himself restoring firearms, although it may have cost a few marriages.

There is, at the root of all of this, a passion. For years I pondered the question of why I, and others, become so emotional about firearms, new and old. Almost always, the passion is directed at finer guns. They could be the largely hand-fitted, hand-finished Winchesters of 1900, or Colts of the same era, or the best bespoke Purdeys and Lancasters. Or, they could be medium-quality boxlocks of the years before 1914. Different guns appeal to different people, but there are common threads.

The common thread here is hand labor—the skill and knowledge that flows from a craftsman's head, through his fingers, into the gun that he is making. That magical quality stays with the gun throughout its life, and that life can be very, very long—virtually infinite, in fact. These guns are made with steel and wood, crafted in a vise with a file, tempered by fire. A thousand years from now, that gun can still be shooting, or made to shoot once again, provided a man exists with the skill and the knowledge and the vise and the file and a piece of steel.

This magic simply does not exist with a gun fashioned from polymer, stamped out by a machine. No matter how well it might function in the short term, it is still a product of a disposable age. Fine guns are not disposable. They are made to last forever.

A man and his dog go out to hunt grouse, and he takes with him a hundred-year old English shotgun. He may be that gun's sixth or seventh owner. Each of these participants —dog, man, gun, bird—is an essential element in a timeless ballet, but each participates within its own cycle. A grouse may live three seasons, a dog may hunt for ten; the man will hunt for 50, but the gun can go a-birding for a century, and the grouse as a species outlasts them all.

This metaphysical reality of hunting is one of the things that intrigues serious bird hunters so much, and gives us all a feeling of participating in something much larger, and older, and more important than ourselves. There is an element of immortality about it.

With this in mind, a man who orders a bespoke shotgun from Holland & Holland today is setting in motion a train of events that will long outlast himself and his children. A century from now, a man whose father is not yet born will lift down that gun and say, "This was ordered in 2008 by . . . ." Immortality, of a sort. And a gift to posterity.

Similarly, intervening in the life of a gun a century after it was made, after it might have fallen on hard times, fallen into the hands of barbarians who cut back its barrels or left it to rust behind the henhouse door, is also acting with an eye to posterity. The man who restores that gun to its former glory and sets it once again on the right path is becoming part of its history, which is already older than the man himself.

Does all this sound too esoteric? Too romantic? Perhaps it is. But a man who hunts ruffed grouse in the forests of southern Ontario or northern Minnesota has a lot of time to think about such things, and most of us do. On those rare occasions when you have a bird or two in hand and can hold it and study it as you sit on a log, sipping some icy creek water, you reflect on its life and your own. I believe it was Gene Hill who said "The birds we kill fly on forever." If you sit on that log, and remember the shot, and recall in detail the flight of the bird as it left the ground and you swung your gun after it—if you remember that truly, then the bird truly does fly on forever.

Every wingshooter has some shots that stick in his or her memory. Not necessarily the best shots they ever made, or the most difficult, or the most dramatic. Sometimes it is the surroundings that make the memory, and the shot is just an exclamation mark. Sometimes, it puts into perspective part of your life that is completely unrelated—the death of your father, the end of your marriage. Sometimes it is just a combination of blue sky, and a chilly breeze, and flaming maple leaves, and oncoming winter, and an exultation so gripping that you can do nothing but hold the warm, dead bird close to you, throw back your head, and watch the clouds crowding before the wind in the deep-blue sky. Skies are never so blue as on a sunny October day.

And sometimes, if you are lucky, you will look down at the gun in your hand and reflect on how many times it may have felt this exultation flow from other hands. In Scotland, on a big grouse drive; later in Ontario, on a backwoods farm; now in southern Georgia, with wild quail bursting from the briars.

Here begins the passion for fine old guns, and for restoring fine old guns.

Blacking the Bits:
Exploring the nooks & crannies of gunmaking

It is almost 160 years since Casimir Lefaucheux appeared in London with his break-action gun and inspired the modern age of the English shotgun. In 160 years, it is not surprising to find intriguing blind alleys, mysterious bits and pieces of information, arcane terminology, and odds and ends of things that should be discussed but have no logical home.

One such is the peculiarly British system of pairs of guns. Other countries have made, and do make, guns in matching sets, but the custom originated in Britain in response to its unique culture of driven shooting in the late 19th century. As with many words and phrases in the English language, the term "matched pair" has been over-used and misused and is, as a result, largely misunderstood.

Pairs of guns are used in driven shooting to increase the shooter's fire-power. While he is swinging and shooting one gun, his loader is recharging the other. Gun and loader hand guns back and forth without looking at one another; the gun's eyes are on incoming birds, the loader's on the shotguns themselves. Ideally, the two guns that make up a pair are absolutely and completely identical down to the last detail, including weight, balance, trigger pull, and even the grain in the walnut stocks. The theory is that there will be no differences whatever in the way the two guns feel, however minuscule, to affect the shooter's swing.

Ideally, the guns are ordered at the same time, the forgings from the barrels come from the same lot, the stock blanks are cut side by side from the same tree, the guns are assigned consecutive serial numbers, and they are built concurrently by the same craftsmen. When completed, one gun (with the lower serial number, usually) will have a gold-inlaid '1' on its frame, barrels, and forend. This is to ensure the parts do not get mixed up because, although they are supposed to be identical in every way, when dealing with the microns of British gunmaking, the parts themselves are not interchangeable. There are exceptions to the numbering rule, too. There is one instance on record of a man ordering a pair but insisting the distinguishing numbers not be visible from the outside—that they be hidden away on the action and barrel flats, and the inside of the forend iron. That way he could not be affected even psychologically by knowing which gun he was shooting.

Making a pair of guns identical in every way is extremely painstaking work and most gunmakers add a surcharge of 10 to 20 per cent when a pair is ordered. Not least of the problems is obtaining a suitable pair of stock blanks. There is more at stake than merely matching the grain; the grain of two pieces of wood will never match exactly, of course, but they can come extremely close in color, flow, and figure if they are adjacent blanks from the same tree. Two such blanks will have the same density and hardness; when cut to size, they will not only be very close to the same weight, but they will also tend to dry at the same rate and react to moisture the same way.

In the walnut business, sets of blanks suitable for pairs, threesomes, foursomes, and moresomes are greatly prized and can be extraordinarily expensive if the wood is highly figured. I have heard of a pair of blanks selling for $10,000. The blanks need to be cut from the same tree, at the same time, and then kept together for years as they season; when you increase it to three, or four, or six blanks, it becomes even more difficult. In 1987, in Spain, I saw a set of six identical AyA No. 1 guns that were being made for an executive of one of the large Basque banks in Bilbao. And a few years ago, gunmaker Peter Nelson undertook to make several sets of nine identical guns for some extremely wealthy clients. Obtaining nine virtually identical blanks from which to make nine guns is well beyond difficult.

* * *

Two guns manufactured to be identical are commonly referred to as a "matched pair," but to the purist, this is not technically correct. Such a set of guns is simply "a pair." A matched pair is one in which the second, matching gun is created later with the goal of duplicating gun number one. Since the first gun was never intended to be part of a pair, it would have no numerals inlaid on its parts, but these would be added when the second gun was built.

Then we have composed, composite, and companion pairs—each a variation on the same theme. A composite pair, according to Geoffrey Boothroyd, would be two guns by the same maker, but with serial numbers some distance apart; the second gun would be ordered and built to the same specifications as the first. The difference between a matched pair and a composite pair is that in the latter case, gun number one would not be marked as such.

The composed pair, Boothroyd says, is the arcane instance of gun number one being made to duplicate number two. This could occur when the original

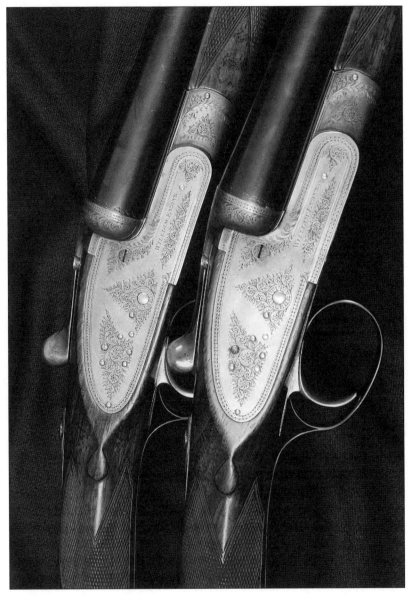

A pair of William Evans 16 bores, indistinguishable but for the gold '1' and '2' inlaid into the forend, the barrel rib, and on the top lever. Ideally, the two guns should move through production together, with each operation performed on each gun by the same craftsman. Making two guns virtually identical is very demanding, and most gunmakers charge a 10 to 20 percent premium.

number one is lost or destroyed, and the owner is trying to recreate the pair.

Finally, a companion pair is two identical guns made to match two other identical guns, thereby giving the owner a foursome. They might be numbered '3' and '4.' Or not, as the case may be. Again, according to Boothroyd, the terminology is used this way even if all four guns were ordered at the same time and have consecutive serial numbers. Obviously, a loader cannot manipulate four guns at once, so normally only two would be in use on any given shoot.

Sometimes, a client will have three identical guns made. This is called a garniture and follows the same steps as a pair. A man with a garniture of guns would generally have two loaders.

Pairs and matched pairs constitute a rich field for anyone interested in the historical aspects of gunmaking. Over the years, pairs are broken up by death, accident, or bankruptcy, and two guns—twins at birth—can find themselves at opposite ends of the earth. Considering the wanderings of landed gentlemen during the days of the British Empire, it is not surprising to find a #1 gun in South Africa, keeping leopards out of the sheep pen, while #2 is in Canada, keeping a trapper in ptarmigan. Often, when a man had two sons, each would get one of the guns and they would gradually become separated as they passed down through two branches of the family.

When war was declared in August 1914, some British officers took their sporting guns with them to France. In those halcyon days, a British officer carried only a revolver, a sword, or a swagger stick, depending on his branch of the service, so going over the top with a Purdey game gun was not a completely ridiculous notion. One such officer said that carrying his London best lent "a touch of distinction to a rather vulgar occasion." Another said he felt it gave the war a more sporting feel.

In 1974, author Anthony Price built an entire mystery novel (*Other Paths to Glory*) around one such junior officer, killed in an obscure part of the Battle of the Somme. In the story, the officer goes to France with a pair of Charles Lancasters in a leather case, and is carrying gun #2 when he and his entire company disappear without a trace, marching into the darkness as the battle unfolds. The story revolves around the resurfacing, years later, of that very gun. What makes it particularly interesting is that the scenario is not really far-fetched considering events that actually occurred during the war.

Geoffrey Boothroyd reported that he became interested in the exact terminology of pairs while looking through an auction catalog. He defined matching, composite, composed, and so on, after consulting with the auctioneer. Auction houses have their own arcane terminology to describe arti-

On pairs, numbers are inlaid into each component (frame, barrels, and forend) to ensure the right parts are reassembled into the right gun. Although supposedly identical, the parts are not interchangeable, were never intended to be, and accidentally mixing them can have unpleasant consequences.

cles of antiquity, not just guns, but not all auction houses will necessarily use the same terms or even agree on what a particular term means. Anyone buying a gun, or thinking of bidding on one, and seeing the term pair, matched pair, or any variation with the word pair in it, should ask for an explanation. About the only foolproof method of knowing what you are dealing with is to see if the serial numbers are consecutive.

Steve Denny agrees that a pair should be a pair, and that a matched pair is one in which the second gun was made later to match the first. Beyond that, he says there is no agreed-upon lexicon among English gunmakers to describe sets of guns. There are just too many possibilities and permutations.

"Here at Holland's, we have guns that come in for various alterations," he said. "A man might have a gun and buy another, and send the second one in with instructions for us to make it feel as much as possible like the first. That could mean restocking as well as changing the barrels to try to create something akin to a pair.

"Another man might just send two guns and tell us to make them feel as similar as possible."

When he was with E.J. Churchill, getting their reconstituted gunmaking operation off the ground, Steve approached an acquaintance who was in the business of making parts for Formula One race cars. The parts were all produced on the most high-tech of machinery, to tolerances of a micron. Steve took him two actions, made as a pair in the 1930s, which Steve described as "perfect in every way – as good as the old Churchill ever made." When they met later, his friend, having measured the individual parts of the actions on his ultra-modern gauges, opined as how he could train a chimpanzee to make actions like that—"in no way" were they identical. They're the same weight, I'll give you that, he told Steve, but by his standards of precision they were not even close. That, however, is not what matters. What matters is whether the guns feel identical to the shooter.

The very fact that the major components of the guns are numbered to ensure the pieces do not get mixed up is evidence that they are not interchangeable, and not expected to be. Steve Denny tells another story of a client with a pair of guns who sent them back, complaining that one gun often doubled while the other refused to fire the second barrel. At the factory, however, they could not recreate these phenomena. Then someone hit on the idea of switching the parts around, mixing up the numbers, and sure enough, with mismatched numbers, the two guns began to misbehave as described. The owner accepted the guns back with an embarassed silence.

At various times, some have advanced the idea of taking a fine double and duplicating the individual parts on computerized machinery capable of producing copies that are identical down to a micron or two. Although to the best of my knowledge no one has seriously tried it, you might or might not get a gun that would work. At the very least, it would probably require some hand finishing, and there remains the question of how long it would continue to function, and how reliably. The concept of duplicating parts fails to take into account that hand-made guns do not have all their bits manufactured, laid out in sequence, and then bolted together into a gun; instead, the gun is an assemblage of individual mechanisms that all work in harmony. Each mechanism is created piece by piece and the parts coaxed to work together as they are gradually filed, fitted, filed a little more, and then tested again.

The lore and legend of pairs has intrigued generations, especially those trying to trace the other half when they own one of the two guns. Curiosity about what might have happened to a gun's brother over the course of a century could easily become an obsession.

For those in this situation, there is a possible solution: In England, an organization—a gun dealer, really—called Matched Pairs attempts to link lost guns, or at least their owners, together. The owner of a gun that is obviously one of a set can register with Matched Pairs to try to trace the other. Sometimes, this is done with an eye to acquiring the other and reuniting the two; other times, it is just curiosity. If too much time has passed, the chances of the two still being identical are pretty slim; stocks get altered, bent, and cut down; chokes get opened up; guns are restocked and rebarreled. Still, I think if I were in that situation, I, too, would want to know where my treasure's other half had ended up. And, if I found it living in penury, eking out a living whacking rats in a henhouse, I would probably mortgage whatever was handy to rescue it. Such are the perils of being a romantic.

* * *

Pairs of guns are just one manifestation of the highly individual nature of the British custom gun business. Another is guns made to suit a person's physical peculiarities. One frequently sees offered for sale a gun with a drastic bend to the stock, allowing it to be placed against one shoulder while the barrels are aligned with the opposite eye. This can be done for a number of reasons: A right-handed man with a left master eye, or a man who has lost an eye, to give two examples.

After the Great War, many soldiers came home missing limbs, missing eyes, or partly crippled, and the gunmakers did their best to fit them with guns that accommodated their disabilities as much as possible. A one-armed man, determined to resume shooting, might order a gun considerably lighter and with shorter barrels, that could be swung with one hand; another, missing a left (lead) hand might order a gun with a special forend or appendage on the barrels in which to link his artificial hand or hook. Given the bespoke nature of the gun business, and the extraordinary skills of the gunmakers themselves, making such guns was not really difficult.

Left-handed shooters were accommodated in several ways: By making a standard gun with cast-on, or making a complete mirror-image gun in which every function is the reverse of the standard, or making a gun somewhere in between.

The mirror image is a fascinating thing to behold, because literally every function is the opposite. The top lever moves to the left to open the gun, rather than to the right, so parts of the internal bolting system are also reversed. The left barrel will be customarily the more open, and be fired by the forward trigger; the right barrel will have tighter choke, fired by the rear trigger. The triggers themselves will be reversed, with the forward trigger on the left. The trigger guard will have its protective bead along the left edge rather than the right.

In some cases, but not all, the lock plates of a sidelock gun will be curved very slightly to match the cast of the stock. This is more common with back-action locks where the plate extends along the wrist, but it was also done with bar-action plates. Usually, it can be seen by putting a straight edge along the plate and looking for a crack of daylight. This becomes a factor if you want to bend the stock from one cast to the other, or restock the gun entirely. Similarly, the tang and the trigger guard will have a curve, but this can usually be corrected. These are things to watch for when buying a gun.

My James Erskine hammer gun was made originally for a left-handed person, but the only left-handed manifestations are the cast of the stock and the curve of the back-action lock plates. Oddly enough, the tang comes straight back, placing it noticeably closer to the right side of the grip than the left. This illustrates the danger of fooling with such a gun without knowing what you are doing, or leaving a fine double in the hands of a gunsmith who is accustomed to replacing springs on pump guns and not much more. Trying to alter something without being aware of all the possible ramifications can begin a domino effect of one problem after another.

When buying a gun, looking for signs such as these and knowing what you are getting into can save a great deal of time, money, frustration, and disappointment along the way.

* * *

James Purdey is a name famous far beyond the gun business. People who know nothing about guns know that a Purdey is reputed to be the best, the finest, the *nonpareil*. Mystery writers routinely write Purdeys into their plots and, depending on the context, possession of a Purdey can demonstrate that a character is a man of taste, a social climber, an *arriviste*, or a man with more money than sense. This places Purdey in a select group that includes Rolex watches and Rolls-Royce motorcars.

The Purdey name in gunmaking is nearing 200 years old, and during that time, not surprisingly, there have been a few attempts to counterfeit a Purdey gun. George Caswell says that in his three decades in the business, he has encountered a few counterfeit guns, but not very many. Certainly, there is no wholesale fraud in fine guns the way Rolex watches are counterfeited by the Chinese. There are various reasons, one being the strict controls on firearm movement internationally, and the other being the difficulty of making a gun that remotely resembles a Purdey at any price that would make it economically viable. After all, had it been possible to do that, some legitimate gun-

It is impossible (short of a can of paint and a man skilled with a brush—which has happened) to find two stock blanks that are absolutely identical. The stocks on this William Evans pair are very close, although the author has seen stocks both better and worse than these.

maker would have done so long since! Then, of course, there is the question of counterfeiting the proof marks.

Traps for the unwary lie in the thousands upon thousands of cheap guns turned out in Europe a hundred years ago, and then emblazoned with names that were similar enough to dupe the innocent. A man may know that a James Purdey is the finest of guns, but what does he do when he encounters a "J. Purdy" or a "James Purdie"? The Belgians were notorious for this around 1900, and to a lesser extent the Spanish.

At a small gun show in Illinois in 2005, I saw a shotgun for sale on a dealer's table. It was a coarsely made sidelock gun with broad scroll engraving of the most nondescript kind; the wood was poor and wood-to-metal fit nonexistent. Carved into the lock plate was the name W. Richards. The dealer was asking $10,000 for it, and had a small sign laboriously filled out giving some details about the history of Westley Richards. I looked at it closely, and when I made eye contact with the seller, his expression suggested I should just move on. Which I did. One thinks of this type of overt fraud as belonging to another century, but it shows that if you come across such a gun—whether bargain-priced or not—it pays to look very carefully. An examination of the proof marks would probably tell the tale, but of course I did not ask to do that.

The British gun trade produced, by comparison with the Belgians or Spanish, no junk. In fact, Steve Denny says, the demand for cheap guns in England in 1900 was filled in the same way it was in America: By importing them wholesale from Belgium. By now, almost all of the Belgian junk has been flushed out of the British market through the cleansing process of re-proof, and requirements that guns be in proof when they are sold.

Such guns might or might not have British proof marks. When a gun is imported to England, it must undergo proof unless it has already been proofed in a country whose proof and proof laws are acceptable. Spanish proof is acceptable in Britain—Spain has some of the toughest proof standards of anyone—but Belgian proof has not always been acceptable, and so a Belgian-made gun might well have British proof marks.

Encountering a gun like the bogus Westley Richards at a country gun show presents its own problems. You are unlikely to be given a three-day grace period in which to have the gun inspected, as you would buying from a high-end, professional gun dealer. On the other hand, anyone who writes a check for $10,000 for such an obvious piece of junk—and it was, even from ten feet away—probably deserves what he gets.

At various times, guns with names like Barker (Parker), W. Richards (Westley Richards), Purdy (Purdey), Riggby (Rigby), and so on, were imported to both America and the United Kingdom. One still encounters them. Regardless of the name, any I have seen have been so ramshackle it was obvious they were imposters.

There is another side to this coin, and W.J. Jeffery is the best example. The Jeffery name is routinely misspelled as Jeffrey, or even Jeffries, even in advertisements for fine guns and by writers who should know better. That aside, in the English trade there were many makers with the name Jeffery (12), as well as Jeffrey (1), Jeffries (1), and Jefferies (2). So a gun with a variation on this name may be a Belgian imposter, or it may be a perfectly legitimate obscure English gun accidentally or intentionally misrepresented as a product of the illustrious William Jackman Jeffery. Of the others, George Jeffries was the most prominent gunmaker, with a couple of patents to his name.

* * *

The first rule for anyone interested in British guns is "never say never." There are very, very few rules, pieces of accepted wisdom, or items of com-

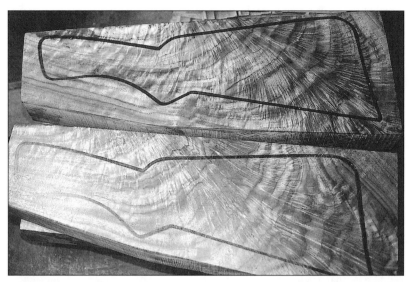

Two blanks, cut from the same tree, adjacent to each other, dried and seasoned together, and now waiting for the right order from the right customer. These blanks originated somewhere in Turkey. There is great competition among gunmakers for the best matching blanks, whether two, three, four, or as many as nine. The finest pair of matching blanks can sell for $10,000, with the buyer assuming all risks if the stockmaker cuts into one and finds an irreparable fault that renders the wood useless.

mon knowledge for which there are no exceptions. Walk into a shop with a few dozen English guns on the rack and you are almost certain to encounter something new, something you have never seen, even something you were certain never existed.

While almost every gunmaker, large and small, had his preferences and idiosyncracies, each was a custom shop, making guns to the specific order of his customers. Literally from the days of Joseph Manton, competition among English gunmakers was intense. Pressure to produce something new, different, or better was driven by the need to attract and keep clients. The English gun trade was free-market capitalism at its most admirable and most ferocious. When Europeans bemoan the ruthless model of Anglo-Saxon capitalism, this is it in a nutshell.

So, when a customer walked in off Bond Street desiring a new gun, the gunmaker might try to sell him this action or that, convince him of the merits of their patent ejectors or single trigger, but when the time came to write down the order, with very few exceptions, the client got what the client wanted.

In this book are photographs of guns and features found on some guns that I, for one, did not know existed. There is a Holland & Holland sidelock with sideplates scalloped like a Rigby; there is a Henry Atkin with a standard action (i.e., not the "spring opener" Beesley); there is a Boss that is neither a sidelock nor a best gun, in spite of Boss's claim to be a "maker of best guns only." The Boss is a John Robertson boxlock, made for Boss in Birmingham, so technically they do not violate their rule. But still . . . .

The Robertson boxlock is a fine example of a sleeper. Were one to come across such a gun at a show and look up the name in Boothroyd's directory of British gunmakers, one would find a short bio of John Robertson himself, but no mention of a boxlock with his name on it. In the section on Thomas Boss, you would find more information about Robertson, his career, his patents, and his success in turning Boss into a top-tier gunmaker, but again, no mention of a boxlock. This is not to criticize Geoffrey Boothroyd; it simply shows that there are always new things to see and learn about. These secrets are one of the fascinations of the English trade.

Sometimes, if the gunmaker was a prolific inventor like Frederick Beesley, you might find features that exist nowhere else. Beesley sold off his first few successful patents, including the action used by Purdey, but his later ones he kept for himself and installed on his own guns. A buyer finding a Beesley for sale might find an unusual safety, or ejector, or who knows what, that he has never seen before, never heard of, and can find no reference to anywhere in the literature. A Beesley with such a unique Beesley feature may very well be one of a kind, and the same is true of many other English gunmakers.

One can be misled by catalog entries for some of the gunmakers if one reads the specifications of a particular model and takes them as gospel. For the high-end gunmakers, a catalog entry was (and is today) only a starting point. From there, the client can upgrade the walnut, change the triggers, dictate the choke configuration and barrel length, request a rounded action rather than standard, and of course alter the engraving. When the gun leaves the shop, it bears no resemblance to the photo in the catalog from which it originated. Since English gunmakers rarely engrave the model name on a gun, a prospective buyer a century later is left trying to piece together a puzzle and determine exactly what gun he is being offered. Even if the model name is engraved on the gun, it may look nothing like a photo of that model found in a book.

This is the reverse of the dilemma discussed earlier—either being offered a counterfeit, or a gun with a similar name by a different maker. In this case, one runs the risk of turning down a fine gun because it has features one does not expect, or a name one does not recognize.

There is no easy answer for this. One cannot tour around a gun show with a wheelbarrow full of reference books. Nor can the average American (or anyone else) easily and quickly absorb the knowledge of someone like Steve Denny, Jack Rowe, or George Caswell, who, collectively, have spent several lifetimes in the business and handled literally thousands of different guns. All the reading in the world is no substitute for holding guns in your hands and learning how they feel.

There is an intuitive aspect to this that goes beyond the absorption of facts and figures about gun production, standard models, engraving patterns, and so on. Take, for example, the John Robertson boxlock mentioned above. Held in your hands, the gun feels right. It is not a Boss game gun by any means, but it is a very fine-handling boxlock with excellent balance and feel. And really, assuming a gun is sound and safe to shoot, isn't that what counts? I have handled a few Purdeys that felt awful in my hands, and many that felt good, but not one that felt as magical as a Boss. Would I buy a Purdey strictly for the name, even if it did not feel good to me? Only as an investment, and only if it was a remarkable bargain, and even then I would think twice.

A knowledge of British proof marks is a good starting point for ensuring that you don't get taken, and also that you do not pass up a great deal. Beyond that, when you are handed a gun with a name you don't recognize, you are much like a detective who comes onto a fresh crime scene and attempts to piece together the event. Much of it is instinct, putting two and two together, looking for something that is out of place, or something that should be there but is not.

Before I ever reach that stage, however, I have to pick up the gun, balance it in my hands, let it speak to me, bring it to my shoulder, move it back and forth. Bring it down, and then back up again. If it does not feel just right, then I put it down and move on. What's the point of going farther? If a gun feels wrong—heavy, ill-balanced, leaden—there is really not much that can be done about it. A seven-pound gun cannot be turned into a six-and-a-half-pound gun without major alterations, and usually not even then. A light gun is built to be light from the time the forgings land on the actioner's bench. A beautifully balanced gun with 30-inch barrels does not get that way as an afterthought. Those qualities are built in from the beginning.

Certainly one can restock guns, shorten barrels, drill wood out of the butt to lighten it or add some lead to make it heavier. One could even, at hideous expense, have a new set of chopper-lump barrels made. But all of those are stopgaps—attempts to put a patch on a problem after it has been created.

Therefore, if a gun does not feel magical to me when I pick it up, I usually don't bother looking for the name or trying to figure out if it is a good deal for the price or not. I already know the answer: No matter how low the price, for me, that gun is not a good deal.

This brings us back to the very beginnings of this book, and the new interest in English guns shown by Americans throughout the 1980s and into the 2000s. They are looking for guns with wonderful workmanship and exquisite handling qualities, not merely guns with names that lend some status. Those handling qualities, to a great extent, can be found on a wide range of guns, not just hyper-expensive jewels from the top-tier names.

The very first step in finding such a gun, one that will fill that spot in your heart but not empty your wallet or void your marriage, is to handle as many British guns as you can, ignoring the name, the hype, and even the price. Like looking at a litter of silky little setters, chances are you won't have to pick one. The right one will pick you.

Part Two:
Guns & Gunmakers

George Caswell

Jack Rowe

Guns & Gunmakers

During the 150-year life of the modern British fine shotgun trade, literally thousands of shops, large and small, have made guns, commissioned guns, or put their names on the barrels of guns purchased from others. These companies ranged in size from large mass-production factories such as Vickers and W.W. Greener, to the larger custom shops like Holland & Holland, to hardware stores in small villages that handled two or three guns a year.

In this section, the major names are listed along with their approximate years of operation at each address; this information helps to date a gun, because the address was often engraved on the rib. As well, the dominant products of each company are listed. Finally, where possible we have assessments of each maker's guns from two experts in the field: gunmaker Jack Rowe and gun dealer George Caswell.

Caswell, who owns Champlin Arms in Enid, Oklahoma, is one of the most knowledgeable dealers in the United States when it comes to British guns of all types. Over a career that has spanned decades, Caswell has bought and sold more than 15,000 double rifles, as well as thousands more shotguns. When it comes to obscure English names, the value of English guns, and the quirks and characteristics of each name, no one in this country is more expert than George Caswell.

John F. Rowe—Jack, as he is universally known—is an English gunmaker, trained in Birmingham, who emigrated to the United States in the 1980s and settled in Oklahoma. Rowe's knowledge of gunmaking and English guns generally is encyclopaedic and he is often consulted before a prospective buyer finalizes a deal for an English shotgun. Jack describes himself as the "eldest English-trained guy in this country," and notes there are only about a half-dozen of his generation of Birmingham gunmakers left.

In many instances, Jack refers to a maker having its guns "made in Birmingham." This does not necessarily mean the guns were completely made and finished there. Rather, many smaller makers would buy anything from a barreled action to a complete gun in a semi-finished state, and finish it themselves—stocking, fitting, engraving, and so on. For example, he notes that few Scottish makers had the resources to make a gun completely, from the ground up, and the same was true of some London gunmakers. By the time H&H bought out W&C Scott in 1985, for example, H&H and Scott were the last two barrel makers in the country, between them supplying the entire trade.

In each section, where either George Caswell or Jack Rowe has an opinion about a particular maker or his products, or their relative value, that opinion has been directly attributed.

Much of the historical company information in this section is drawn from the works of Geoffrey Boothroyd and Nigel Brown.

Boothroyd devoted his life to cataloging, preserving, and recording every available detail about the British gun trade. He wrote newspaper and magazine columns for many years, and in most cases these columns were compiled into a series of anthologies (see Bibliography), as well as *Boothroyd's Revised Directory of British Gunmakers*. The directory has 412 pages listing every gunmaker or dealer whose name might be stamped on a gun; this information was meticulously gathered during a career that lasted half a century.

Nigel Brown was, for many years, a legal advisor and secretary of the Gun Trade Association in the United Kingdom. His *British Gunmakers, Vols. 1 & 2* covers every listing in the trade, both in London and throughout the country, for the last two centuries.

The lists in both of these works are exhaustive and detailed, covering thousands of gunmakers and shops involved in the British trade. Our purpose here is to include only those names whose products are most likely to be found in an American shop, and provide information that will be useful to a prospective American buyer. The dates and addresses listed have been drawn from both Boothroyd and Brown, and reconciled if possible where there is a conflict.

* * *

ARMSTRONG & CO.

Little is known about Armstrong & Co., which was located in Newcastle-upon-Tyne around 1900. The first listing appears in 1886, at 10 Neville Street, and the last around 1917, at 115 Northumberland Street.

There is nothing exceptional about Armstrong & Co. It is included here for two reasons: One, we have a surviving example of an Armstrong gun—an Anson & Deeley boxlock with sideclips and a blind Greener crossbolt belonging to Robert Kolesar. Two, Armstrong & Co. is a proxy for thousands

A mid-quality 12-bore boxlock by Armstrong & Co. Note blind Greener crossbolt and sideclips.

of similar small firms that existed throughout England and Scotland in the years before the Great War.

Their guns are not London bests, by any means, but by today's manufacturing standards they are exceptional, exhibiting signs of hand workmanship and great care in their creation by skilled craftsmen.

ARMY & NAVY

The Army & Navy Co-operative Society Limited was set up in 1871 to supply all the equipment a young officer would need going overseas or out to the colonies on service. This included guns, rifles, and every manner of gear. Because it was founded by a group of officers, the managers were less concerned with price than they were with ensuring that every item with the name "Army & Navy" was top quality. After all, an officer's life might depend on it. Being a co-operative, goods were sold at very low prices and members received a share of the profits at the end of the year.

The original store was at 105 Victoria Street in London and by 1901 there were branches in the main cities of India—Bombay, Delhi, Calcutta, and Karachi. The company remained in business for more than a century and maintained a gun department in their store at 60 Victoria Street until 1964.

In 1978, Army & Navy (by then a general retailer) was acquired by House of Fraser, and the original Army & Navy was renamed House of Fraser Victoria. It is now the only department store operating in the Mayfair district of London. The records of the Army & Navy Co-operative Society are deposited in the archives of the University of Glasgow.

Army & Navy retailed a wide range of brand-name firearms, including Greener, Smith & Wesson, Colt, and Remington, as well as guns made to order with its own name. According to Boothroyd, in 1907, a best A&N sidelock cost £45, a plain sidelock could be had for as little as £13, and Anson & Deeley boxlocks cost from £7 to £12.

Jack Rowe insists that all Army & Navy guns were made in Birmingham, but Michael McIntosh knows of at least a half-dozen double rifles made by the London firm of John Wilkes, and the author has seen a single-shot manufactured by Charles Lancaster. This is one of the intriguing aspects of Army & Navy, and makes an A&N gun or rifle an excellent buy simply because one may be buying a fine name under a different label.

Jack Rowe:

> *The company had no gunsmiths as far as I am aware, and the guns were all made in Birmingham. Webley & Scott made a lot of their shotguns as well as the double rifles. The boxlock double rifles made for them by Webley were the finest to be found anywhere. Their best grade of sidelock is as well made as any high-grade gun bearing the names of top London makers.*

George Caswell:

> *They are basic but serviceable guns, generally made by Webley and of very good quality. Most were plain to begin with and are often well-used. They come on the market frequently, and there is no premium or discount on their price.*

ASPREY

Asprey is the most famous name in the British jewelry trade, and their shop in New Bond Street is to Mayfair what Tiffany is to Manhattan. Asprey's is now 227 years old; it was founded in 1781, and opened its shop in New Bond Street in 1847. Asprey later acquired property on Albemarle Street, parallel to New Bond Street, which allowed their shop to stretch between the two.

Over the years, some of Asprey's wealthiest clients have come from the oil-rich Middle East. Bespoke gold jewelry is an Asprey specialty, and in 1983, Asprey produced their first presentation gun, a Smith & Wesson revolver, extensively engraved and inlaid in gold for an Arab client. From there, it was a short step to opening a gun room in 1989, offering custom shotguns and rifles.

Asprey was involved in the early stages of the bidding for Holland & Holland when that company was purchased by Chanel, and Edward Asprey told me in 1993 that the decision to open an Asprey gun room was an indirect result of losing H&H to Chanel. Asprey hired away many H&H craftsmen, who built the Asprey guns from workshops in their homes.

The company manufactured guns of only the very highest quality. Their standard shotgun was a sidelock self-opener with blind pins in the locks. Asprey also made double rifles and bolt-action rifles. Relatively few guns were made, and most ended up in the hands of people like the Prince of Wales, the first President Bush, and General Norman Schwartzkopf.

Asprey's closed their gun room in 1996. Recently, the last three guns produced, still in the white, were completed by former Asprey craftsmen and sold by Christie's, the auction house.

> 1847 – Present: 165-169 New Bond Street
> 1991-96: Asprey Gun Room, 23 Albemarle Street

Jack Rowe:
> *Guns made by this company were best guns only.*

HENRY ATKIN

Henry Atkin the elder was a gunmaker who started with James Purdey in 1814, and was reputed to be the first craftsman Purdey hired. He stayed with them for 50 years. His son, also Henry, joined Purdey and was apprenticed to his father. In 1866, Henry the Younger went to work for William Moore before setting up on his own in 1877 (although there are records of him being in business some years before that at an address in Chelsea).

Atkin signed his guns "from Purdey," which caused some problems with his former employer but, since James Purdey signed his own guns "from Manton," he did not have a very solid argument. Henry Atkin died in 1907.

From the beginning, Atkin made very high quality guns. His "spring opener" is essentially a Beesley action, the same as used by Purdey. In 1960, the company amalgamated with Grant & Lang; from that point on, if a gun was ordered from Atkin Grant & Lang with a sidelock spring-opening action, it was sent out with the Henry Atkin name.

AG&L went through its own tumultuous history (see below) before ceasing to trade in 1980. It has now been resurrected by Ken Duglan, who apprenticed with Atkin Grant & Lang in the 1970s. Duglan continues operations, including making new guns and refurbishing old ones, at his shooting ground outside London.

> 1877: 18 Oxenden Street
> 1890: 12 Jermyn Street
> 1890-1918: 41 Jermyn Street
> 1918-52: 88 Jermyn Street
> 1952: St. James's Street
> 1960: Amalgamated with Stephen Grant & Joseph Lang to
> become Atkin Grant & Lang.

Jack Rowe:
> *Guns made by this company have always been of the highest quality. Their finest gun was the Atkin "Spring Opener," a gun similar to the Purdey with only the ejector mechanism being different.*

George Caswell:
> *The company is noted for its "spring open" action, and Atkin's general quality is excellent. In a best sidelock, I have found Atkin guns to be one of the better values. They typically command a 5 to 10 percent premium. One thing to watch for is condition, as many Atkin guns appear to have been used extensively.*

ATKIN GRANT & LANG

This company was formed from the merger of Henry Atkin with Stephen Grant & Joseph Lang, Ltd., in 1960. It was located at 7 Bury St. in St. James. In 1971, E.J. Churchill joined the group, it became Churchill, Atkin, Grant & Lang, and stayed in the same premises until 1976 when it moved to 61 Pall Mall.

The company ceased to trade in 1980, but was later resurrected by Ron Solari, who was located in Lincoln's Inn Fields, London. The name is now owned by Ken Duglan, who operates the company from his shooting ground outside London. Although he does not have a factory *per se*, Duglan has gunmakers who make new guns and refurbish old ones.

In recent years, Duglan has made a practice of buying old Henry Atkin, Stephen Grant, and Joseph Lang guns, or any of the other companies that

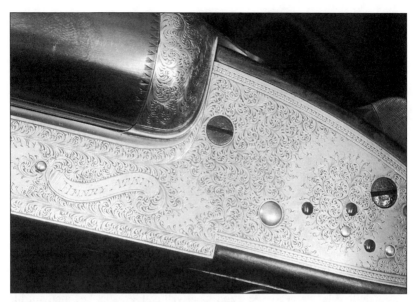

Henry Atkin best 12-bore sidelock, unusual in that it is not built on the Beesley action with its "spring opener."

Henry Atkin, number one of (probably) a pair. Note Churchill rib.

were absorbed by AG&L, and refurbishing them to new condition. He has reconditioned many fine old guns this way and, because they are done on his premises, the alterations are considered "factory."

The amalgamated company never made guns with the name "Atkin Grant

& Lang." Rather, they made guns with the names of the original companies on them—Henry Atkin "spring opening" sidelocks, Stephen Grant (mostly sidelever) guns, and Joseph Langs of various descriptions.

FREDERICK BEESLEY

Frederick Beesley was one of the most inventive gunmakers in the English trade. At the age of 15, he was apprenticed to William Moore (who had been a stocker for Joseph Manton) and worked for James Purdey before setting up on his own. In 1879 he patented a self-opening hammerless (sidelock) action, and the following year sold the design to Purdey. They have used the Beesley action, virtually unchanged, ever since.

Beesley himself continued in the trade, making guns and inventing and patenting various mechanisms. He was a prolific and successful inventor, designing boxlocks, safety mechanisms, an improved version of the self-opener, and an over/under. Some of these patents were sold to other gunmakers, including James Woodward and Cogswell & Harrison, but many of his later ones he preferred to keep and use himself. Because of this practice, surviving Beesley guns may incorporate some unusual features.

After the patent expired on the Purdey action, Beesley preferred it for his own guns. He died in 1928; his son carried on the business until 1939, when he retired, and it was absorbed into Grant & Lang. In 1980, Churchill, Atkin, etc., was closed down and the owners sold off many of the gunmaker names it owned, including Hellis, Beesley, and Watson Bros. This became, for a time, Hellis, Beesley & Watson. In 1986, it was renamed Frederick Beesley Gunmaker and continues in business, in Buckinghamshire. The Watson name was acquired by yet another group in London and, reconstituted, is once again making guns.

This is typical of the tangle caused by the absorption of different names by other companies throughout the early 20th century, and the subsequent spinning-off of those names to become new companies, albeit with no connection to their predecessor beyond that.

> 1879-93: 85 Edgeware Road
> 1893-1900: 3 St. James's Street
> 1900-39: 2 St. James's Street

Jack Rowe:
> *Beesley made some very fine guns. He made an O/U sidelock, but not*

many. It was a rather heavy gun with a big action. The lock that fired the lower barrel was made to work upside down to direct the force of blow to the striker in a direct line, the idea being to avoid misfires often caused in O/U guns with angled strikers. I repaired the only matching pair of these guns that Beesley made, but I have never seen any others. They are rare guns; not many were made. There was another Beesley, not to be confused with Frederick Beesley, but I have not seen a high-grade gun made by the other one.

George Caswell:
I've never seen a bad Beesley. He was noted for his innovation and the overall quality of his guns is excellent. They do not appear in the market very frequently, and when they do, they command a premium of about 20 percent.

BENTLEY & PLAYFAIR

Bentley & Playfair was formed in Birmingham in 1846, and later opened a London office at 60 Victoria Street. The company made all grades of guns, both boxlock and sidelock. It later amalgamated with Isaac Hollis to become Hollis, Bentley & Playfair. Isaac Hollis and Charles Playfair were shareholders in Birmingham Small Arms (BSA) when it was formed in 1861.

BIRMINGHAM SMALL ARMS (BSA)

BSA was established in 1861 to manufacture military weapons, with much of its output going to the United States. Its shareholders were members of the Birmingham Arms Trade, a gunmakers' trade association. The company survived the severe gun-trade slump following the end of the War Between the States. For the next several decades, BSA underwent various corporate reorganizations but prospered making Snider, Enfield, Martini-Henry, and other military weapons.

In the 1920s, BSA began making boxlock shotguns on Anson & Deeley actions, in both ejector and non-ejector models. There were three grades: The lowest grade was very plain with a blued frame, the mid-range gun had some engraving, and the top grade was fully engraved. Stocks varied according to grade.

Jack Rowe:
These guns were about 80 percent machine made, and assembly was farmed out to outworkers in the Birmingham trade. I recall one old-timer

telling me years ago that the outworkers welcomed this work, as it was so well machined that they could make big money on it. I have repaired many of these BSA guns over the years, and can confirm that they are well made, robust, and if one should come your way, hang on to it. BSA guns are now showing up in the USA.

JOHN BLANCH & SON

John Blanch worked with John Manton before establishing his own firm in 1813. In 1826, he moved to 29 Gracechurch Street; when his son William joined the firm in 1848, it became John Blanch & Son. The company relocated to Cullum Street in 1915, then moved several times before it was bombed out in 1942 and, to all intents and purposes, ceased to trade in new bespoke guns.

The company continued after 1942, however, doing trade work. At one point, it occupied the same premises as Cogswell & Harrison, for whom it did considerable work.

> 1826-1915: 29 Gracechurch Street
> 1915-1928: 20 Cullum Street
> ?: 96 York Road
> 1931: 40 Pall Mall
> 1933-42: 6 Mitre Street

Jack Rowe:
> *Very under-rated guns by a good maker. I have never seen an original gun by this maker that was in any way poorly made. Most of what I have seen have been back-action sidelocks similar to the Holland & Holland Grade C, or Dominion model.*
>
> *In the 1970s, the Blanch name was being used by a dealer in London using the Cullum Street address. These guns were made from Spanish-barreled actions, imported, proofed at either the London or Birmingham proof house, and stocked, engraved, and finished in England. They should not be confused with the original Blanch guns.*

George Caswell:
> *Blanch was particularly noted for making back-action guns, and the quality was very good. I have seen a couple of very nice Blanch guns with excellent detailing and very nice engraving. Blanch guns are seldom seen, but there is no premium paid for the Blanch name.*

THOMAS BLAND & SONS

Thomas Bland began in Birmingham in 1840; in 1872, the son of the founder, Thomas Jr., opened a branch in London. The Birmingham end of the business closed after the Great War, but the company continued in London until 1990, when the name and company records were purchased by an American, Glenn Baker, of Pennsylvania.

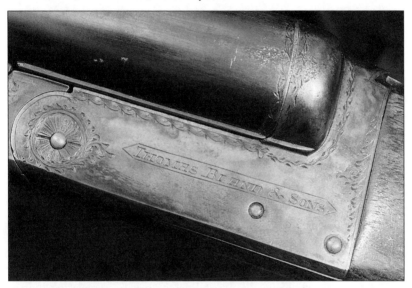

Thomas Bland 12-bore boxlock, made around 1965. The 1960s were a sad time for English gunmaking. This is undoubtedly a solid gun, but not a pretty one.

Through the latter half of the 19th century, Bland made a wide range of shotguns, rifles, and pistols, and took out patents for various inventions, including a rifle sight and a three-barreled gun. Bland made 4-bore "Field" patent guns, keeper's guns, waterfowl guns, and just about anything else you could name.

> 1840-1918: 41-43 Whittall Street, Birmingham
> 1872: 106, The Strand, London
> 1886: 430, The Strand
> 1900: 2 William IV Street
> 1919: 4-5 William IV Street
> 1973: New Row, St. Martin's Lane

Jack Rowe:

A fine old firm of gunmakers, now moved to the USA. My experience of their guns is that they made mainly middle-grade to cheaper-grade guns, with much of their trade done in the empire, India, and the colonies.

George Caswell:

Bland guns are mostly working or field-grade guns, and waterfowl guns. They appear fairly regularly, but a lot have obviously been heavily used. While the quality is good to very good, Bland guns tend to be heavy.

C.G. BONEHILL

Christopher George Bonehill was a Birmingham gunmaker who contributed to the trade in many ways, and was widely respected, not just for his guns but also for his pioneering efforts in the way they were made.

C.G. Bonehill was obviously a man of talent, ambition, and drive. Born in 1831, he apprenticed with one Mr. Aston (there were 15 in the trade, and no one is sure which one it was) at the age of 13, and after completing the seven-year apprenticeship set up on his own in 1851, when he was only 20 years old. His first shop was in the St. Georges district of Birmingham; in 1870, he moved to 33 Charlotte Street, and a few years later acquired the old National Arms and Ammunition Company plant in Belmont Row, where he established the Belmont Fire Arms & Gun Barrel Works.

Early on, Bonehill saw the possibilities of machines replacing human hands in the manufacture of guns, and much of his effort was directed towards this. Because he was also active in the politics of the trade, through gunmakers' associations, and was a Guardian of the Birmingham Proof House for 28 years, he was very influential with other gunmakers.

C.G. Bonehill believed that guns could be made on machines, with interchangeable parts—a laudable goal in some ways—and actually succeeded in doing this to a point. He even made a model called the Interchangeable, but to what extent this was really true is difficult to tell. Not surprisingly, Bonehill's main market for this type of gun was the U.S., but his exports to the U.S. were effectively ended in 1890 with the punitive McKinley tariffs that made such imports prohibitively expensive.

Because he began in business the very year the break-action gun was introduced in Britain, Bonehill made a wide range of firearms, including all kinds of rifles and shotguns, both sporting and military, and even air rifles in later years. With the introduction of the Anson & Deeley action, Bonehill

C.G. Bonehill Belmont Interchangeable Hammerless 12-bore boxlock.

more or less standardized on that basic design, although he continued to make a range of sidelock guns as well. Much of his effort at machine production was concentrated on barrels. He developed a pattern of machined block (similar to the European monobloc) into which his barrels were inserted after being turned on a lathe.

Because of his innovations, Bonehill guns are both interesting and widely respected in the trade. The company went out of business gradually, finally ending in 1962. The company records and ledgers, piled in a corner of the shop when it was cleaned out, were destroyed.

> 1851-70: St. Georges, Birmingham
> 1870-75 (approx.): 33 Charlotte Street
> 1875-1922: Belmont Row
> 1922-62: 4 Price Street

Jack Rowe:

Bonehill was in business for many years and made everything from hammer guns through to sidelocks. They made a gun called the Belmont Interchangeable. The parts were supposed to be interchangeable with other guns. I don't know if they are—I've never tried. The Belmont was a medium-quality boxlock of Bonehill's own design (not an A&D) and had the notation

"Three Bells Steel" engraved on the barrels. I have never seen this make of steel on any other gun.

Bonehill's sidelocks were well made, but I have yet to see one that would come up to what I call best London standards.

George Caswell:
Bonehill's general quality is good. They appear fairly regularly and there is no premium paid for the name. Most Bonehill guns I see were well used.

BOSS & CO.

Boss is one of the truly legendary names in British gunmaking, always included as one of the top three and considered by many the best of them all. The company's motto is "Maker of Best Guns Only," and while this may not be strictly true (Boss marketed a line of made-in-Birmingham boxlocks with the name John Robertson), it is close enough to the truth that the exception proves the rule.

Just as a brilliant composer will be found to have had a chaotic, tragic life, completely belied by his music, so Boss's early history gives little indication of the single-minded dedication to quality that marks the company's work. Thomas Boss led an unsettled existence, the company moved around, changed hands, and by the end, little of Thomas Boss was left except the name, the quality, and the name that had itself become a byword for quality.

Boss's father, William, worked for Joseph Manton, and Thomas was apprenticed to his father in Manton's firm. Manton kept him on after he became a journeyman, and probably around 1812 he struck out on his own. The company letterhead states "Established 1812," but the company itself does not date from that year—hence the conclusion that this is the year Boss left Manton. At various times he performed out-work for James Purdey but was not, contrary to belief, ever a Purdey employee. He set up shop in various places, but never stayed for long. Thomas Boss died in 1857.

In 1860, Boss's widow took Stephen Grant (later founder of his own renowned firm) as managing partner, and in that year the company took the name "Boss & Co." Grant left to set up on his own in 1867. Control of Boss later passed to two nephews named Paddison. In 1891, John Robertson was brought in as a partner and the company finally began to find the direction that defined its existence for the next century. Robertson was a gunmaker and inventor, apprenticed in Scotland and later employed by Westley Richards.

Although Robertson is now given credit for many innovations that define

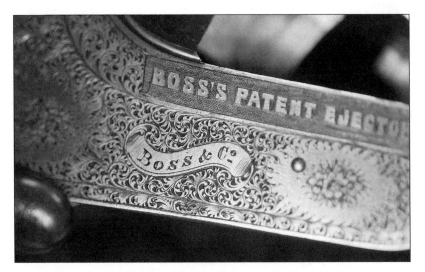

Boss & Co. 12-bore sidelever game gun.

Boss (the over/under and single trigger especially), Boss was never renowned for individual inventions so much as for the consistent, overall brilliance of its gunmaking. This was Robertson's greatest achievement. He cannot have been an egotist, since he never attached his name to Boss, and so dwells in relative obscurity while Thomas Boss is revered as a great gunmaker.

Since the firm dates from the earliest years of fine English gunmaking, it is not surprising to find Boss hammer guns, Damascus-barreled guns, and sidelocks of various descriptions, as well as the later over/under. It is generally agreed that Boss really began making "best guns only" on its adoption of a hammerless sidelock mechanism, but the guns that predate that are still very fine indeed.

The Boss game gun is a side-by-side, often with a rounded action, with a distinctive rose and scroll engraving pattern, its own sidelock mechanism, and a feel and balance that can only be described as exquisite.

The over/under is truly legendary. Geoffrey Boothroyd says it is not a gun, it is a work of art. George Caswell says a Boss O/U is "an incredible piece—possibly the best."

Boss also made double rifles (including, in the 1990s, the only O/U .470 on a Boss action). They are revered, rare, and hideously expensive.

Boss & Co. moved around so often it is very difficult to compile an exact record of where they were and when, and for how long. Herewith, an attempt:

c. 1816: 3 Bridge Street, Lambeth
c. 1827: 33 Edgware Road
c. 1833: 1 Lower Grosvenor Street
1835: 14 Clifford Street
1837: 76 St. James's Street
1839: 73 St. James's Street
1908: 13 Dover Street
1930: 41 Albemarle Street
?': Cork Street
1982: 13 Dover Street

Jack Rowe:
   They are best guns; you will not find better. The boxlock, sold under the John Robertson name, was made in Birmingham and was itself "best" quality.

George Caswell:
   Boss guns are always top quality—excellent plus. Especially desirable are their rounded-action guns, and guns in smaller gauges. They appear fairly regularly, and a Boss commands a 30 to 40 percent premium.
   It is not well known, but Boss used dovetail lumps as well as chopper-lump barrels, and many guns rebarreled by the company have dovetail lumps.
   Most Boss owners are astute gun people who take pride in owning one.

CHARLES BOSWELL

Charles Boswell was a small London firm with a checkered history that never produced many guns compared to some larger firms, but did make guns that were high quality. Boswell was born in 1850, apprenticed to Thomas Gooch in Hertford, and set up his own shop in Edmonton, outside London, mostly doing repairs. He became an excellent trap and live-pigeon shooter, and this led to considerable work from other shooters. He finally opened a shop in The Strand in 1884.

The period of greatest production was between 1887 and 1914. Boswell became prominent in the London gunmakers' association, but sometime during this period he had a falling out with the Proof Master in London and took to sending his guns to Birmingham to be proofed. The existence of Boswell guns with Birmingham proof marks has led to the conclusion that he was a Birmingham maker, or had his guns made in Birmingham. This is not true.

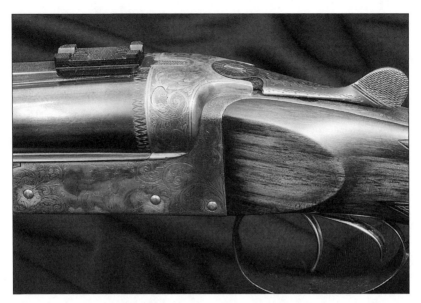

Charles Boswell double rifle in, of all calibers, .32-40. A well-made rifle, and Boswell had a good reputation. The engraving leaves much to be desired.

Boswell's early connection with trap and live-pigeon shooting continued, with the company making many extremely fine pigeon guns. It seems the abolition of live-pigeon shooting in Britain, combined with the Great War, helped to bring about a general reduction in business for Charles Boswell, and from 1918 until their final demise in 1941, they made relatively few guns.

In 1941, the company was bombed out and family connections with the firm ended in 1944. The Boswell name continued in the gun business, however. In 1958 the name was acquired by Interarmco, with an address at 168 Piccadilly (the address of Cogswell & Harrison, also part of that conglomerate), but it ceased to trade in 1963. In 1980, the name was acquired, reportedly, by Frank Malin, who tried to make guns in Canada. That venture lasted only a few years. The Charles Boswell name and records were then acquired by an American.

Boswell double rifles are not uncommon. The single ugliest English double rifle the author has ever seen was a Boswell .450 boxlock on the rack at E.J. Churchill in 1998. The action was deeper than it was wide, the forend looked like a door wedge, and the engraving could have been scratched on with a nail. More recently, I have seen some very nice Boswell double rifles.

1884: 126 The Strand
1921-31: 7 South Molton Street
1931-41: 15 Mill Street

Jack Rowe:
> *I have seen very few Boswell sidelocks, but those I have seen have been truly best-quality guns. I have encountered many Boswell boxlocks, all A&D, all made in Birmingham.* (Ed. Note: Or at least proofed there.)

George Caswell:
> *Boswells are working guns. J.A. Hunter's famous .500 NE 3" was a Boswell. The general quality is good to very good. They appear fairly regularly and command no premium.*
> *Notably, Boswell guns are heavy compared to other makers.* (Ed. Note: These may well have begun life as live-pigeon guns, which are notably heavier.)

A.A. BROWN & SONS

Albert Arthur Brown began his career in the Birmingham trade, largely providing out-work services to other gunmakers. In 1929, he is listed on Whittal Street, where he remained (albeit changing shop addresses) until just before the Second World War. Around that time, his two sons, Albert Henry and Sidney Charles, joined the firm and it became A.A. Brown & Sons.

The company was bombed out during the war, and afterwards took in what work they could, gunmaking and otherwise, to stay afloat. Most of their work was still in the trade rather than retail. In 1960, A.A. Brown moved into premises adjacent to Westley Richards, for whom they provided gunmaking services of various kinds, and stayed there until 1974, when they moved to Snake Lane, Alvechurch, outside Birmingham.

Other companies for which A.A. Brown has made guns include Holland & Holland, John Harper, and Alexander Martin, including Martin's "ribless" pattern side-by-side.

A.A. Brown retired in 1957, but the firm is still in business and still family owned, now operated by Robin Brown, who joined the company as an apprentice.

The company moved gradually into the making of entire sidelock guns for retail sale to clients, and has the machinery and skills necessary to make a gun in its entirety. Today, A.A. Brown offers best-quality sidelock side-by-side shotguns, with 95 percent of the work done in-house, as well as other machining services to the trade. They also modify and sell a lower-priced Beretta over/under.

Jack Rowe:
A.A. Brown is one of Birmingham's finest gunmakers. I remember when they were in Sand Street, Birmingham, at that time making the ABAS air pistol as well as shotguns. In the 1950s and '60s they made some sidelocks for Westley Richards, and at that time were even in the same premises as WR. These guns were well made, of quality equal to any London gun. I know they also made guns for H&H as well as sidelocks under their own name. Their Supreme and Supreme DeLuxe models are equal to H&H in every way.

DAVID MCKAY BROWN

D.M. Brown is a relatively new company, located in Glasgow. Although Brown is slightly outside the scope of this book, he should be mentioned because of his connection with two older Scottish firms, Alex. Martin and John Dickson.

David McKay Brown apprenticed with Alex. Martin in 1957, later moved to Dickson in Edinburgh, and continued to perform a great deal of out-work for Dickson even after setting out on his own in 1967.

Today, David McKay Brown is located in Glasgow and produces shotguns and rifles, both side-by-side and over/under. He is renowned for his Dickson round-action guns and for the exquisite quality of his products, which are uncompromising bests.

1967: 39 Portland Place, Hamilton, Lanarkshire
1980: 32 Hamilton Road, Bothwell, Glasgow

Jack Rowe:
Brown makes his version of the Dickson round action, and also a round-action over/under. Both are very well made guns, equal in quality to the Dickson guns.

George Caswell:
McKay Brown guns are a modern round action, excellent to excellent-plus quality. They are fairly common, but not many reach the second-hand market. They command a 20 percent premium in price.

These guns are noteworthy for their very well done, modern engraving patterns, and overall they are a real complement to the modern age of best guns.

BSA – *SEE* BIRMINGHAM SMALL ARMS

WILLIAM CASHMORE

William Cashmore was a Birmingham gunmaker, in business from 1835 until its last directory listing in 1960. Cashmore specialized in trap, live-pigeon, and other competition guns, as well as fowling guns. They held several patents, and much of their production was exported to Australia and the United States.

As might be expected, Cashmore patents tended toward increasing strength and durability in guns used for competition. Catalogs from around 1900 included testimonials from such notables as Annie Oakley and Doc Carver, as well as listing the various championships, from Tasmania to the Grand American, won by Cashmore guns.

> 1847-57: 33 Newton Street
> 1858-1900: Steelhouse Lane
> 1910: 130 Steelhouse Lane
> 1920: 132 Steelhouse Lane
> 1940: 25 Whittall Street
> 1955: 59 Bath Street
> 1960: 121 Steelhouse Lane

Jack Rowe:
> *Cashmore made mostly boxlock guns on Anson & Deeley actions. All the ones I have seen have been in the medium to high grades. They are very well made—I have yet to see a bad one.*

E.J. CHURCHILL

Churchill is one of the great names in British gunmaking, with a long and involved history. The company dates from 1891, when Edwin John Churchill left the firm of F.T. Baker to set up on his own.

From the beginning, Churchill was heavily involved in live-pigeon shooting, and fitting and making competition guns. Churchill brought his son into the business, but he died very young, and in 1899, his nephew, Robert Churchill, joined the firm. Robert was never a gunmaker, but he was many other things: instructor, showman, ballistics expert, and a bit of a maverick.

It was Robert Churchill who came up with the idea of the short-barreled gun as the answer to all problems, and the Churchill XXV (for its 25-inch barrels) became a fixture of the gun trade. It sparked all kinds of controversy, including wars of words between proponents and opponents in the sporting press of the time. Churchill also espoused the raised, narrow-filed "Churchill" rib as an aid to sighting with a short-barreled gun.

The great barrel-length controversy took place in the 1920s. Previously, blackpowder guns required longer barrels for complete combustion, and were heavier in order to dampen recoil from substantial loads. Churchill championed both shorter, lighter guns, and lighter loads in them. As an instructor, he also originated a shooting theory in which there is no conscious lead—also a controversial idea. But Robert Churchill was a short, pugnacious man who seemingly thrived on conflict, and he did get results. He is credited with helping to make 26-inch barreled guns popular in the United States—a trend that began in the 1920s.

An interesting sidelight: Edwin Churchill became involved in the field of forensics because his shop in Agar Street was close to Charing Cross Hospital, where many shooting victims of London gang fights were taken for treatment. The police would take extracted bullets to Edwin for identification, and Robert Churchill followed in his footsteps. Until his death in 1958, Robert Churchill was frequently called upon as an expert witness in criminal cases involving shootings of all kinds.

After the Second World War, there was a great contraction and consolidation in the British gun trade. After Robert's death, the company was reformed as Churchill (Gunmakers) Ltd. It was acquired by Interarmco, became associated with Cogswell & Harrison, later amalgamated with Atkin Grant & Lang, and finally ceased trading in 1980. The final stock of Churchill guns was sold off and the Churchill name acquired by Don Masters. Masters made guns under the E.J. Churchill name, but the waters were further muddied in the 1990s when a new Churchill gunmaking firm was founded by Steve Denny, working for a company owned by Edward Dashwood and Mark Osbourne. Eventually, ownership of the name was sorted out and E.J. Churchill was once again in business making sidelock side-by-sides and, for a brief time, an over/under gun. The venture did not prosper for a number of reasons, and died, to all intents and purposes, about ten years later.

Sorting out the various incarnations of E.J. Churchill, and the premises they occupied, would require an entire book. For the purposes of this one, suffice to say that a Churchill gun identifiably made before 1958 would be more desirable than one made after, and later guns should be carefully inspected by an expert to ascertain their origins. This is not to say that guns made either by Don Masters or the later E.J. Churchill are anything but good, only that the name has appeared on many different guns over the years.

The author had the privilege of shooting both the first clay bird with E.J. Churchill gun number 10,000 in 1998, and later that year, the first feathered creature as well (a woodcock). It was a spectacular gun and worthy of the Churchill name in every way. Eventually, the handful of guns made by E.J. Churchill while Steve Denny was in charge may come to be regarded as the finest Churchills of all. They were notable for their spectacular walnut stocks and extremely fine engraving.

Robert Churchill's theories aside, short-barreled guns have shortcomings. The trend since 1990 has been back toward longer barrels, and the Churchill XXV has fallen out of favor in the used-gun market. They command a lower trade value, and may be obtained for a lower price—a point to remember for those who may still like short barrels and want an English gun.

Jack Rowe:
Guns from the original company, both sidelocks and boxlocks, are well made, good quality guns. Many of the boxlocks were made in Birmingham.

George Caswell:
Churchill guns appear in the market regularly. They are very good to excellent quality, and command about a five percent premium. The lightweight XXV with its 25-inch barrel is very unpopular with most upland hunters.

COGSWELL & HARRISON

The origins of Cogswell & Harrison are lost in the mists of time. The company itself claims to have originated in 1770, with Benjamin Cogswell, but this is impossible to substantiate. Boothroyd says Cogswell began in business as a pawnbroker, and became involved with guns that way. His son then brought Edward Harrison, a well-known shooter, into the business in 1837.

C&H made a wide range of shotguns, rifles, and pistols over the years, and went through the travails one might expect as the arms trade changed, and wars and economic crises came and went.

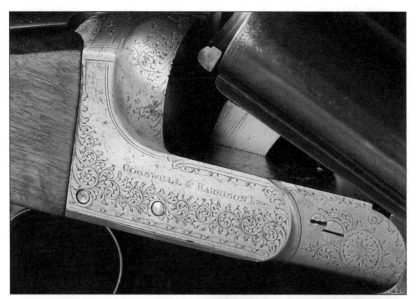

*Cogswell & Harrison Avant Tout
12-bore boxlock.*

For sheer complication, it would be hard to beat Cogswell & Harrison's history. The firm moved around, its principals changed, partnerships were formed, dissolved, and re-formed, new products were introduced and dropped, and many commercial dead ends were explored. Throughout it all, the company's products were generally good to very fine. Today, Cogswell & Harrison double rifles are fairly common, and they are reasonably well respected.

Of all the London firms, Cogswell & Harrison probably has the most spotty reputation. At times, their products were great; at others, less than great (and sometimes considerably less). How can one put it more diplomatically than that?

Because the company is so old, one sees every conceivable type of firearm with the name engraved on the barrels. They expanded into other lines, such as fishing, selling tackle and equipment from their shop in Piccadilly, and even making tennis rackets and golf clubs. In 1957, the company was taken over by Interarmco, underwent various incarnations, and is once again in business under the direction of Michael Cooley and Alan Crewe. They own the company name and records, and can provide certificates of origin for Cogswell & Harrison guns.

Jack Rowe:
> *One of the oldest gunmakers in the UK. Over the years they made so many models. Their Extra Quality Victor sidelock gun is as good and well made as any of the best London makes. Of the boxlocks, the Avant Tout, an earlier model, is a well-made A&D. Later boxlock models were the Blagdon and Konor. The Konor (unusual for English guns) had sideplates. Both of these models were made in Birmingham at my old place of employ, S. Wright & Sons. Having worked on many of them, I can vouch that you will not find a better-made boxlock anywhere.*

George Caswell:
> *Cogswell & Harrison made quite a number of models, with an equal range of quality from fair, to good, and some very good. They are quite common and command no premium. Many were different than other A&D guns, with a unique cocking and ejector system. Also, many Cogswell & Harrison guns appear to have been semi-mass produced.*

GEORGE COSTER & SON

Coster was a well-known name in gunmaking in Glasgow. According to Geoffrey Boothroyd, Julius Coster (originally Koster) emigrated from Germany. The family Anglicized its name, probably because of anti-German sentiment. George was the son of Julius.

At one time, Julius was in partnership in Edinburgh as Coster & Hunter, and moved to Glasgow around 1898. George was in business after the Great War.

The family were well-respected gunmakers, specializing in barrel work. Because of this, their name may appear on the rib of a rebarreled gun made by someone else (as in the case of an E.M. Reilly owned by the author).

c. 1926: 145 West Nile Street, Glasgow

Jack Rowe:
  I have only ever seen one gun by this maker, a boxlock, and it was well made.

JOHN DICKSON & SON

John Dickson of Edinburgh is undoubtedly the most famous of all the Scottish gunmakers and almost a cult name among shotgun enthusiasts. The Dickson round action (a true round action, too, not merely a conventional action with the corners rounded off) is a trigger-plate design that commands as much as the finest London sidelock.

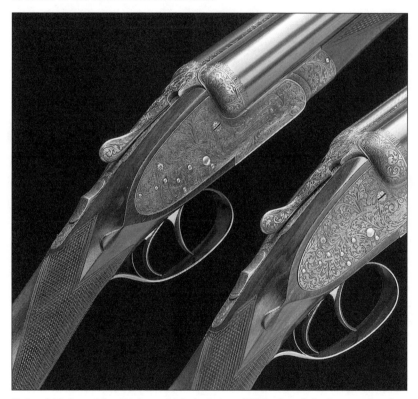

Pair of 12-bore John Dickson sidelock ejectors. While famed for its round action, Dickson made all manner of guns and rifles.

Photo Courtesy Steve Davis and Bill Orr

As well, Dickson made some guns as over/unders that were essentially their side-by-side design, rotated 90 degrees, with barrels that opened to the side rather than down. An oddity is the Dickson three-barrel gun (a variation on the round-action SxS). And, of course, Dickson made conventional sidelock guns and double rifles.

As with almost all the British makers in business for the better part of two centuries, Dickson's history is long and complicated, and involves many mergers, acquisitions, and moving of premises. The first John Dickson began as an apprentice in 1806, and was located at various addresses until 1840, when John Dickson & Son is definitively listed at 60 Princes Street. In 1849, he moved to No. 63, and remained there until 1929.

During this period, Dickson filed patents (from 1880 to 1887) related to its triggerplate lock and round-action gun.

In 1923, the last John Dickson died and the company passed into other hands. In 1938, Dickson absorbed two other famous Scottish gunmakers, T.E. Mortimer and Joseph Harkom, which had amalgamated 15 years earlier. In 1947, James MacNaughton was added, and in 1964, the business of Alex. Martin (which had earlier absorbed Alex. Henry).

In this way, the most famous names in Scottish gunmaking all came under one roof.

In the 1990s, there began almost a divestiture in which other investors purchased the rights to individual names (most notably MacNaughton) with the intention of making those specialty guns once again. One such group acquired first the MacNaughton name, then Dan'l Fraser, then purchased the Dickson company itself and renamed it Dickson & MacNaughton, but still located in the old Dickson premises on Frederick Street.

There the company remains, still making guns and, according to reports, intending to make specialty guns (not unlike the approach of the original Atkin Grant & Lang) under several of the component names such as MacNaughton and Martin.

> 1840: 60 Princes Street, Edinburgh
> 1849-1929: 63 Princes Street
> 1929-37: 32 Hanover Street
> 1937: 21 Frederick Street

Jack Rowe:
> *Of course, Dickson is most famous for their round-action gun. They are well made but, being in a class of their own, it is difficult to compare them to a London best sidelock. The work inside these guns is of a quality equal to a London gun.*

John Dickson 16-bore round-action ejector gun.
Photo Courtesy Steve Davis and Bill Orr

Dickson sold other grades of guns, both sidelocks and boxlocks. Some of these were made in Birmingham. Their Capital model boxlock was made by S. Wright & Sons, and was a fine, well-made gun.

George Caswell:
In quality, Dickson guns qualify as excellent to excellent-plus. They are not common in the market, but not rare either, and command a premium of 20 to 30 percent. One thing to watch for is condition and possible alterations, since many Dickson guns in this country were early pieces.

Overall, the Dickson is an impressive gun that seldom, if ever, is a disappointment to its user. There is a definite magic to a Dickson: Put one on the rack with many other types and it will be the first to be handled by anyone who knows anything about guns.

JAMES ERSKINE

James was the most prominent of a family of Erskines that practiced the gun trade in the Scottish town of Newton Stewart for more than 200 years. The family traces its roots to 1716, when Charles and Robert Erskine are listed on the rolls of the Jacobite Army. Charles married a blacksmith's daughter, inherited the business, and his son Thomas set up nearby as a gunmaker.

Thomas's two sons, James and John, apprenticed with Williams of Liverpool and returned home to Newton Stewart. Together, they built a successful business and were highly skilled, winning a bronze medal for a pair of muzzle-loading shotguns with recessed hammers, at the fabled Great Exhibition of London in 1851. Possibly as a result of this, the brothers began building guns for some prominent people, including HRH the Duke of Saxe Coburg Gotha.

James Erskine became famous for two things: The exceptional quality and beauty of his Damascus barrels, and an eponymous cartridge-loading machine. James died in 1891, but his son William carried on the business. He was the last male descendant of the Erskine line. In 1907, he moved the business to Dumfries, where he continued until 1946 when, at the age of 80, he retired.

Until 1907: 62 Victoria Street, Newton Stewart
1907-46: 6 Loreburn Street, Dumfries

Jack Rowe:
I have seen only a hammer gun by them, but I believe later (boxlock) guns were made in Birmingham.

WILLIAM EVANS

William Evans is a famous London name that has been in business for more than a century, but Evans himself, and the company he founded, are quite different than the usual London gunmaker.

First, although he worked for Purdey, then at H. Holland, and later Holland & Holland, Evans himself was not a gunmaker. He was, for lack of a better term, a salesman. Which makes it odd that, when he began business

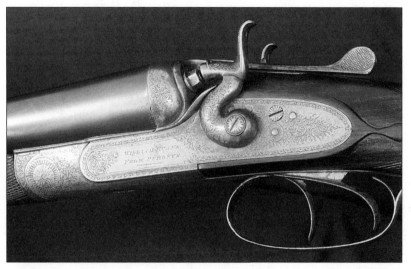

William Evans 12-bore hammer gun. Evans guns were made in the trade, either in London or Birmingham.

on his own, he affected the former journeyman's habit of signing his guns "From Purdeys." This was a legitimate practice for a gunmaker, who could claim to have learned the trade and follow the standards of his former employer. Whether it was appropriate for a salesman is another question. Purdey apparently thought not, but since it all happened 120 years ago, the point is probably moot.

At any rate, in 1883, after learning the trade in the front office of Purdey and H&H, William Evans set up shop in Buckingham Palace Road. Arriving on the scene just as hammerless guns were taking over, Evans immediately began making both boxlock and sidelock shotguns and rifles. That is to say, guns and rifles appeared with the name Evans on the rib or barrels; the guns themselves were made in the trade, since Evans did not, and never has had, a factory like Holland's on Harrow Road.

Jack Rowe says most, if not all, Evans guns were made in Birmingham. Today, Evans guns are made in the trade in London by craftsmen working from their own shops.

Although he was not a gunmaker, William Evans was of an inventive turn. In 1905, he and a man named Corrie patented a single trigger, and it was offered as an option until at least the 1920s. As well, Evans was able to boast of royal warrants as gunmaker to HRH the Duke of Connaught and HRH Prince Arthur of Connaught. Evans also had their own shooting grounds.

> 1883: 95a Buckingham Palace Road
> 1885: 4 Holden Terrace, Pimlico
> 1888: 4 Pall Mall Place
> 1896: 63 Pall Mall
> 1945 to present: 67a St. James's Street

Jack Rowe:
> *Evans is a London store. Their guns were all Birmingham-made, and by several makers. Webley & Scott made both boxlocks and sidelocks for them, and their sidelocks were as good as any by the London top names. I have not seen their more recent guns.*

George Caswell:
> *Evans offered a wide variety of guns and rifles, ranging in quality from very good to excellent. They appear for sale quite often, and command a premium of 10 to 15 percent as a quality London name.*

DANIEL FRASER

Daniel (or Dan'l, as it is more commonly spelled) Fraser was a Scottish riflemaker, primarily, although he did make shotguns. Fraser apprenticed with Alexander Henry, then set up on his own in partnership with his brother John (as D&J Fraser) in 1878. He patented his famous falling-block rifle action in 1880. The Fraser name continued in the Scottish trade for more than a century, following a serpentine path that is impossible to summarize except to say, famous and long-lived as the Fraser name might be, it was never a force in shotgun making, and so is outside the scope of this book.

GEORGE GIBBS

George Gibbs was a Bristol gunmaker who distinguished himself in several areas, most notably rifles, although he made fine shotguns as well. The firm was established in 1830 as J&G Gibbs, later became George Gibbs, then Gibbs & Pitt, then George Gibbs again. At one point, the company also had a London office.

Gibbs is one of those English makers known primarily for its rifles (like Jeffery and Rigby) and is preeminent in the field of hardkicking elephant tamers. Gibbs made Sir Samuel Baker's first huge-bore gun in 1840, following the 19-year-old Samuel's specifications for a gun that would fire a four-ounce conical bullet propelled by a full ounce (437 grains) of blackpowder. When blackpowder turned to smokeless, Gibbs introduced its famous .505 Magnum (now more commonly known as the .505 Gibbs) in 1911.

During the brief period of partnership with Pitt, in 1874, the company produced the handsome, intriguing, and undoubtedly strong Gibbs &

Gibbs & Pitt's 1874 Patent Action with snap underlever.

Pitt's Patent Action, a boxlock (for lack of a better term) with the safety on the side and the locks on a platform in front of the trigger guard. The action is a snap-action lever. Boothroyd says Gibbs made about 10,000 such guns, but that number seems high.

George Gibbs died in 1884. The company was acquired by I.M. Crudgington of Bath in 1963, and they continue to build bespoke guns and rifles under the Gibbs name. Through its long history, Gibbs had many different (and sometimes multiple and simultaneous) addresses.

1830: 4 Redcliffe Street, Bristol (as J&G Gibbs)
1841-50: 141 Thomas Street
?: Clare Street
1858-90: 29 Corn Street
1890-1924: 39 Corn Street
1931: 37 Baldwin Street
1942: 51 Baldwin Street (temporary, due to war damage)
1952-89: 3-4 Perry Road, Park Row
Current: 37 Broad Street, Bath

Jack Rowe:
  Gibbs was better known for double and magazine rifles than for shot-guns, but they did make some very nice high-grade sidelock and boxlock guns. The Gibbs sidelocks I have seen have been of the highest quality, and I would not hesitate to buy one.

WILLIAM GOLDEN

There were three Goldens in the gun trade in and around Bradford and Huddersfield, Yorkshire—Charles Golden, and two sons, William and Charles. Although the two sons are listed as being in business in the latter half of the 19th century, a Golden exhibited at the Great Exhibition in 1851.

Jack Rowe:
  I have seen very few of this maker's guns, but all have been boxlocks, made in Birmingham, of all different grades, and all well made.

STEPHEN GRANT & SONS

Stephen Grant began his gunmaking career as an apprentice in Dublin before moving to London, where he is believed to have worked with Charles Lancaster before going to work for Thomas Boss. When Boss died in 1857, his widow elevated Grant to the position of managing partner, a position Grant held for ten years. In 1867, he set up on his own at 67a St. James's Street (a premises now occupied by William Evans). In 1889, his two sons, Herbert and Stephen, joined him and the company became Stephen Grant & Sons.

Stephen Grant was a conservative gunmaker, not quick to adopt either new ideas or designs. He was, however, a man of consummate taste and dis-cernment, and this shows in the guns that bear his name, both hammer guns and hammerless. They are graceful, seductive guns—elegant, austere, and flawlessly made. In the last quarter of the 19th century, Grant guns came to the attention of royalty, and Stephen Grant & Sons could boast of royal warrants from Queen Victoria, the Prince of Wales (later Edward VII), and several other European royal houses.

After the Great War, Grant moved to 7 Bury Street, St. James, and the firm was taken over by the Robsons, father and son. WRH Robson became a director in 1925. The Robsons set about their own private amalgamation of the London gun trade, acquiring Joseph Lang in 1925 (to become Stephen Grant & Joseph Lang, Ltd.), then Harrison & Hussey, Charles Lancaster, Watson Brothers, Frederick Beesley, and, finally in 1946, Henry Atkin. At that point, the company became Atkin Grant & Lang.

But back to Stephen Grant. The company had several signature features, the side-lever opening mechanism being the best known. As well, Grant guns are known for their beautifully carved fences.

> 1867: 67a St. James's Street
>
> c. 1918: 7 Bury Street

Jack Rowe:
> *Stephen Grant was noted for its side-lever guns and continued to use this mechanism long after others had abandoned it. Some Grant guns were also made with Baker patents as used on Charles Lancaster 12/20 guns, and were quite light. Grant fences are very distinguished, with fluting resembling a long, oval leaf running across the fences diagonally.*

George Caswell:
> *Stephen Grant guns have excellent overall quality, with great style on the fences. They are fairly hard to find, and command a 15 to 20 percent premium. Grants are among my personal favorites. Every one I have looked at has had superb style and workmanship.*

STEPHEN GRANT & JOSEPH LANG, LTD.

In 1925, the two established firms of Stephen Grant & Sons and Joseph Lang & Son amalgamated to become Stephen Grant & Joseph Lang, Ltd. (commonly known as Grant & Lang). Lang moved from its Bond Street location into Grant's premises at 7 Bury Street, which became a hub of the London gun trade for many years.

Under succeeding generations of the Robson family, Grant & Lang (and later Atkin Grant & Lang) were a major force in the trade, and something of a haven for a succession of companies that found themselves in difficulty through, first, the Great Depression, and later, the Second World War. Grant & Lang absorbed Harrison & Hussey (1930), Charles Lancaster (1932), Watson Brothers (1935), Frederick Beesley (1939), and finally, in 1960, Henry Atkin, at which point it became Atkin Grant & Lang.

EDWINSON GREEN

Edwinson C. Green was one of a family of Birmingham gunmakers who set up in business in Cheltenham in 1863. He was associated with the firm until his death in 1927, at the age of 89.

Edwinson Green is best known today for his inventions, the most famous of which is an over/under design adopted (briefly) by James Purdey before they absorbed Woodward. Green filed his first patent in 1871, his last in 1913, and several were joint patents with other members of his family.

The company made several guns that are curiosities today, including a three-barrel design. According to Geoffrey Boothroyd, Edwinson Green also made a round-action boxlock that, aside from the name, is identical to the Dickson.

W.W. GREENER

William Wellington Greener could make fair claim to being the most colorful character in British gunmaking history—a title for which there is no small number of candidates.

W.W. was born the son of William Greener, himself a well-known gunmaker who held a warrant from HRH Prince Albert, consort to Queen Victoria. William Greener worked with John Manton before establishing a business in Birmingham in 1844. He is credited with inventing the first "expansive" bullet (a bullet that expands in the rifle's bore to grip the rifling). Greener also wrote three major books on guns and gunnery. He went to his grave in 1869 still convinced of the superiority of muzzleloaders—a view that led him into vocal and public conflict with his second son, W.W. It reached a stage where, for some years, father and son refused to speak.

William Wellington believed strongly in breechloading systems. When his father died, he was cut out of the will, but raised the money to buy his father's gunmaking shop, changed the sign from "W." to "W.W." and carried on, producing the mechanisms his father hated from his father's own premises. W.W. then went on to eclipse his father in virtually every way, from gunmaking to inventing to writing books.

A Birmingham gunmaker from the ankles up, W.W. Greener became perhaps the strongest proponent of the boxlock action, both the Anson & Deeley and his own Facile Princeps design. His most famous invention is the Greener crossbolt, a fastener now used on double guns around the world. There was virtually no facet of firearms and firearms use that Greener did not delve into, influence, or improve. He was an expert in rifle shooting and developed some of the finest target rifles of his day. He saw the transition from blackpowder to smokeless and embraced it wholeheartedly. As much like his father as he was in some ways, in others—particularly his willingness to embrace change—he was completely unlike him.

By 1890, he was able to claim that his factory in Birmingham was the largest maker of sporting arms in Britain; by 1921, when W.W. Greener died at the age of 87, it was the largest in the world.

Today, W.W. Greener is most remembered for his book *The Gun and its Development*, a massive effort that went through nine editions and countless reprints, and is a standard reference for writers and students of firearms to this day.

As for Greener's guns, they were all admirable and some were breathtaking. The fabled "St. George's Gun," with its deep-relief engraving of St. George and the dragon, is considered by many to be the finest boxlock shotgun ever created. The vast majority of Greener's shotguns and rifles were boxlocks, although he did make some sidelocks and, his mass-production factory aside, the hand-made guns were excellent.

The Greener factory stood proudly on St. Mary's Row in Birmingham from start to finish. After W.W. Greener's death, his sons carried on the business, but it shrank steadily. Finally, in 1965, W.W. Greener was acquired by Webley & Scott. In recent years, W.W.'s great-grandson, Graham, reacquired the rights to the name, wrote a book about his famous family (*The Greener Story*) and began making guns, in a small way, once again.

It should be noted that, at the height of its production, Greener was a major exporter to all parts of the world, including the United States. So, unlike many English makers whose products have appeared here only recently, a used Greener could have been here for a century or more. The most famous Greener used here was a 10-gauge custom double that Doc Holliday may or may not have wielded to such effect at the gunfight at the OK Corral. If so, it was an early Greener, since that encounter took place in 1881.

Jack Rowe:

It would take a book just to cover this one maker. Greener made so many guns—boxlocks mainly, some on A&D actions, but most on their own Facile Princeps. They absorbed the firm of Joseph V. Needham (in 1874), and many of their A&D guns bear the Needham name. Greener did make some sidelocks, but the number was very small compared to the boxlocks. The quality of all Greener guns was of the highest degree.

JOSEPH HARKOM & SON

Harkom was a London-born gunmaker who relocated to Edinburgh. He died in 1891 and his son ran the company until his own death in 1923, when it was absorbed by T.E. Mortimer. Mortimer was in turn taken over by Dickson. Early listings of Harkom in Edinburgh refer to either James or Joseph; in all likelihood, they are one and the same.

> 1837: 15 Leopold Place, Edinburgh
> 1838: 30 Abbeyhill
> 1840: 31 West Register Street
> 1856: 32 Princes Street

Jack Rowe:

Another Scottish maker. I have seen very few of their guns, mostly hammer guns, but all that I have seen were of high quality and well made. I believe they were all Birmingham-made; very few of the Scottish makers had the work force and facilities to make a complete gun.

JOHN HARPER

Harper was a common name in the Birmingham and provincial gun trade from the late 19th century into the 20th, with no fewer than 17 being listed at various times. John Harper was in business from 1902 to 1975, first on Steelhouse Lane (1902-11), then at 28 Whittall Street (1912-39), 3 Price Street (1940-53) and 63 Price Street (1954-75).

Harper made chiefly boxlocks of good quality, and at least some were made for him by A.A. Brown. There were any number of gunmakers listed in England during this period that were similar to Harper—small, one- or two-man operations, having basic guns made for them in Birmingham, which they then finished in their own shops.

John Harper 12-bore boxlock.

The gun shown, owned by Robert Kolesar and partially refurbished by him, is an excellent example of the kind of English boxlock available today at a fraction the cost of a London best, yet a far better gun overall than any new mass-production side-by-side.

HARRISON & HUSSEY

This firm was a brief alliance between two well-travelled names in the London gun business. Both Harrison and the Husseys, father and son, formed partnerships with various other makers at different times. None lasted long, and the character of H.J. Hussey, and his son H.H., certainly had something to do with it. H.J., who was in partnership with James Lang as Lang & Hussey, was driven out of the business after some illicit dealings came to light.

Claude Harrison, former manager of Cogswell & Harrison's Bond Street shop, and the son, H.H. Hussey, formed Harrison & Hussey in 1919; the company lasted until 1930, when it was acquired by Grant & Lang.

Jack Rowe:
   This was the last-but-one in the Hussey partnership saga (the last being Ogden, Smiths & Hussey). Throughout all the partnerships, they kept the name Imperial on their best sidelock guns. I don't think they made any guns

other than bests. It is interesting to note, too, that they also used serial numbers beginning with 14xxx throughout. I believe their guns were Birmingham made, since the style of action and lock work was very similar to the Army & Navy best sidelocks. They may well have come from the same maker. I would rate all their guns as equal to any of the prestigious London names.

CHARLES HELLIS & SONS

Charles Hellis is one of those London firms with a history that can only be described as checkered. Hellis is first recorded in business at 21 Shrewsbury Road in 1888 as an antique dealer; six years later, at the same address, he is a gun dealer; in between, apparently, he dealt in live pigeons, supplied for trap shooting, and this led him into dealing in firearms.

In 1897, the firm relocated to the more fashionable address of 119 Edgeware Road. Charles died in 1905 and the business was carried on by his son, who himself died in 1932.

Although Hellis sold guns bearing its own name, it was known chiefly as a supplier of cartridges and as an active dealer in second-hand guns, a trade that most 'name' London gunmakers eschewed until forced into it by the cold hand of economic necessity.

In 1956, Hellis was acquired by Henry Atkin, which later merged with Grant & Lang. As many incorporated gunmaker names were divested by Atkin Grant & Lang, the Hellis name was subsequently linked to Beesley and Watson; apparently, guns are once again being manufactured under the Hellis name.

Jack Rowe:

Hellis was a gunshop on Edgeware Road. I don't know if they ever actually made guns there. The only Hellis guns I have seen personally were, without a doubt, made in Birmingham. They made (or had made for them) various grades of boxlock and sidelock guns. In actual fact, before and after the Second World War, many were made for them by the firm of S. Wright & Sons (my old employer).

In 1948, Ralph Crump started a gunmaking workshop in Birmingham for Hellis; I knew him well, and did some filing up (shaping fences and actions) for him.

Hellis made some very high quality boxlock and sidelock guns. The firm still exists, the name having been bought out of the AG&L group, and is making some fine guns at present.

George Caswell:
  Hellis guns are very good. They are distinguished by using small side-plates on boxlock guns, with the sideplates in sunken panels. They seldom appear in the market, and command a small (five percent) premium. Current and recent Hellis guns are well made and very nicely finished.

ALEXANDER HENRY

Alex. Henry was a riflemaker, established in Edinburgh in 1853. The first Henry patent for falling block rifles was registered in 1865. Henry rifles are found in a vast array of configurations. Although rifles are outside the scope of this book, the company is included because of its close connections with other Scottish firms.

The company was acquired by Alex. Martin, which later amalgamated with John Dickson.

George Caswell:
  Alexander Henry made falling block rifles with Henry rifling, and the quality was excellent to superb. They are uncommon, and command a premium of 25 to 35 percent. Because nearly all of them date back to before 1900, condition is a factor. However, I don't know if it is possible to find a bad Henry; they are exceptional guns.

HOLLAND & HOLLAND

Holland & Holland is so prominent and well known that it is almost outside the scope of this book. Like Purdey, people who know little or nothing about guns know the name Holland & Holland. Many books have been written about the company, its history, its guns and rifles, its cartridges, and the famous people who have used them.

Since its acquisition by the Chanel group in 1989, H&H's line of clothing and accessories has been expanded, with shops established on fashionable streets in such disparate places as Moscow and Beverly Hills. This has brought the distinctive logo into the consciousness of people who wouldn't know a bird gun from a bird bath.

Briefly, the company was founded in 1835 by Harris John Holland, a tobacconist in Holborn who was a fine shot and amateur gunmaker. His guns impressed his pigeon-shooting friends, who encouraged him to become a full-time gunmaker. He started at a disadvantage: First, he had never worked for Joseph Manton, the spiritual father of the fine gun trade, and he was in competition with men who had—men named Purdey, Lancaster, and Boss, among others. And second, at the time, the London gun trade had 90 gun-makers listed, and the business was intensely competitive. The fact that he survived is evidence of Holland's ability.

Harris Holland had no sons, so he took his nephew, Henry William Holland, first as an apprentice, later as a partner, and in the 1870s (the date is vague) the firm became Holland & Holland. Previously, Holland guns were marked "H. Holland."

From that time, the list of the company's accomplishments is almost endless. Henry Holland formed a loose alliance with Sir Samuel Baker, one of the great heroes of the Victorian age, and Baker's experiences in Africa shaped H&H's big-game rifles and cartridges.

H&H is unique among London gunmakers in one way: It is the only company that is always mentioned as one of the big three in both rifles (with Rigby and Westley Richards) and shotguns (with Purdey and Boss). This gives the company almost a split personality, but in no way takes away from the quality of its products. Over 150 years, H&H has produced almost every type of rifle and shotgun, and all are highly regarded.

Among its shotguns, the Royal stands pre-eminent, at least in the public mind. This is Holland's flagship sidelock double, in both rifles and shotguns. It uses an H&H-pattern lock, which has become the world standard for double guns. Its self-opening mechanism is the one generally used in Spain, Belgium, and Italy. Hand-detachable locks, originated by H&H, are also widely used and a sign of quality. Everywhere one looks, in every country that aspires to produce fine sidelock guns, one sees the term "H&H-style" or "H&H-pattern"; many (especially the Basques) even incorporate the word "Holland" into their model names.

The Royal is the standard, but equally fine, in different form, were the Dominion grade rifles and shotguns, which employed a back-action sidelock. There were also boxlocks, some made for H&H in Birmingham, particularly after it purchased W&C Scott in 1985.

Naturally, with such fame and range of products, H&H firearms appear frequently in many forms, and all command a premium for the name alone. But they do so legitimately: The products bearing the name are consistently fine.

H&H is still in business, with its shop in Bruton Street, Mayfair, and its factory on Harrow Road. It has shops in major cities, such as New York. It is now owned by the Chanel group, and makes over/under and side-by-side shotguns, and double, bolt action, and single-shot rifles. Its shooting ground, at Northwood, outside London, is thriving under the direction of Steve Denny.

A potential buyer needs to be careful on one point: There were other gunmakers named Holland in the business, including one named David in Gloucestershire until 1870, and a father and son, both named Henry, in Oxfordshire until 1870. In the latter case, a gun could be legitimately marked "H. Holland" yet have no connection with the famous firm.

1835-66: 9 King Street, Holborn
1866-1960: 98 New Bond Street, Mayfair
1960: Bruton Street (first #13, then #31-33)

Jack Rowe:

In my estimation, number one of the English gunmakers. Some will disagree, but in any event, one of the top three. All the top models of guns were made in their London factory; other models, such as the Dominion or 'C' grade, and the Northwood boxlock, were made in Birmingham. Interesting to note that the 'C' grade was made by two men in Birmingham: James Pople and Harry Bennett.

Some boxlock guns were made for Holland's by Webley & Scott in the 1960s that bore just the initials H&H. All these guns, however, were shot and regulated by them in London. Good guns by a maker you can trust; that sums it up.

George Caswell:

This company is noted for so many things: the Royal, the .300 and .375 belted magnum cartridges, hand-detachable locks. The overall quality is excellent. They appear regularly in the market, and command a 20 to 30 percent premium.

The .375 H&H cartridge has done more to spread the company name to the masses of people owning guns than perhaps any other innovation from any other British maker. I feel H&H guns and rifles have contributed more to the British trade than those of any other maker, partly because of their long history, and partly because of the range of models.

ISAAC HOLLIS & SONS

Hollis was a Birmingham maker, in business from 1861, manufacturing a wide range of shotguns, rifles, and pistols of varying grades. Hollis mass-produced cheaper models for the South African market, as well as higher-grade guns for other gunmakers to sell under their own names. Particularly, Hollis supplied Crockart of Blairgowrie, a well-known Scottish maker.

At various times, Hollis joined with Bentley & Playfair to become Hollis, Bentley & Playfair (notably from 1915-1930, and again from 1935 onward). The company also had offices in both London and Birmingham, although it was a Birmingham maker.

> 1908: Lench Street, Birmingham; 28 Victoria Street, London;
> 9 New Bread Street, London
> 1920: 16 & 17 Loveday Street, Birmingham
> 1935: 91 & 92 Lower Loveday Street (as Hollis, Bentley &
> Playfair)

Jack Rowe:
From this maker I have seen only medium-grade hammer guns, boxlocks, and cheaper-grade sidelocks. No doubt he made some better-grade guns, but I have yet to see any.

George Caswell:
Hollis made guns that sold under the names of various other companies. I believe most Bentley & Playfair guns were from Hollis. The quality is fair to good. They seldom come onto the market, but command no premium.

H.J. HUSSEY LTD.

More on the tangled affairs of the Hussey family: Henry Joseph Hussey was an assistant manager with Holland & Holland until about 1895, when he left to join the firm of James Lang (Gunmaker), first as manager, then as a partner. The firm became Lang & Hussey. Three years later, Lang & Hussey, and Lang's old firm, Joseph Lang & Co., were amalgamated by an investor, Henry Webley. Webley became chairman, with H.J. Hussey as managing director, and the name changed to Lang & Hussey Ltd.

Five months later, Hussey resigned. According to Nigel Brown, he had been secretly auctioning guns belonging to the firm and its customers, and pocketing some of the proceeds. He was forced out, agreeing that if he re-entered the gun business, he would do so totally honestly, and would never refer to his past association with Lang & Hussey. That firm later reverted to the name Joseph Lang & Son.

A month later, his son, H.H. Hussey, who also worked with Lang & Hussey, was dismissed. The son went into business, temporarily, on his own. In business for himself, H.J. Hussey immediately broke his word to Lang, claiming past association on his letterhead, but was brought up short by their solicitors and apparently then stuck to the straight and narrow. In 1914, his son joined him in the business, and it became Hussey & Hussey. H.J. Hussey died in 1918, and with one son in the British Army and the other a prisoner of war, the firm was set to fold until Claude Harrison joined and it became Harrison & Hussey.

Throughout all this travail, surprisingly enough, Hussey made fine guns. Although he was an acknowledged rogue, he was also a fine craftsman. In 1997, the author had the pleasure of shooting red grouse with a Lang & Hussey gun, one of a matched pair that were two of the most striking shotguns I have ever seen.

For the record, the firms with which the Husseys were associated over the years include Lang & Hussey, H.J. Hussey Ltd., Hussey & Hussey, Harrison & Hussey, and Ogden, Smiths & Hussey.

> 1898: 81 New Bond Street
> 1908: Ryder Street
> 1914: 88 Jermyn Street (as Hussey & Hussey)

For Jack Rowe's comments, *see* Harrison & Hussey.

W.J. JEFFERY & CO.

William Jackman Jeffery was born in London in 1857 and entered the gun business in 1885, first as a salesman with Cogswell & Harrison, then with P. Webley & Son. After a disagreement with Webley, he went into partnership with a man named Davies (Jeffery & Davies); in 1891, the firm became W.J. Jeffery & Co., the name it retained until it was purchased by Holland & Holland in 1959.

Jeffery was an inventive man and from the beginning gravitated more to rifles than shotguns. His inventions generally relate to rifles, and the firm is famous for its cartridges, especially the .404 Jeffery, 450/400 3" (Jeffery), the .500 Jeffery, and the .600 Nitro Express. When bolt actions came onto the scene, Jeffery naturally began building magazine rifles as well.

W.J. Jeffery died in 1909 and the business was carried on first by his brother, Charles, and later a nephew, F. Jeffery Pearce.

Because of the number of gunmakers listed in England named Jeffery, Jeffrey, Jeffries, and Jefferies, buyers should be especially careful when buying what purports to be a W.J. Jeffery.

> 1890: 60 Queen Victoria Street (initially as Jeffery & Davies)
> 1898: 13 King Street (additional premises)
> 1914: 26 Bury Street (closing Queen Victoria and King Street premises)
> 1927: 9 Golden Square
> 1955: 5b Pall Mall
> 1959: Acquired by Holland & Holland
> c. 2000: Name acquired from H&H by private investor; Jeffery resumed production under the direction of Paul Roberts

Jack Rowe:

Jeffery is a well-known name for boxlock and sidelock guns, and double rifles. This maker did not manufacture the guns he sold in London. To my knowledge, they were all made in Birmingham. S. Wright, where I worked in my youth, made best-quality boxlocks for Jeffery, and other makers also made various grades of boxlocks, sidelocks, and double rifles.

Generally, all Jeffery guns were well made and good quality.

George Caswell:

Jeffery is noted for rifles more than shotguns. The quality is generally very good. Their rifles are found with Krupp steel barrels, and doll's-head extensions are common. They appear in the market regularly, and command a premium of about 20 percent. I have always liked a Jeffery gun or rifle; they are very consistent quality.

CHARLES LANCASTER & CO.

Charles Lancaster was a charter member of the Manton class—craftsmen who learned the trade and, more important, espoused the demanding aesthetic principles propounded by Joseph Manton. When they left Manton to set up their own shops, these men—James Purdey and Thomas Boss among them—made guns to the Manton style and quality.

Lancaster was Manton's barrel maker. His work came to the attention of Colonel Peter Hawker, the famous shooter and author, who advised him to set up on his own should Joseph Manton retire. Lancaster did not wait for

W.J. Jeffery & Co. plain 12-bore boxlock ejector from the company's Golden Square, Soho, days (1927-55). Jeffery made all grades of both sidelock and boxlock guns and rifles.

that event: He set up shop in Drury Lane in 1811, supplying barrels to Manton and the rest of the London trade, and moved into the making of complete guns in 1826 at 151 New Bond Street. Barrels supplied to other makers during this time were marked "CL."

By 1843, Lancaster had been awarded his first royal warrant (from the Prince Consort), and many more were to follow. Charles Lancaster died in 1847 and the business was carried on by his son, Charles William (C.W.) In 1855, a second son, Alfred, joined the company, but left in 1859 to set up independently as A. Lancaster, Gun & Rifle Manufacturer.

At this point, the affairs of the Lancasters become tangled. For 20 years, there were two Lancasters in London, competing with each other, especially in live-pigeon shooting. Alfred was located at 27 South Audley Street (near the current premises of James Purdey), then in 1886 moved to 50 Green Street, off Park Lane near Grosvenor Square, then as now an ultra-fashionable address. So obviously, he was successful.

While they were together, the brothers took out joint patents for a number of inventions. From their father, they inherited a deep interest in barrel-making, and many of their innovations relate to rifles and rifling, and even artillery. Charles William himself (in 1850) patented the famed Lancaster oval-bore rifling, a system that achieved some success over the next few years. Alfred was no less gifted, with patents of his own.

C.W. Lancaster died in 1878, and Charles Lancaster was acquired by Henry A.A. Thorn, who was to become to Lancaster what John Robertson was to Boss—its guiding light. In 1890, Alfred Lancaster died. His unfinished work was taken over by W.J. Jeffery, who completed the guns and rifles. In 1892, Henry Thorn acquired A. Lancaster and reunited the two companies as Charles Lancaster & Co.

Incidentally, the immensely successful book *The Art of Shooting* (1889) was actually written by Thorn, although it says "by Charles Lancaster." The book went through 14 editions, the last in 1985.

The firm of Charles Lancaster was active in shotgun innovations as well as rifling. Lancaster made one of the first (more or less) centerfire, self-contained cartridges for breechloaders, although it was not terribly successful and was quickly supplanted by the Daw/Schneider design of 1862. The existing Lancaster guns were easily modified, apparently, which shows how close the two ideas were.

Lancaster claimed to have originated the 2-inch 12-bore when, in 1898, it introduced its "Pygmy," a cartridge intended to deliver 12-bore patterns with a 20-bore load. Since Nobel already listed its 2-inch "Parvo" cartridge, and the Pygmy was actually 2 1/4-inches, the claim is dubious (like Greener's Dwarf). Regardless, the idea only became popular—and then very mildly— many years later.

Then, in 1925, Lancaster introduced its 12/20 shotgun, the same idea approached from the angle of the gun rather than the cartridge. The 12/20 is a 12-bore built on a 20-gauge frame, reducing weight and improving handling. Naturally, it requires a lighter load if it is to be shot comfortably for long periods.

Finally, Lancaster experimented extensively with multi-barrel guns, both pistols and shotguns. They made four-barrel guns in various configurations, and many army officers bought their four-barrel pistols until they were replaced by six-shot revolvers. Various shotguns, including three-barrel (side-by-side-by-side) 20-bore and 12-bores (one barrel atop two) still exist.

Like many gunmakers in London and Birmingham, Charles Lancaster made guns for the Army & Navy stores. Often, these were discreetly marked "Cs.L." somewhere on the frame, to show the true maker.

In 1932, Charles Lancaster amalgamated with Grant & Lang, and the name disappeared until 1989, when it was purchased by a consortium that included the lock maker Joseph Brazier, and began making guns once again.

Brazier left the consortium in 1996.

As a firm, Charles Lancaster & Co. enjoyed a fine reputation, with the usual coterie of enthusiasts who will insist "better than a Purdey!" just as they will for Boss, Woodward, and several others. Whether this is true, who can really say? They were all in the stratosphere.

> 1811-18: 10 Craven Buildings, Drury Lane
> 1822-24: Coach & Horse Yard, Great Titchfield Street
> 1826: 151 New Bond Street
> 1855: 2 Little Bruton Street (reverse frontage to Bond Street address)
> 1904: 11 Panton Street (as Charles Lancaster Ltd.)
> 1925: Mount Street
> 1932: 7 Bury Street (with Grant & Lang)

JOSEPH LANG & SON

Joseph Lang is one of the oldest and most established of the London gun-makers, with impeccable credentials and ancestry and many innovations to its name.

The original Joseph Lang did not work for Joseph Manton, but he did marry James Purdey's daughter, and he acquired and sold off Manton's remaining stock in 1826 when Manton went into bankruptcy. One cannot ask for better connections than that.

In 1851, after Casimir Lefaucheux exhibited his break-action shotgun at the Great Exhibition in London, Joseph Lang was first out of the gate with his own design, a pinfire, not long after. This is one of the seminal events, not only in the history of the London trade, but in all of firearms history.

Lang was deeply involved thereafter in the development and refinement of the various components that eventually comprised the classic London gun, although he has no notable patents to his name.

Lang had two sons, Joseph and James. After Joseph the Elder's death, the sons ran the business until 1887, when they had a falling out and James went on his own as James Lang (Gunmaker). The original company, incidentally, only became Joseph Lang & Son in 1875, with Joseph the Younger running it until the great reshuffling that occurred under Henry Webley in the 1890s.

James Lang, now on his own, eventually ended up in partnership with H.J. Hussey, and the story of that ill-fated pairing is told elsewhere (*see* H.J. Hussey). Investor Henry Webley took over first Lang & Hussey, then the original Joseph

Lang, and eventually (in 1901) reverted to the name Joseph Lang & Son.

The company is credited with one other invention that changed the world: It is believed that, around 1907, Lang developed the .470 Nitro Express and released that cartridge to the trade, to be chambered by anyone. It became, by far, the most successful of the nitro-express cartridges.

An innovation that was not so successful was the rather bizarre Vena Contracta gun. H. Phillips, shooting editor of *The Field*, is credited (if credited is the word) with this one: A 12-bore whose barrel contracted to 20-bore within the first third of its length. The goal was to reduce weight, but all it did was increase recoil, and performance was mediocre at best. Most of the Vena Contracta guns were subsequently rebarreled.

Ironically, given their later association, this ill-fated design is often confused with Lancaster's eminently sensible and successful 12/20.

In 1925, Joseph Lang & Son amalgamated with Stephen Grant & Sons to become Stephen Grant & Joseph Lang, Ltd.

After that merger, and through the subsequent absorption of other well-known firms such as Lancaster, Watson Brothers, and so on, the company made guns under the names of its individual component companies. So a side-lever gun would be a Stephen Grant, a 12/20 a Lancaster, and so on. The Lang name appears to have been a catch-all to include double rifles and shotguns, both sidelock and boxlock, that were generic designs. While they are well made, they have acquired over the years an image of being something less than other London bests.

For some reason, one sees more refurbished Joseph Lang guns than those of other makers.

> 1821: 7 Haymarket
> 1853: 22 Cockspur Street, Charing Cross
> 1890: 10 Pall Mall
> 1898: 102 New Bond Street (the former James Lang premises)
> 1925: 7 Bury Street

Jack Rowe:

Lang guns made under the Lang name were of the finest quality. Lang also made a boxlock of their own design about the time Anson and Deeley were working on theirs. Not many were made, as it was not as viable as the A&D. Lang also made a sidelock, with the locks removable by way of a key. A novel idea, until someone lost the key and wished to remove the locks. I have never seen this on any other make of gun.

George Caswell:
One of the oldest firms, whose products are very good to excellent. They are reasonably common in the market, and command a premium of five to 10 percent. Because many that we see were very early pieces, a buyer needs to pay close attention to condition.

LANG & HUSSEY

There were two incarnations of the name Lang & Hussey, the second of which added "Ltd." to the name. The first, a partnership with James Lang (late of Joseph Lang & Son) lasted from 1895 to 1898, and the second for just five months during the year 1898 when Joseph Lang & Son was added to the group. Hussey was forced out for what amounted to embezzlement. Although the partnership was over, the firm retained the name Lang & Hussey Ltd. until 1901, when it reverted to the name Joseph Lang & Son Ltd.

JAMES MACNAUGHTON & SONS

MacNaughton was a Scottish inventor and gunmaker whose small firm had an influence on gunmaking out of all proportion to its size.

MacNaughton filed his first patent, in 1867, for a forward-sliding, drop-down double barrel design. This became known as the MacNaughton Lockfast.

In 1879, MacNaughton obtained patent number 2848, which covered a design for a round-action side-by-side with its lock work on the trigger plate. This design set the stage for every similar mechanism that came later, some of which are still made today. Nigel Brown says this basic design became "to all intents and purposes the private property of the Scottish gunmakers." John Dickson patented his version in 1887, and David McKay Brown patented an over/under variation in 1992.

MacNaughton used this basically wonderful design as the foundation for guns that were elegant, stylish, and unique in some aspects. Aesthetically, they are a triumph.

It became known as the "Edinburgh Gun," and was characterized by a bar-in-wood action (a legacy of the hammer era) in which the stock extended far forward, covering much of the metal frame. Cocking was done by a lever. The gun won a gold medal for design at the 1886 Edinburgh Exhibition, and the first one was sold to Sir Derrick Dunlop; this gun was sold at auction in 1998 and acquired by the (now reconstituted) MacNaughton company.

James MacNaughton died in 1905 at the age of 66, at which time the firm became known as James MacNaughton & Sons and moved to 36 Hanover Street.

In 1947, the business was taken over by John Dickson. For a while, they continued to make MacNaughton guns from the remaining stock of parts, and as long as MacNaughton's craftsmen were available to do the work. Finally, it was absorbed into Dickson's own business. In 1995, a firm called Logie Gunmakers, which included Barry Wilcox, acquired the Mac-Naughton name and records from Dickson, and then later acquired Dickson itself, and renamed the firm Dickson & MacNaughton. It is currently located on Frederick Street, Edinburgh.

> 1864: 33 George Street, Edinburgh
> 1869: 26 Hanover Street South
> 1905-40: 36 Hanover Street
> c. 1897-1909: Perth (branch outlet)

Jack Rowe:
> *MacNaughton was the inventor of the round action. It can be distinguished from the Dickson by its longer top lever (the operation of which cocked the gun). Some also had a panel cut out of the center of the top lever, to view a small window in the top strap. Through this window, you could see if the tumblers were cocked. Nice guns, but rather old-fashioned compared to the Dickson. If you can find one in good condition, it's a keeper.*

George Caswell:
> *Delightful guns, with workmanship excellent to excellent-plus. They seldom come onto the market, and when they do, they command a 20 to 30 percent premium. One must be careful of condition, however, and the possibility of alterations.*
>
> *But, they are superb guns. I know of a late pre-war bar-in-wood round action that is in exceptional condition and is a delight to handle.*

MANTON & CO. (CALCUTTA)

Manton of Calcutta is an English company in origins only, but is included because of its connections with John and Joseph Manton, and the fact that its products were made in England and often resurface in such disparate parts of the world as Australia, America, and South Africa.

In 1825, the year before Joseph Manton went bankrupt and only a few years before his death, Frederick Manton travelled to India and opened Manton & Co. at 10 Lall Bazaar, Calcutta. These were the early days of the British Raj and India was a prime market for firearms of all kinds.

Manton guns were made in Birmingham and the company issued an elaborate catalog of shotguns, rifles, pistols, and all kinds of related equipment in every grade and form. Jim Corbett, the celebrated hunter of man-eating tigers, refers more than once to "Manton's, in Calcutta" and seems to have been a regular client.

The company continued under Manton family management until 1846, when it was taken over by W.R. Wallis. At one point, it had an outlet at 116 Jermyn Street, London, and continued in business well into the 20th century.

Being a large company with a long history, many guns were sold with the name "Manton & Co." on the rib, and many of these in turn were shipped to Australia and other destinations after 1947, when India became independent, and in another wave in the 1960s when hunting was banned and firearms were confiscated wholesale. Many guns and rifles belonging to maharajahs and other Indian notables left at the same time, but it is doubtful any of these masterpieces came from Manton's, which catered mostly (like the Army & Navy stores), to military men and civil servants abroad in the service of the empire.

The author has seen only one Manton of Calcutta rifle, a .470 double owned by Derek Hurt. Although a mid-grade boxlock that has been undoubtedly well used over its lifetime, it is still delivering dependable service under the harshest of conditions—typical of a Birmingham gun of that era.

Jack Rowe:
This should be considered a store, not a gunmaker, although they did have a workshop on Whittall Street in Birmingham, which made some of their guns and double rifles as well. Their guns and rifles I have seen have all been of lower or medium grades, which is understandable given the Indian market.

ALEXANDER MARTIN

This firm was founded in 1837 in Paisley, Scotland, and later moved to Glasgow. Although Alexander Martin is best known for its rifles, especially target rifles, it also made shotguns and even sold fly-fishing tackle from its store.

Martin shotguns were noteworthy for their use of Celtic-style engraving. Martin also produced a shotgun without ribs between the barrels. Like the round action, a shotgun with its barrels connected by spacers at breech, muzzle, and mid-barrel was something of a Scottish specialty. This reduced weight and supposedly eliminated a possible source of rusting. At least some of the later Martin ribless guns were made for them by A.A. Brown in Birmingham.

Martin's shop in Glasgow was closed around 1970 and the business was absorbed into John Dickson.

Jack Rowe:

A Scottish firm, also well known for fly-fishing tackle. Their guns, at least the later ones, were all made in Birmingham. I have only seen boxlocks bearing this name, but all of them, even the lower grades, have been very well made.

George Caswell:

Alex. Martin was noted for its target rifles. Overall quality is very good, and their ribless shotgun is worth looking for. Martin guns appear very seldom, and command a premium of five to 10 percent. Their more recent boxlock guns are well made, and of nice quality and appearance.

MIDLAND GUN COMPANY

Birmingham is in that part of England known as "The Midlands," hence the name for this Birmingham company founded in 1885. It was known to those in the trade as "the Midland" throughout its life.

The company made a wide range of firearms of all types and issued a large catalog that, as one might imagine, was highly sought after by gun lovers around the world. The company survived until 1952, when it was bought out by Parker-Hale. All the Midland records were lost, probably because of bomb damage to the factory in 1942.

After the takeover, Parker-Hale used the Midland name on various firearms, including some imported shotguns and sporting rifles made from converted Springfields.

Because Midland made a wide range of shotguns (see Jack Rowe's comments below) they have a reputation as a maker of mid-range and utility guns, when in fact many were quite fine pieces. This being the case, Midland guns are often under-estimated and under-priced.

1889: 77 Bath Street
1890: 81 Bath Street
1900: 81 Price Street

1910: 77 Bath Street
1930: 76 & 77 Bath Street
1937: Demon Works, Bath Street
1945-65: 74 Whittall Street

Jack Rowe:

If you had the time, I could write you a book about "the Midland," as we called it in the trade. Cutting it short, they made all grades from the very best-grade sidelocks to the cheapest grade of boxlocks. They also made a single-barrel gun called the Knockabout, similar to the single-barrel hammer guns made by Harrington & Richardson, Iver Johnson, and other American firms.

The Midland also made guns for many of the provincial gunmakers. The factory in Bath Street was built to house individual section workers. They worked for themselves and paid rent to the owner, John Craythorne. He planned it that way, and one of the conditions was that he would have first call upon them to do work for the Midland Gun Company.

Unfortunately, the factory received a direct hit from a German bomb in 1942, and all that remained was a portion of the building, the yard at the rear, and a few buildings at the bottom of the yard. The Midland kept going in these remaining buildings until it was bought out by Parker-Hale.

A lot of the old stock of boxlocks in the white were auctioned off, and have since appeared in the market as finished guns bearing the names of other makers.

George Caswell:

Overall, these are basic guns and rifles—pretty decent, inexpensive working guns. The quality is generally good, but most were hard-used and a buyer should pay close attention to condition and be especially cautious of improper repairs. They are fairly common and command no premium.

MORTIMER & SON

Mortimer is a very old name in British gunmaking, dating back to 1753 with three sons of a London grocer becoming gunmakers and succeeding generations entering the business.

Although it is primarily remembered today as a Scottish company, T.E. (Thomas Ellsworth) Mortimer began as a London gunmaker. His father, T.J. Mortimer, had a shop at 21 St. James's Street from 1818 to 1821, and was Gunsmith-in-Ordinary to King George IV. T.E. was born in 1807 and probably apprenticed with his father.

T.E. Mortimer left London and opened a shop on Princes Street in Edinburgh in 1835. His son joined the business around 1862, and it became Mortimer & Son. Mortimer absorbed Joseph Harkom in 1923, and was absorbed in turn by John Dickson in 1938.

Author's note: I have seen one Mortimer, a lovely old boxlock 12-bore with 30-inch barrels, light weight and excellent balance. Alas, some ham-fisted cretin had bored out the 2¹/₂-inch chambers to something approaching 3¹/₂ inches, in the interests of reducing recoil by eliminating the forcing cones. The result was a gun out of proof, possibly dangerous, and no bargain. It had been a lovely gun to begin with, though.

> 1835: 78 Princes Street, Edinburgh
> 1840: 97 George Street
> 1854: 86 George Street

Jack Rowe:
> *Another Scottish maker. I have never seen many guns bearing this name. All have been either hammer guns or boxlocks, all were made in Birmingham, and all have been good quality.*

WILLIAM S. NEEDLER

William Needler was a gunmaker in the port city of Hull for most of the 19th century. He was born in 1820, apprenticed in London, and moved to Hull in 1841. At the time, Hull was a major whaling port, and Needler produced a wide range of firearms up to and including harpoon guns.

Needler guns on display in the Hull museum include a couple of rifles with the names of two Arctic whaling ships, the *Venerable* and *St. George*, stamped on the breech. These were presumably part of the ships' stores. There is also a matched set of double-barreled percussion pistols, also from whaling ships. A Needler harpoon gun with percussion ignition, on display in Hull, was destroyed by bombing in the Second World War.

Except for the whaling connection, William Needler is neither unique nor particularly noteworthy, there being hundreds of similar gunmakers throughout the land in the 1800s. However, George Calef, a friend of the author, acquired a Needler hammer gun (see color section) with Damascus barrels, with which he is in love, and rightly so. It is a beautiful example of the kind of hammer gun that was made for, and sold routinely by, English provincial gunmakers—graceful, deadly, and with a gorgeous walnut stock.

If ever there was a bargain shotgun, this is it.

W.W. Greener, being into anything that fired a projectile, naturally made harpoon guns as well. On Needler's death in 1895, his firm was taken over by Greener and the Needler shop on Silver Street became the Hull branch of W.W. Greener.

PETER NELSON

Peter Nelson is an English gunmaker who apprenticed with Purdey as an action filer in 1953, building over/under and side-by-side shotguns, trap guns, and rifles. He went to work for Hartmann & Weiss in Hamburg in 1971, returned to the United Kingdom to open a branch of Hartmann & Weiss in 1974, and then struck out on his own.

When the world's greatest gunmakers gather and discuss who is the best of them all, Peter Nelson's name invariably comes up (as do those of Gerhard Hartmann and Otto Weiss, his friends and former colleagues).

Peter Nelson is the most meticulous and demanding of craftsmen, very difficult to work for, but then a genius usually is. Away from his shop, Peter is friendly, genial, and unassuming. When examining a gun, however, he is an unforgiving perfectionist. In his small shop in the south of England, Peter produces only a few guns a year and those go straight into the world's finest collections.

Nelson makes over/unders on the Boss pattern, and side-by-sides in both Purdey and Boss styles, as well as rifles. It is almost impossible even to order a gun or rifle from Peter Nelson, and there is little or no chance the average person will ever actually see one, but any book that includes the greatest of British gunmakers must include Peter Nelson.

Jack Rowe:
   My old friend Peter. He is a very fastidious gunmaker. Everything has to
   be right on a gun, and his work is meticulous. I have done work for him, I
   know how critical he can be, and he is not widely liked as a result. But any
   gun bearing his name is the very best.

W.R. PAPE

William Rochester Pape was a provincial English gunmaker, much like any of hundreds of others, but with one great claim to fame: He was the inventor of choke boring. Pape's patent of May 29, 1866 (#1501) pre-dates any other, including Fred Kimble's development in America, which is generally dated around 1870.

Pape was a good gunmaker and a very inventive one. His guns won the London gun trials in 1858, '59, '66, and '75, and he held many patents for ejectors, strikers, and bolting systems. Pape's choke-boring system was developed and refined by W.W. Greener (who was not above claiming to have invented it himself).

Pape started his gun business in Newcastle-upon-Tyne in 1857 and retired in 1888, the year his company won its last award (a Diploma of Merit at the Glasgow Exhibition). He died in 1923. What remained of his company was re-formed in 1935 into the firm of Bagnall & Kirkwood.

PARKER-HALE

This Birmingham company is primarily remembered as a riflemaker and supplier of accoutrements and equipment for target shooting, but it published an extensive catalog and for part of the 20th century, at least, offered name-brand shotguns and a few Birmingham-made A&D boxlocks under the Parker-Hale name.

The company was founded by A.G. Parker around 1910. His nephew, A.T.C. Hale, later joined the company and in 1936 it became Parker-Hale. From that point until the 1990s, it was managed by members of the Hale family.

At one point, Parker-Hale offered shotguns made by BSA, Webley & Scott, and Vickers. They later added A&D boxlocks in three versions, made in Birmingham. In the 1980s, Parker-Hale also imported sidelock guns bearing the Parker-Hale name from Ignacio Ugartechea in Spain. Some of these guns were in turn brought into the United States and Canada by Parker-Hale's American importers (Precision Sports in the U.S., and Safari Arms in Canada).

WILLIAM POWELL & SON

William Powell & Son is often referred to as "the Purdey of Birmingham," and dates from 1802, making it 12 years older than Purdey itself. The company began with a partnership between William Powell and Joseph Simmons, and one of their early contracts was to produce military muskets, some of which were used at the Battle of Waterloo.

On Simmons's death in 1812, the firm became just William Powell. His son later came into the business, which took the name William Powell & Son in 1847.

W.R. Pape 12-bore ejector boxlock. William Rochester Pape was the inventor of choke boring.

From the beginning, Powell stressed fine finishing of both guns and rifles (hence the Purdey comparison). The company prospered through the percussion and pinfire eras, and contributed several inventions and patents, most notably their "lift-up top-lever snap action," but none were generally adopted.

The Powell family was active in the gun trade in Birmingham, through both the trade association and the proof house, and was highly regarded. In recent years, there have been two developments that should be noted. Powell always sold a wide variety of clothing and shooting accessories from its shop in Carrs Lane, and in the last years of the 20th century took to catalog sales as well. This business grew to become the company's dominant source of revenue.

In 1987, to combat the rapidly escalating cost of an English double, Powell began importing partly finished guns from the Basque Country, which were finished in their shop to their customers' specifications. These guns were known as the Heritage Line.

As this book went to press, it was announced that Powell's gun business had been purchased by Mark Osbourne, former part-owner of E.J. Churchill, and had passed out of family ownership.

c.1802-12: High Street, Birmingham (as Powell & Simmons)

1812-22: High Street (as William Powell)

1822-25: 3 Bartholomew Row

c.1832-47: High Street and Carrs Lane (originally Cares Lane)

1847: Carrs Lane (as William Powell & Son)

1976: 35/37 Carrs Lane

(The company has remained at the same premises on Carrs Lane since 1832, but over the years the numbering has changed from #9 to #11, and then to #13 in 1870, and finally #35 around 1901. The company added #37 in 1936.)

Jack Rowe:

Powells are good guns, both sidelock and boxlock. I knew Bernard Powell, father of the current (now former) owners. They are still making guns and, if you have a Wm. Powell, you have a good, well-made gun. This firm should not be confused with Williams & Powell of Liverpool.

George Caswell:

The Powell snap-action is seen occasionally. Their quality is good to very good, and their post-war guns particularly are very good. They do not appear in the market often, but they built a lot of guns over many years, and they command about a five percent premium. I have seen some very nice modern Powells.

JAMES PURDEY & SONS

James Purdey is the pre-eminent name in the British gun trade, regardless of claims (however legitimate and justified they may be) of other firms. In the public mind, whether they know anything about guns or not, a Purdey is simply the best—and not just the best in the United Kingdom, but the best in the world.

This reputation is not undeserved. Since 1814, James Purdey has been synonymous with the finest in gunmaking. James Purdey apprenticed with Joseph Manton, paid tribute to Manton with the statement "but for him we would have been a pack of blacksmiths," and took over Manton's premises at 315 Oxford Street in 1827, when Manton went into bankruptcy.

Purdey's sons joined the business, which became James Purdey & Sons in 1877, and the company moved into its current premises at 57 South Audley Street in 1882.

There have been many milestones in the company's history. The most significant was Purdey's invention of the double underlug, which became the industry standard bolting system. The second was the adoption, in 1880, of Beesley's patent sidelock hammerless action. The Beesley action has been associated with Purdey ever since.

During the late 1800s, Purdey was a prominent riflemaker as well, and is credited with coining the term "express" to describe the new high-velocity rifles they helped pioneer. Purdey developed its share of cartridges, both blackpowder and smokeless, although none became widely used.

Purdey makes sidelock guns exclusively. In the 1920s, they briefly made an over/under on the design of Edwinson Green, but it was heavy and awkward, and few were made. In 1948, Purdey took over the business of James Woodward and adopted the famous Woodward over/under design, which it manufactures (with some modifications) to this day.

As might be expected with any gunmaker approaching two centuries in business, Purdey has had its poorer periods along with the good. Immediately after 1945, for example, and into the 1950s, some Purdey guns were produced that were nondescript (at least compared with earlier Purdeys) in terms of their quality of walnut and engraving. Partly, this had to do with what was available to them at the time, and the prevailing tastes.

Overall, however, Purdey has maintained a standard of style and workmanship that is the envy of other gunmakers, even such legendary firms as Boss, Woodward, and Holland & Holland. A Purdey hammer gun is a joy to handle, and their later over/unders, especially in smaller gauges, are a revelation.

Today, Purdey is still in business in South Audley Street, still making guns, and is part of the Vendôme group of companies.

1813: 15 New Grey Coat Place, Tothill Fields, London (residence)
1816-27: 4 Prince's Street
1827-77: 314-315 Oxford Street (later 314)
1877-81: 289 Oxford Street (premises renumbered in 1881) as
    James Purdey & Sons)
1882: 57 South Audley Street

Jack Rowe:
    What can one say? On a par with H&H. Everyone knows the history. Best hammer guns. Best sidelocks. Also a few boxlocks in the last part of the 1800s. These were made in Birmingham—I believe they were designated grade 'E.' Nevertheless, very well made guns. I would sum it up as: The best there is.

George Caswell:

Purdey's Beesley self-opener and the later over/under are two of the best guns ever made. The quality is always superb. Purdeys appear in the market often (and forever) and command a premium of 40 to 50 percent. A Purdey gun never dies, but one should be careful of badly re-done or improperly restored guns. There are a few fake Purdeys and a few back-door Purdeys. I have seen both, but few.

Even non-gun people know what a Purdey is. I know several people who are not students of the gun, but success in life has elevated them to owning a Purdey. They don't know why it is better, why they bought it, or what for, but they feel that on their occasional visits to the shooting fields they merit being seen with a Purdey.

E.M. REILLY & CO.

Edward Michael Reilly was a London gunmaker, born in 1816, who entered his father's gunmaking business in 1848. Their shop was at 502 Oxford Street. By 1861, the firm was called Edward M. Reilly & Co., which later evolved into E.M. Reilly & Co. The firm was located in Oxford Street throughout its existence, but the numbers changed, sometimes because the company moved and sometimes because the buildings were renumbered.

For a while, in the 1880s, Reilly also had an outlet on Rue Scribe in Paris —an indication of how successful the company was.

Although it is not a household name, E.M. Reilly was well respected and its products were used by two of the most famous hunters of the Victorian Age: Sir Samuel Baker and Frederick Courteney Selous. Baker used a pair of E.M. Reilly 10-bores to back up his monstrous "Baby"; reading of this, and seeking to emulate the much-admired Baker, Selous took a Reilly 12-bore with him on his first venture to Africa, but the gun was stolen shortly after he landed.

E.M. Reilly lasted until 1917, when it was bought out by Charles Riggs & Co., which sold shooting accessories. The Reilly name disappeared from gunmaking.

Reilly is known to have made hammer guns and boxlocks, most of which were probably made in Birmingham and finished at the shop in London. Its boxlocks ranged from very basic to genuine bests.

Jack Rowe:

Long since out of business. I have seen many of their hammer guns, and

E.M. Reilly 12-bore boxlock non-ejector, probably made toward the end of Reilly's existence. The gunmaker was absorbed by another company around 1917, and the name disappeared.

a few boxlocks, and some really big-bore hammer guns and boxlocks. All were good quality and well made. E.M. Reilly is an under-rated gunmaker.

JOHN RIGBY & CO.

John Rigby is one of the greatest gunmakers in history. It claims to be the oldest gunmaker in the English-speaking world (and probably is). It could also claim to be (or to have been, at times) the greatest riflemaker in England.

None of these claims is undisputed, but none of them is ill-founded, either. Given the company's extraordinary history, it is not surprising to find the odd conflict.

To start with, for years Rigby has claimed that it was founded in Dublin in 1735. Nigel Brown says this is not true—that the actual year was 1775, and that 1735 was a misprint in some early printed material that has become accepted truth. He points to an advertisement placed by the company in 1935 that states the real year, and celebrates 160 years in business. Brown also writes that John Rigby was not born until 1758, and died in 1818.

So, whether Rigby is in fact the oldest gunmaking company in the English-speaking world is possibly open to question.

Countering this, Geoffrey Boothroyd points to the fact that the first John

Rigby (there were several) owned some gunmaking patents that were filed as early as 1754, so he (or someone) was obviously in the business before 1775.

At any rate, Rigby was founded in Dublin and began by making duelling pistols. From that point, the company made every type of firearm imaginable. They opened a London office in 1866 and sold off the Dublin end of the business to Truelock & Harris in 1892.

From the beginning in London, Rigby concentrated on rifles more than shotguns, and all its innovations are rifle related. They are, however, vastly impressive: Rigby introduced the .450 Nitro Express in 1897 (or 1898, depending on the source), ushering in the nitro-express era. It was Rigby that first prevailed upon Mauser in Germany to make a magnum-sized action, and Rigby introduced the .416 Rigby, one of the greatest of all magazine-rifle cartridges, in 1911.

Rigby's double rifles and shotguns were both sidelocks and boxlocks. Rigby sidelocks have a distinctive scalloped or humped shape to them, but this feature was not exclusive to Rigby.

In 1984, Paul Roberts bought a controlling interest in John Rigby, and eventually moved the company to Great Suffolk Street. In 1998, Roberts sold Rigby to Geoff Miller, who moved it to Paso Robles, California, where it continues in business making both shotguns and rifles.

Jack Rowe:
> *A maker more noted for rifles than shotguns. Nevertheless, Rigby made many fine shotguns. Many shotguns bearing this name were made by Webley & Scott and other Birmingham makers. Good guns and rifles by a good maker.*

George Caswell:
> *Rigby is best known for double and bolt-action rifles, and one of the most noteworthy features of its double rifles is the rising (third) bite. Overall quality is excellent. Rigby rifles are fairly common in the used-gun market, but not Rigby shotguns. They command a premium of 20 to 30 percent.*
>
> *The real Rigby existed before the Second World War. Some post-1950 shotguns were actually made in Spain or Belgium, then proofed in London with the London address. Most post-1945 Rigbys, especially the sidelocks, cannot be compared to the original Rigby.*

W&C SCOTT

It is impossible to imagine the English gun trade from 1880 to 1980 with-

John Rigby was one gunmaker that made the use of Old English lettering almost a trademark.

The renowned John Rigby "rising bite" third fastener is found on many of the company's double rifles. It is an expensive feature, and very difficult to make, but very effective. Note the trademark "leaf" fences on this double rifle.

out W&C Scott in its many permutations and incarnations—on its own or in partnership first with Webley and finally, briefly, with Holland & Holland.

The firm began with William Scott of Birmingham, who set up shop in 1834. In 1840, he was joined by his brother, Charles, and the name changed to William & Charles Scott. William married Susan Middleditch, and when his two sons later joined the business it became W&C Scott & Son. The eldest of the two sons was William Middleditch Scott, inventor of the Scott spindle, one of the pivotal inventions that made possible the modern side-by-side shotgun.

The company concentrated on making higher-quality double shotguns until 1897, when it merged with Richard Ellis & Son, and P. Webley & Son, to become Webley & Scott Revolver & Arms Co.

At this point, the story of W&C Scott ends, at least temporarily. Webley & Scott became one of the world's most famous names in gunmaking. The Webley revolver was a mainstay of the British Army through many wars and skirmishes, the company branched out into other engineering ventures, including automotive parts, and became a supplier of guns, gun parts, and services to other gun companies large and small, famous and obscure.

The W&C Scott name was kept alive within the larger company with a line of shotguns, but sales were slow after 1920 and production ceased in 1935. The remaining W&C Scott & Son shotguns were disposed of gradually, with the last one sold in 1950. At the same time, however, Webley & Scott was making shotguns, rifles, and handguns, and so there is a certain amount of confusion over what was what during those years.

In 1965, Webley & Scott absorbed W.W. Greener, a sign of just how dire things had become, not only for the Birmingham gun trade, but for English gunmaking in general. Webley & Scott was acquired by the Harris & Sheldon Group in 1973 and ceased making shotguns in 1979. The shotgun side of the business was divested and reconstituted under the name of W&C Scott (Gunmakers) Ltd., which introduced a line of boxlocks and one best-quality sidelock, the Blenheim. In 1985, W & C Scott was acquired by Holland & Holland. The Blenheim was abandoned and the works set to producing the Cavalier line of boxlocks for H&H.

With the purchase of H&H by Chanel in 1989, the Birmingham works were closed down and all production concentrated at the H&H factory in Harrow Road.

Jack Rowe:

Scott made both boxlocks and sidelocks in so many models it would make a long list, and in all grades of guns, too. They made two O/U guns—two guns, not two models—and both were completely hand-made by Rowley Bloomer, a well-known gunmaker who worked for Webley & Scott his entire working life. We shall never see his like again.

An interesting note is that Hoffman Arms was the U.S. agent for Webley & Scott in the 1920s, and purchased barreled actions from them for their own use. Many Hoffman guns are in fact W&C Scott guns, finished and engraved in the U.S.

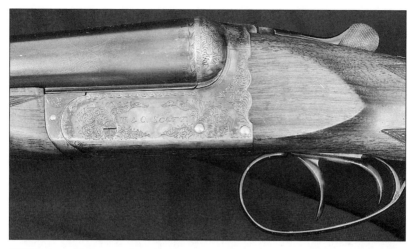

W&C Scott & Son 12-bore boxlock. Scott made all kinds of double shotguns and rifles, ranging in grade from very good to excellent. One of the most dependable names.

George Caswell:

The Premier model is noteworthy, and their square-cut crossbolt is worth looking for. Early W&C Scott guns are excellent, and the more modern guns are still very good. Some have quite elaborate engraving. They made many models, and I have seen a wide range of weights within the same gauge, varying from model to model.

They appear regularly in the market and command a five to 10 percent premium. High-grade Scott guns are very well made and there are quite a number in the United States. I consider them one of the better values in British guns.

J&W TOLLEY

James and William Tolley were Birmingham gunmakers, first listed in 1859. The company was absorbed by Holloway & Naughton sometime around 1911.

In the intervening 50 years, Tolley did a bit of everything in the gun trade, advertising rifles, shotguns, and pistols. They made some very large bores intended for the African market, including a double 4-bore, and claimed the Persian royal family as patrons.

Tolley at times had a shop in London as well as Birmingham, but their ventures into the London trade were not particularly successful and never lasted long.

1859: 22 St. Mary's Row, Birmingham
1878: Loveday Street
1925: 10, 12, 14 Vesey Street (with Holloway & Naughton)

Jack Rowe:
  Tolley made Anson & Deeley boxlocks, sidelocks, and hammer guns.
  Those I have seen have been lower and mid-grade guns. If they made a best
  gun, I have yet to see one.

VICKERS, SONS & MAXIM

Vickers is a name more usually associated with military ordnance and
machine guns than with sporting guns, but for a time in the 1920s and '30s they
did venture into the sporting market. They advertised a sidelock (the Imperial)
in both ejector and non-ejector models, a boxlock, and a single-barrel gun.

These sporting guns were probably made for Vickers by William Baker in
Birmingham, and they incorporated some unusual features. For example, the
sidelock employed coil springs rather than the usual leaf or V-springs. This
lock was a Baker invention.

Vickers was located in Kent.

Jack Rowe:
  Vickers was best known for military weapons, and operated in Crayford,
  Kent. They made a sidelock with Baker patent locks—locks with few mov-
  ing parts and a coil mainspring. Not considered a best gun, though a robust
  gun and well made.

WATSON BROTHERS

The first Watson, Thomas William, married the daughter of Birmingham
gunmaker William Tranter, and took over the business of the early Victorian
gunmaker, Durs Egg, at 4 Pall Mall, in 1878.

Watson handed over the business to his two sons and it became Watson
Brothers in 1885.

Watson Brothers was noted for making small-bore guns, especially for
ladies and children. They offered a hammerless model called the Carlton,
which boasted both a new method of cocking the tumblers (half on opening,
half on closing, making both "imperceptible") and a new safety that bolted
both tumblers and hammers.

On the death of the last surviving Watson brother in 1935, the firm was taken into the Grant & Lang fold.

An interesting sidelight: One of the Watson workmen was the stocker Ebenezer Hands. He continued working with Grant & Lang until his death in his 91st year. Hands was still working at the bench in the 1960s when Les Paul, a gunmaker now living in Ontario, apprenticed with Henry Atkin and worked with him. Hands apparently "signed" each of his stocks with a tiny teardrop carved into the comb.

In the 1980s, the Watson name was divested from Atkin Grant & Lang, teamed with Hellis and Beesley for a time, and then sold to Michael Louca, formerly of Purdey's, who now makes guns in London under the Watson name.

> 1878: 4 Pall Mall
> 1894-95: 31 Cockspur Street
> 1896-1930: 29 Bond Street
> 1930-35: 13a Pall Mall

George Caswell:
Watson made many small-bore game guns. The quality is very good, and many of them have very unusual engraving. They do not appear often, and command a premium of about five percent. I have encountered some very nice, well-made Watson guns.

P. WEBLEY & SON

The other half of the famous firm of Webley & Scott began with Philip Webley around 1834, when he completed his apprenticeship at the age of 21 and was joined in business by his brother James. In 1838, Philip married Caroline Davis and amalgamated with her father's existing gunmaking business. It was located at 84 Weaman Street in Birmingham, which later became the site of the Webley factory.

At first, Webley concentrated on handguns. His two sons joined the business in 1859, and it became P. Webley & Son. In 1865 the elder son, Thomas William, obtained a provisional patent for a method of converting pinfire guns to centerfire. Webley probably began building shotguns around this time. The younger son, Henry, later acquired (as an investor) Lang & Hussey and Joseph Lang & Son.

By 1873, Webley was producing rifles and shotguns in a major way, and received a medal for its work at the Vienna Universal Exhibition that year.

Webley's greatest contribution to the world of double guns is the Webley screw-grip treble bite, a means of bolting a gun using a combination of the Purdey double underlug and a rib extension which is an interrupted thread. As the top lever closes back over the extension, it cams it down and holds it tight. This action was patented by Webley in 1882 and later used on all manner of rifles and shotguns, both boxlock and sidelock, and continued in use after Webley merged with W&C Scott. As well, Webley supplied the action (or supplied guns built on that action) to other gunmakers in Birmingham and London. Some of the best known are Army & Navy and William Evans.

According to Geoffrey Boothroyd, lower-grade Webley guns were sold with no name on them, but the best guns were signed P. Webley (as with the Webley gun shown on the dust jacket, and in the color signature of this book). When Webley established a London presence in the early 1890s, the guns were signed P. Webley, St. James, London, and after they opened a showroom on Shaftesbury Avenue in 1893, that address was given.

In 1877, Webley acquired the firm of Tipping & Lawden, and some guns bearing that name are actually Webleys.

P. Webley merged with W&C Scott in 1897.

Jack Rowe:

The Webley name was used only on their best-grade guns. I can say that every gun I have seen bearing the name P. Webley has been a best boxlock. I have seen only one hammer gun with the Webley name, and never a sidelock.

WEBLEY & SCOTT LTD.

This firm was the result of the merger in 1897 between P. Webley and W&C Scott. After the merger, a certain amount of rationalization took place, including the closing of some showrooms. In 1906, the company adopted the name Webley & Scott Ltd. All shotgun manufacturing was concentrated in Scott's factory on Lancaster Street, while Webley's Weaman Street works were given over to the making of revolvers and other military items.

In 1919, in the post-war economic collapse, the Lancaster Street works was closed, followed by the old Webley Shaftesbury showroom a couple of years later. The company relocated its London presence to 55 Victoria Street, where it remained until the Great Depression struck in 1929.

During this period, Webley & Scott encountered other difficulties. Changes to firearms regulations both limited their sales at home and opened these markets to cheaper foreign guns. The company turned its engineering expertise to other fields, such as automotive parts.

Webley & Scott began making a series of shotgun models designated by number—the 400, 500, 600, and 700 series guns. The 400 was made until 1924, replaced by the 500 and 600, which were made until around 1952. The 700 series was introduced in 1949, and was the basis for the company's shotgun production until it stopped making shotguns altogether in 1979. The 600 series was the first in which component parts carried code numbers, prefixed "G6/".

After 1945, the company underwent a series of corporate reorganizations. Webley & Scott had a flourishing business in airguns, and the name was retained for those products after shotgun manufacturing was discontinued. The shotgun side was spun off as W&C Scott and acquired by Holland & Holland in 1985. At that time, W&C Scott had the only barrel-making operation in the country aside from Holland's own.

In 1991, W&C Scott Gunmakers Ltd. in Birmingham was closed and some of the staff and equipment transferred to the H&H factory in Harrow Road. The surviving Scott records are now in the possession of Richard Gallyon in Norfolk.

Jack Rowe:

> *If you have several years to spare, and enough paper, I could write a book on them. This firm made best sidelocks for William Evans, among others. They made hammer guns and boxlocks in so many models it's hard to list them all. They supplied the trade with barrel tubes and barreled actions. They also produced some of the finest gunsmiths, many of whom left to work in the trade and became well known. Ron Collings, the engraver now working in the U.S., is a Webley man. I did some time with that firm myself. Suffice to say, any gun, if made by Webley, regardless of grade, is for the money a damned good gun!*

George Caswell:

> *Webley & Scott is best known for its boxlock, which was a standard in the industry. The quality ranges from good to very good, although some of their single triggers left a bit to be desired. They appear regularly in the market, and command a premium of maybe five percent.*
>
> *One thing to watch for is quality of repairs. Many of these guns were well used and then altered or repaired by people who were not competent to do it.*
>
> *In my opinion, however, no other make of boxlock created more first-time*

owners of British guns in the U.S. than Webley & Scott. Many people learned the features of weight, balance, and quality in a game gun from owning a Webley & Scott, and they converted many people from the American double.

WESTLEY RICHARDS & CO.

Today, when people think of custom gunmakers in Birmingham, the name that most often comes to mind is Westley Richards. While many of the larger Birmingham names have disappeared (Greener and Scott, to name two), Westley Richards continues to thrive as one of the prominent names in English gunmaking.

The firm was founded in 1812 by William Westley Richards, a member of a prominent and successful Birmingham family whose members included everything from lawyers to jewellers to barrel makers.

William was just 22 went he started his business, and the very next year, he and his father were instrumental in setting up the Birmingham proof house. The site of his first shop, behind 82 High Street, was fortuitous because it afforded room for a shooting range for testing his products—a practice the company continued for the 86 years it occupied the premises.

The founder was succeeded by his son, Westley, who was an ambitious man and a hard taskmaster. During the period of greatest ferment in the English gun trade, Westley Richards was deeply involved in all kinds of developments, from refining Whitworth rifling, to developing the first Enfield rifle, to his "monkeytail" carbine, which in 1858 became the first breech loader to be adopted by the British government.

Through the middle years of the 19th century, Westley Richards (through an associated company) was heavily involved in supplying military arms and ammunition both in England and abroad.

The company did not entirely neglect shotguns and suitable actions for them. In 1862, Westley Richards patented a doll's-head rib extension combined with a top lever, a bolting system that was widely copied in the trade.

The greatest single patent associated with Westley Richards is the Anson & Deeley boxlock, which was invented and patented by William Anson and John Deeley, two Westley Richards employees. Westley Richards naturally adopted the boxlock action as its own (although it continued to make sidelock guns), and further refined the A&D action with its famous "drop lock" variation.

When combined with WR's patented doll's-head bolting system, the A&D boxlock provided an extremely strong platform for the large double

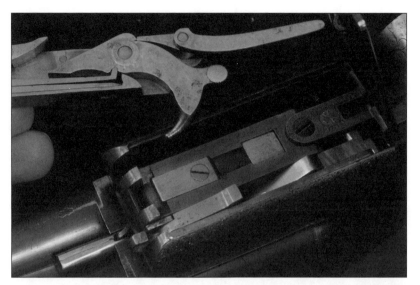

Westley Richards detachable locks are exact and finely finished. Guns and rifles with this feature command a price comparable to a London sidelock.

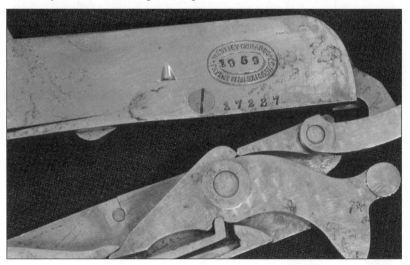

rifles that were then coming into use, and that would evolve into the nitro-express rifles.

In 1896, having outgrown its premises, John Deeley (then managing director) purchased property in Bournbrook and built a new factory. This area is now part of greater Birmingham.

Westley Richards was active in the rifle trade, especially double rifles and

Westley Richards 12-bore best boxlock. Westley Richards is one of the most respected of all British gunmakers. The Anson & Deeley boxlock was a Westley Richards invention.

An early Westley Richards 12-bore boxlock utilizing only the Westley Richards patent doll's-head fastener, and no underlugs.

bolt actions, and contributed its share of cartridges for African hunting, including the .476 Nitro Express and .425 Westley Richards. The company's double rifles were highly regarded then, and are even more highly regarded now.

Many events took place over the first half of the 20th century, not related to shotgun making but still having an impact on Westley Richards. The depression that followed the Great War resulted in a severe reduction in their business and work force.

In 1946, Westley Richards was put up for sale, and purchased by Captain E.D. Barclay. In 1957, he sold his holding to Captain Walter Clode. From this point on, the business affairs of Westley Richards become increasingly tangled and complex, but really do not warrant a lengthy explanation. Suffice to say, the company survived and, in 1987, Walter Clode's son Simon entered the business and continues running it to this day.

Westley Richards is still in business in Birmingham, still making shotguns and rifles, and has a presence in the United States as well, with a retail outlet in Bozeman, Montana.

Jack Rowe:

Again, it requires a book to do this firm justice. So many models, so many grades of guns and double rifles.

This firm produced some of the finest men in the gun trade, fine craftsmen. At one time, an entire family—the Payne family—worked there. I knew one of the last, Horace; his brother was a stocker and still worked there. Then there was the Lillie family. Three generations of the same family worked there as barrel makers, and their initials can be found on a wide range of barrels from WR guns. Frank Lillie (FL), Harry Lillie (HL), and Jack Lillie (JL). What firm can boast that? Three generations of the same family stretching from before the 20th century up until the Second World War. I had the pleasure of knowing Jack Lillie.

So what can one say about Westley Richards? Their guns and double rifles, of whatever grade, are universally well made.

George Caswell:

Westley Richards is notable for the A&D action and the droplock version of it. They have made a large range of models and grades, with the quality generally very good. They appear regularly in the market and command about a 10 percent premium.

One should beware of guns that were well used and improperly restored. Some post-WWII single triggers are not very good. The pre-WWII droplocks were well built and of excellent quality (and today command as much as a London best sidelock). Westley Richards's low-end guns were just that.

JOHN WILKES GUNMAKER

John Wilkes is another old company, highly respected within the trade, but not widely known outside it. The firm began in Birmingham in 1830, later moved to London, and remained in the Wilkes family until the 1990s.

The original John (actually Joseph) Wilkes prospered making guns for sale to America during the Civil War. When the war ended, he mortgaged his business to the hilt, withdrew all the money, and absconded to America. His three sons, Joseph, John, and Tom, were left to pick up the pieces. John re-established the family firm, and began the tradition of naming the eldest son John, and the second son Tom. When the Wilkes family finally sold the business a few years ago, the last John and Tom Wilkes retired.

During its 170-year history, the company had premises in Birmingham, then London. At first, John Wilkes worked with J.D. Dougall, but established his own operation in 1894, in Lower James Street off Golden Square in Soho. The Birmingham branch of the business was finally closed in 1933.

During this period, John Wilkes made a wide range of guns and rifles, of all grades. Generally, the lower grades were made in Birmingham, the higher grades in London. Although Wilkes did sell guns to retail clients, they were largely a trade gunmaker, and estimate that at least half of their production over the years was sold within the trade.

Wilkes produced components for other gunmakers, such as Woodward, and made entire guns and rifles for companies like Army & Navy. It is generally acknowledged that, after W.J. Jeffery, John Wilkes made more .600 Nitro Express double rifles than anyone else.

> 1894: Lower James Street, Soho
> 1912: 31 Gerrard Street
> 1925: 21 Broad (now Broadwick) Street, Golden Square
> 1927: 79 Beak Street

Jack Rowe:
> *Wilkes made all grades of gun, both sidelock and boxlock, and they were well made, whatever the grade.*

George Caswell:
> *Wilkes was in business in the trade for many years, right up to modern times making modern guns. Their quality is generally very good, with many excellent. Wilkes guns do not appear often, and they command about a five percent premium. I have little experience with their shotguns except for a few recent ones. They are nice guns.*
> *Their pre-WWII boxlock double rifle is one of my favorite actions. They*

particularly liked sideclips on their actions and they are very strong. I have not encountered a bad one. In terms of their action body, I put them right alongside a Webley or a Jeffery.

WILLIAMSON & SON

This firm is included here not because it is particularly noteworthy, but because it is rather a mystery. There were several companies called Williamson & Son in business around 1900, or variations thereof, and I am not sure which one I am writing about.

More than the company, this small section concerns one gun that bears the name Williamson & Son.

At one time, the author owned a lovely old boxlock gun—a best boxlock or very close to it, and certainly the best that Williamson would produce—with 30-inch Damascus barrels, full-coverage, tiny scroll engraving, a lovely stock of fiddleback walnut, and checkered panels behind the frame. This gun was on the rack at West Wycombe Shooting Grounds when Steve Denny was running the gunshop there. It was the kind of gun for which there was no market in England in 1998—a boxlock non-ejector—and I bought it for about $450. A year or so later, I sold the gun in the U.S. for four times that amount (and would eagerly pay more than that to have it back). There is a photograph of this gun in the color section of this book. If the current owner happens to see it, he has my congratulations on owning a delightful gun.

The Williamson & Son boxlock: Obscure, puzzling, but quite lovely.

Jack Rowe:

I know nothing of this firm. I suspect it was a provincial gunshop or hardware store which sold guns made in Birmingham with their name on. Let me know if I'm right. (Ed. Note: You are right, Jack.)

JAMES WOODWARD & SONS

James Woodward was born in London around 1814, entered the gun trade working for Charles Moore in 1827, completed his apprenticeship, and eventually rose to become a partner. The firm was renamed Moore & Woodward around 1843, and relocated to 64 St. James's Street.

Eventually, Moore died or retired, James Woodward's two sons, James and Charles, entered the business in 1872, and it became James Woodward & Sons. And so it remained for 75 years. Management passed first to the two sons, then to a nephew of one of them, who ran the business until the time came for his own retirement, in 1948, and he sold the business to James Purdey.

Woodward was never a large firm and its output was relatively small, but it developed an enviable reputation for producing guns that were extremely finely finished. Woodward was exacting with his own craftsmen and with his suppliers. One barrel maker told of having work refused because there were two or three too few pellets in the pattern. Nigel Brown says that whether this story is strictly true is now impossible to prove, but what is certain is that "best-quality Woodward guns with original regulation of the chokes do throw exceptionally fine and even patterns."

Edwin von Atzigen, a Swiss-born gunmaker who now lives in Ontario and has restored several guns for the author (including the E.M. Reilly boxlock shown elsewhere in this book), says Woodward guns have been consistently "the best-made guns I've ever seen. Better than Purdey, better than Holland & Holland."

Although Woodward made a few hammer guns, double rifles, bolt actions, and falling-block rifles, they are quite rare. The company concentrated on shotguns, especially their legendary sidelock side-by-side game gun and their even more legendary over/under.

The Woodward O/U was designed by C.L. Woodward and two craftsmen named Evershed and Hill, and was patented in 1913. It is acknowledged to be one of the two finest over/under designs ever made in Britain during this era (the other being the Boss).

The company survived the Great Depression and bomb damage to their shop during the Second World War, but by 1948 business was bad and the

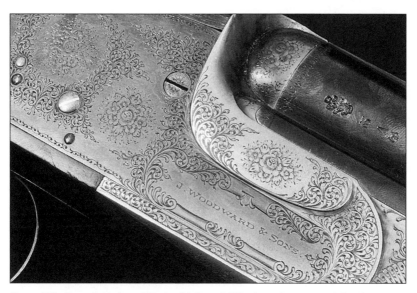

James Woodward 12-bore "Under & Over." Woodward was noted for the austere elegance and extremely fine workmanship of their guns, both side-by-side and over/under.

last Woodward wanted to retire. His first overture to Purdey was rebuffed, but Purdey later relented and bought the rights to the over/under, stipulating that they would not make the Woodward game gun.

> 1843: 64 St. James's Street
> 1937: 29 Bury Street

Jack Rowe:

>   *They made best-quality sidelocks, and I have not seen a bad one yet. I have seen a lot of tired, worn-out old Woodwards, though. They seem to be used hard. Most of the guns I've seen were from the early 1900s—1900 to 1920. All their guns have their signature "arcaded fences," which in actual fact is a "cutaway fence with arcading cut in." There's a name for every basic fence shape. There had to be, because if you sent out a gun for filing up, you had to tell the man what shape you wanted it to be. The same was true with provincial gunshops ordering a gun from Birmingham.*

George Caswell:

>   *Woodwards, both side-by-sides and over/unders, are among the very best.*

The over/under is particularly noteworthy. The workmanship is excellent-plus. Woodward guns are not common, and command a premium of 30 to 40 percent.

Condition is always a consideration, as virtually all the Woodwards we see are from before the Second World War and were well used. It is not easy to find a little-used Woodward.

The great interest in Woodwards lies with serious students of the gun. The occasional buyer knows little about Woodward, but automatically thinks "Purdey." Relatively few Woodwards were made, but they are one of the best.

Appendices

Appendix One: *British Proof*

The United Kingdom has a long history of requiring that firearms undergo proof testing before they are sold. Proofing is carried out at two proof houses: London and Birmingham. The London proof house is the older, dating from 1713; the Birmingham proof house was established in 1813.

Because it is older, and existed when there was no other, London does not have a mark that obviously denotes "London," whereas Birmingham marks have a 'B' somewhere. Not surprisingly, guns with London marks have a cachet not enjoyed by those with Birmingham marks.

Various histories of proof marks have been written over the years. In the 1950s, A. Baron Engelhardt wrote a series for *Gun Digest*, beginning in 1953 (7th Ed.) with an overall history of gun proof and followed by a country-by-country review. British proof historically was covered in 1954 (8th Ed.), and a survey of modern British proof was published in 1962 (16th Ed.). A decade later, Lee Kennett built on Engelhardt's work with a new series that ran from 1968 to 1979. This is very useful for those with a complete collection of *Gun Digest*, but not so useful for those without. Also, being nearly half a century old, it is no surprise that changes have taken place.

The most up-to-date and comprehensive explanation of British proof marks past and present is contained in several appendices to Nigel Brown's monumental two-volume work on British gunmakers.

Obviously, a change to the proof laws today will make no difference to a gun proofed in 1896; however, regulations relating to re-proof, and the marks used to denote it, may well affect an older gun. So, one must be prepared to unravel the proof-mark puzzle with both old and new code books.

The London proof house traces its origins to the days of King James I, the advent of firearms as military weapons, and the granting of royal monopolies on the supply of gun barrels. In 1637, a group of gunsmiths formed the Worshipful Company of Gunmakers of the City of London. The company's charter included a reference to proving firearms, and in 1713 the company built a proof house in Whitechapel for that purpose. It became the London proof house, and is still there on Commercial Road.

A century later, in 1813, the government extended proof regulations to include the entire country and authorized the establishment of a proof house in Birmingham, the heart of large-scale British gunmaking. The Guardians of the Birmingham Gun-Barrel Proof House were the black-country equivalent of the Worshipful Company in London. Because the two houses were operated independently, London proof is sometimes called "Company" proof, and the letter 'C' is used in some early marks. Birmingham proof is called "Guardian" proof, and the letter 'G' is used. To add to the confusion, "Birmingham proof" and "blackpowder" have the same initials: BP.

Proof in Great Britain was then regulated over the course of the next two centuries by a succession of proof laws, first in 1855, then 1868, 1904, and 1925. New regulations were introduced in 1875 to cover choke barrels, and in 1896 for smokeless powder. As regulations have changed, so have the marks required.

The two basic proof marks are provisional proof, done when the barrels are unfinished, and definitive proof when they are completed. There is also an inspection or "view" mark, which includes a 'V.' During the transition from blackpowder to smokeless, there was a confusing period in which marks for semi-smokeless powder proof were also used.

Generally speaking, the older a gun is, the fewer marks it will have (unless it has been re-proofed). As technology has advanced, the gunpowders, allowable pressures, configuration of firearms, proofing practices, and marks have also changed. Today, the proof houses apply a plethora of marks indicating all kinds of measurements, including chamber length, proof pressure, bore diameter at time of proofing, and year of proof, as well as the basic marks that show the barrel withstood the proof load and the examiner found no flaws.

Except for the actual proof marks, showing which proof house performed the test, many of these markings are common to both London and Birmingham.

The following explains those marks most likely to be relevant to the guns covered in this book, during the time of particular interest, or which may have been applied subsequently if an older gun was re-proofed. For complete proof marks, including those for rifles, military, and special-purpose firearms and loads, the reader is referred to Nigel Brown's *British Gunmakers*, or the work of Gerhard Wirnsberger, A. Baron Engelhardt, and Lee Kennett.

LONDON PROOF

The basic London proof mark is a crown, with the entwined letters 'G' and 'P' underneath *(Figs. 1&6)*. It is a mark dating from the very early years and in the 18th century it became the definitive London blackpowder proof mark. A crown over a 'V' is the London view mark *(Figs. 1&3)*.

Fig. 1: Damascus barrels from an E.M. Reilly shotgun circa 1892. The two proof marks are London, and show that the barrels received blackpowder proof and visual proof. The 'G' and 'P' interwoven under a crown is the oldest London mark, standing for Gunmakers' Company. It has been the definitive London proof mark since the 1700s. The letter 'V' under a crown is the "view" mark; again, it dates back to the very early days of the Worshipful Company of Gunmakers. The chambers are 12 bore, and the bore diameters at proof were both slightly undersized. The "13" over the "1" indicates a bore diameter of .719. This is the equivalent of 13-bore (.709") plus one 1/100th. The left barrel has choke boring, the right barrel none.

A third mark, found on the barrel itself rather than the flat, is a lion rampant over the script letters 'GP' (although rarely recognizable as such). This is the provisional proof mark, introduced in 1813 and used ever since *(Fig. 2)*. Barrels are proofed twice, the first time very early in their manufacture (provisional proof) and after completion (definitive proof). Provisional proof saves the gunmaker from spending a great deal of time finishing a barrel with a hidden defect.

The London mark for nitro proof is, in heraldic terms, the letters 'NP' surmounted by an "arm dexter in armour, holding a scimitar." This mark was

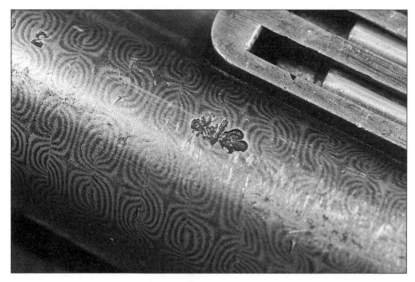

Fig. 2: Closeup of the London provisional proof mark (a lion rampant over the intertwined letters 'GP'), stamped on the barrel wall. This mark is often hard to decipher because the lion is so intricate, the letters so elaborately intertwined, and the mark itself so small.

Fig. 3: Action flat of a London-made E.M. Reilly, showing the single London view mark, a crown over the letter V, dating from the early days of the Gunmakers Company.

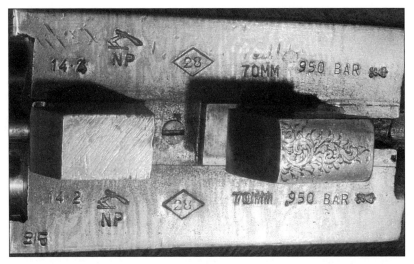

Fig. 4: The barrel flat of a 28-bore hammer gun, originally proofed for blackpowder in Birmingham in the 1880s, re-proofed for nitro powder in London. The markings for each barrel are essentially the same. Looking at the bottom barrel, from left, we have the London date mark (LP over 01) for 2001; 14.2 is the bore diameter in millimeters, nine inches forward of the breech; the London nitro-proof mark (arm and scimitar over the letters NP); 28 in a diamond denotes chamber size; 70mm is chamber length; 950 BAR is the proof pressure; and finally, a crown and script R, to denote re-proof.

introduced in 1904 and has been used ever since *(Fig. 4)*.

Another London mark of particular interest is a script uppercase ℛ beneath a crown. Since 1925, this has indicated that a barrel has been re-proofed sometime after definitive proof took place *(Fig. 4)*.

BIRMINGHAM PROOF

An original Birmingham proof mark that may be encountered on older guns has crossed scepters beneath a crown, with the letters B,P and C in the angles. It was used from 1813 until 1904. Until 1855, this mark was used alone; after 1855, when a separate provisional mark was introduced, this was used to denote definitive proof only.

A similar mark, with crossed scepters, crown, and a V in the bottom angle, was the Birmingham "view" mark from 1813 to 1904 *(Fig. 6)*.

The provisional mark, introduced in 1855 and still in use, is the script letters *BP* intertwined beneath a crown. This mark is found on the barrel, not the flat, and is often illegible, resembling a blob *(Fig. 5)*.

In 1904, a series of new marks was introduced that simplified things considerably. These marks were the letters **BP, BV,** and **NP,** beneath a crown. The first was definitive blackpowder proof, the second a new view mark, and the third definitive proof for smokeless powder (nitro proof). In 1925, two more marks were added to the series: a crown and **R** was introduced to denote a re-proof after definitive proof, and crown and **SP** denotes proofing for a special heavy load.

In 1954, a crown over the letters **BNP** was introduced and became the definitive nitro-proof mark.

IN PROOF, OUT OF PROOF, & RE-PROOF

In the United Kingdom, proof marks on a gun are of vital concern to both the seller and the prospective purchaser because they show whether the gun is still in proof, or whether it must be re-proofed before it is sold. In the UK, it is illegal to transfer a firearm that is out of proof except to a licenced gunsmith or gunmaker—and transfer means to buy, sell, lend, give, or otherwise hand over possession.

What is "out of proof"? A gun can go out of proof either accidentally or deliberately. If, through wear or damage, the bore diameter exceeds the allowable minimum, then the gun is out of proof and must, by law, be re-proofed. Also, major work performed on a set of barrels can render it out of proof; this includes sleeving, installing choke tubes, shortening the barrels or lengthening the chambers.

Once the gun is sent for re-proof, however, other factors come into play. If the proof house finds the gun is off the face, or there is excessive pitting, the examiners may refuse to re-proof the gun until those conditions are corrected. For this reason, extensive work may be involved in preparing a gun for re-proof to ensure that it is not rejected. If it passes proof, it is so stamped, and the re-proof marks are added to the private résumé that every gun carries on its action flats and barrel flats.

The United States has no comparable proof laws, but proof marks on a gun still serve several purposes. Knowing that a gun is technically out of proof can prompt a purchaser to have it checked carefully by a qualified gunsmith, which is advisable with any older gun. The marks also provide valuable clues to the gun's history and to any damage that might have occurred in the past. Finally, they help to determine the gun's age.

*Fig. 5: The barrels of a 28-bore hammer gun, showing Birmingham blackpowder proof. The left (lower) barrel has choke; the right barrel does not. The marks on the bottom barrel, from left, denote: Provisional proof, the original "view" mark, and the original definitive proof mark. The number 30 shows the barrel to be nominally 30-bore at the breech, 33-bore at the muzzle (because of the choke); followed by the words **NOT FOR BALL**. This means of denoting choke boring was discontinued in 1887. The right barrel (top) is nominally 29-bore.*

Fig. 6: The action flat of a James Erskine hammer gun, blackpowder-proofed in Birmingham originally in the 1880s, nitro-proofed in London in 2001. The top mark is the original Birmingham view mark; beneath is the definitive London proof mark, a crown over the entwined letters G P.

BORE (GAUGE) CHAMBERS AND LOADS

Beginning in 1887, as bore (gauge) sizes were standardized in response to the need for shotshells that fit the chambers, the proof houses began stamping on the bore size (12, 16, 20, and so on).

Shotgun bores are not, and never have been, as rigid in their measurements and tolerances as rifle bores, and the proof houses took this into account. For example, a 12-bore is nominally .729 inches in diameter. If the proof house measured the bore and it was .729, then the bore was stamped with a **12**. If, on the other hand, they found it measured .740 (one 1/100th oversized), it would be marked $\frac{12}{1}$. If, years later, a gunsmith measured that bore and found it was .741, he would know it was still in proof; if, on the other hand, it began as **12** and had opened up to .741, he would know it had expanded too much and was now out of proof.

In 1887, a mark was also introduced to show the chamber size (the size of cartridge for which the gun was chambered). This was shown as a number (e.g., **12**) inside a diamond, sometimes accompanied by a **C** or **LC**. **LC** denoted a long chamber. This is not very exact, although it was adequate for the time. In 1925, the proof houses began stamping the actual cartridge length (e.g., **2 1/2"**). The use of accompanying letters was discontinued in 1954, and beginning in 1955 the metric length became optional along with imperial (**65mm** for 2½", **70mm** for 2¾"). In 1989, the proof houses began using metric length exclusively.

Similarly, bore diameter came to be marked in millimeters. Standard 12-bore (.729") is **18.5mm**.

In 1896, with the acceptance of smokeless powders, the words **NITRO PROOF** were used for the first time. For years thereafter, this was often followed by an actual load, such as "1⅛ oz. Max." Sometimes, if a barrel was proofed for a particular load at the owner's request, those details would be stamped on the barrel or barrel flats.

CHOKE BORING

After 1875, and the introduction of choke boring, a mark was used to indicate whether or not a barrel had choke. Eventually this was phased out, but many barrels made during the period that is the focus of this book (1875-1940) will have barrels marked **CHOKE**. If one is marked and the other is not, then the unmarked barrel is cylinder. These marks are on the barrel flats, not the action flats, and there was no differentiation made for degree of choke. In

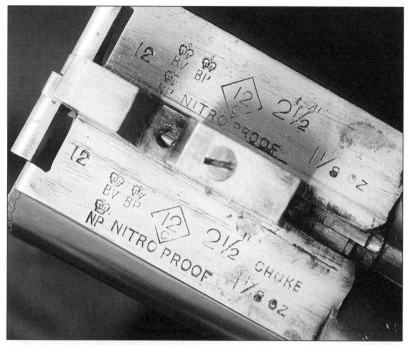

Fig. 7: Barrels of a John Harper boxlock of 20th century manufacture, displaying the complete array of Birmingham proof marks. From left, we see these are 12-bore barrels that have undergone provisional and definitive proof, passed the examiner's viewing, and been nitro proofed. The chambers are 12-bore, 2¹/₂" long, the left barrel has choke, the right does not, and both are proofed for 1¹/₈-oz. loads.

the early days of choke boring, there was full and there was nothing.

Naturally, there was a transitional period as the proof houses figured out exactly how to handle certain questions. Choke boring appeared just around the time that shotguns and rifles were starting to go their separate ways (in fact, choke helped speed that process). Muzzleloaders often served dual purposes and this tradition carried on into the early days of breechloaders. Obviously, however, once gunmakers began constricting muzzles, some of them quite drastically, it became more difficult for one solid lead ball the diameter of the gun's bore to squeeze through.

Between 1875 and 1887, many guns with choke boring were marked on the barrels with the nominal bore size at the breech (e.g., **12B**) followed by **NOT FOR BALL**. If the gun was additionally marked **14M**, this showed that the bore measurement at the muzzle equated to a 14-bore. This was a warning to users not to fire solid projectiles. This practice was abandoned in 1887. It is useful to know, however, because it may help date a particular firearm. After 1887, such guns were marked CHOKE.

A variation was Holland & Holland's Paradox, which had a section of rifling near the muzzle, allowing the gun to be used as either a shotgun or a crude rifle with a projectile. Other manufacturers later came out with their own versions of the principle, such as the Cape guns. These barrels were marked R CHOKE.

Between 1904 and 1954, barrels that were rifled or partly rifled and intended for use with both shot and ball were marked S & B.

PRESSURE

Beginning in 1925, the proof houses began stamping service pressures allowed on the barrel flats, and have followed the practice ever since. However, the transition from imperial measure in tons per square inch to metric measure in kilograms per square centimeter, and later in BAR, led to some confusing usage.

Until 1955, pressure was denoted in tons (either 3 tons, for standard, or $3^{1}/4$, for special heavy loads). For a while, Birmingham added a symbol of an open square and the inch symbol (") to denote "per square inch," but discontinued this in 1984. For a while, pressures were marked in both tons and kilograms. The two usual kilogram measures for 12-bore are 900 kg (standard) and 1200 kg (magnum). Finally, in 1989, a complete transition was made to BAR, or units of barometric pressure. One BAR is equal to approximately 1.02 kg/sq.cm. Standard proof is 850 BAR, magnum is 1200 BAR *(Fig. 4)*.

One notable difference is that the old English system showed service pressures, the metric shows proof pressures. Converting 850 BAR to tons results in the number 6.16, which is double the British proof rating. The actual proof test is the same; only the method of conveying the result is different.

DATE MARKS

Both London and Birmingham have adopted methods of date markings to show when a gun was inspected or proofed. Not surprisingly, the two systems do not resemble each other in the least.

Birmingham began the practice in 1921, suspended it during the Second

World War, and resumed it in 1950. London's code began in 1972.

According to Nigel Brown, the London mark in 1972 consisted of the letters **LPH** and the last two digits of the year **72**. The following year, the letter 'H' was dropped, and henceforth the mark consisted of **LP** only and two digits for the year (e.g., **92**) stamped beneath.

Birmingham's system was far more complex. A letter was assigned for each year, and the year ran from July 1 to June 30, so the letter 'A' was stamped on a gun made between July 1, 1921 and June 30, 1922. This system was used until 1940-41. The codes were stamped in the angles of a pair of crossed swords. The examiner identified himself by a number (either a '1' for the senior examiner or '2', '3', or higher for more junior examiners). The date letter was stamped in the top angle, the examiner's number in the bottom angle.

A – 1921-22
B – 1922-23
C – 1923-24
D – 1924-25
E – 1925-26
F – 1926-27
G – 1927-28
H – 1928-29
J – 1929-30
K – 1930-31
L – 1931-32
M – 1932-33
N – 1933-34
O – 1934-35
P – 1935-36
R – 1936-37
S – 1937-38
T – 1938-39
U – 1939-40
V – 1940-41

On July 18, 1950, the Birmingham proof house resumed applying date stamps but adopted the calendar year. Thenceforth, the mark changed on January 1. Now the letters were stamped in the left and right angles of the crossed swords, and the examiner's number in the bottom angle.

AB – 1950
BB – 1951
BC or CB – 1952
DB – 1953
EB – 1954
FB – 1955
GB – 1956
HB – 1957
JB – 1958
KB – 1959
LB – 1960
MB – 1961
NB – 1962
OB – 1963
PB – 1964
QB – 1965
RB – 1966
SB – 1967
TB – 1968
UB – 1969
VB – 1970
WB – 1971
XB – 1972
YB – 1973
ZB - 1974

In 1975, this code was resumed from the beginning, so duplicate marks exist from 1975 to 84. The mark itself was different, however, with the two letters and the examiner's code number inside a circle.

AB – 1975
BB – 1976
BC or CB – 1977
DB – 1978
EB – 1979
FB – 1980
GB – 1981
HB – 1982
JB – 1983

KB – 1984

In 1985, the proof house returned to the old mark of crossed swords with the letters and examiner's mark stamped in the angles, but changed to using a 'C' in the code.

LC – 1985
MC – 1986
NC – 1987
OC – 1988
PC – 1989
RC – 1990
SC – 1991
TC – 1992
UC – 1993
VC – 1994
XC – 1995
YC – 1996
ZC – 1997

Appendix Two: *Bibliography*

Boothroyd, Geoffrey

- *The Shotgun: History and Development*
- *Boothroyd on British Shotguns*
- *Sidelocks & Boxlocks: The Classic British Shotguns*
- *Shotguns and Gunsmiths: The Vintage Years*
- *Gun Collecting*
- *Guns through the Ages*

Boothroyd, Geoffrey and Susan Boothroyd

- *Boothroyds' Revised Directory of British Gunmakers*
- *The British Over-and-Under Shotgun (1996)*

Brown, Nigel

- *British Gunmakers, Volume One: London*
- *British Gunmakers, Volume Two: Birmingham, Scotland & the Regions*

Garwood, G.T. (Gough Thomas)

- *Gough Thomas's Gun Book*
- *Gough Thomas's Second Gun Book*
- *Shotgun Shooting Facts*
- *Shotguns & Cartridges for Game and Clays*

Greener, W.W.

- *The Gun and its Development*

Grozik, Richard S.

- *Game Gun*

Gun Digest (Edited by John T. Amber)

- 7th Ed. (1953) History of proof in Europe (A. Baron Engelhardt)
- 8th Ed. (1954) History of proof in Great Britain (Engelhardt)
- 16th Ed. (1962) Modern British proof (Engelhardt)
- 31st Ed. (1977) Gun Proof in England (Lee Kennett)

McIntosh, Michael

- *Best Guns*
- *The Big-Bore Rifle*
- *Shotguns and Shooting*
- *More Shotguns and Shooting*
- *Shotguns and Shooting Three*

Martin, Brian P.

- *The Great Shoots*

Stanford, Col. J.K.

- *The Complex Gun*

Wirnsberger, Gerhard (Trans. by R.A. Steindler)

- *Standard Directory of Proof Marks*

Index

Index

A

B

C

D

H

O

P

R

Reilly, E.M.	*47*, 50, 66-67, *126*-27, 145, 147-48, 153, 168-72, *171, 173*-74, 179, 260-*61, 283-84*, 2 VBS, 3 VBS
Patent ejectors	*159*-60, 170-71
Rigby, John, & Co.	21, 27, 44, *79, 87, 89*, 122, *125*, 180, 196, 261-6*3*, 14 VBS
Rising bite	122-*23*, 262-*63*
Patent forend latch	*153*
Riggs, Charles, & Co.	260
Ringer, Robert	*25*
Ripon, Lord	28, 30, 33, 41, 56, 132
Roberts, Paul	262
Robertson, John	*109*, 136, 157, 214-16
Boxlock gun	196, 197
Robson, W.R.H.	233-34
Rowe, Jack	175, 197, 201-2, 204, 205, 206, 208-10, 212, 213-14, 216, 218, 219, 220, 222, 224, 225, 226-28, 230, 232, 233, 236, 237-38, 241, 242, 244, 248, 250, 251, 252, 253, 254, 255, 258, 259, 260-61, 262, 264, 266, 268, 269, 273, 274

S

Scott's patented breech bolting system	*69, 115*
Scott, Charles	263
Scott, William	263
Scott spindle	74, 116, *160*, 264
Scott, W.M.	26, 116, 264
Scott, W&C	42, *75*, 98-*99, 125*, 127, *147, 155, 160*, 202, 240, 262-*65*, 268, 8 VBS
Blenheim	264
Crystal Indicator	99, 12 VBS
Over/under	264
Premier	265
Selous, F.C.	67, 168, 260
Side-clips	124
Solari, Ron	206
Southgate, Thomas	160
Ejectors	*159*-60